Birgit Abegg, Michael Benford

Lehrbuch Communication for Business

Zeitgemäße englische Handelskorrespondenz und Bürokommunikation

Aktualisierte Ausgabe mit Incoterms® 2010

Hueber Verlag

To Rosalind, Rebecca, Jake and David
Für Peter, Pete und Gabi

Note:

All Standard Expressions tables and Phraseology sections can be found in the
Satzbausteine book.

| 4. | 3. | 2. | | Die letzten Ziffern |
| 2018 | 17 | 16 | 15 | 14 | bezeichnen Zahl und Jahr des Druckes. |

Alle Drucke dieser Auflage können, da unverändert,
nebeneinander benutzt werden.
2. Auflage 2012
© 1999 Hueber Verlag GmbH & Co. KG, 85737 Ismaning, Deutschland
Verlagsredaktion: Cornelia Dietz, München
Umschlaggestaltung, Layout und Herstellung: Christiane Gerstung, München
Zeichnungen: Reinhard Blumenschein, München
Druck und Bindung: Firmengruppe APPL, aprinta druck, Wemding
Printed in Germany
ISBN 978–3–19–122617–6

Preface

Communication for Business approaches the task of writing business letters, faxes and e-mails in a new way. It is a package consisting of two books – a *Coursebook* (**Lehrbuch**) with background information, exercises and activities, and a *Book of Tables* (**Satzbausteine**) containing a wide range of phrases and expressions.

In the modern business world, communication, especially in its many electronic forms, has become faster and, as a result of this, more informal. Many messages are simply read on a computer screen and then stored for later reference without ever being printed out. This does not mean, however, that letters are no longer written. The traditional letter still has an important role to play in the business world but now co-exists alongside faster electronic forms.

All these factors have been taken into account in **Communication for Business**. Each written communication activity can take the form of a letter, fax or e-mail and in the *case studies* students are encouraged to work in groups and communicate with each other. Each Unit also contains a *telephone role play* and a *listening comprehension* activity leading to either a letter, fax, e-mail, memo in English or a summary in German.

Students using this book are not invited to translate from German into English and make the usual mistakes. Instead, they are encouraged to use the **Satzbausteine**, which contain a wide range of expressions arranged in such a way that they can be combined to produce grammatically and stylistically correct sentences. The *Letter Plan* in each Unit of the **Lehrbuch** provides a structure for the students to follow when putting their letters, faxes and e-mails together. The different parts of the *Letter Plan* are numbered and correspond to expressions listed in the **Satzbausteine**. The students work their way through the *Letter Plan* selecting relevant points and then turn to the **Satzbausteine** to choose suitable phrases to express them. In this way, they are assured of writing a well-structured letter, fax or e-mail. The more traditional approach to commercial correspondence is, of course, also catered for in the *Phraseology* sections of the **Satzbausteine**, in which English expressions and their German translations are listed.

After work on the coursebook has been completed, the **Satzbausteine** will, of course, still serve an important function as an invaluable reference book for use in the office.

The materials contained in **Communication for Business** have been tried and tested on a large number of students over a period of years and modified accordingly. In this connection we would like to thank the students and colleagues at the Robert-Schuman-Berufskolleg der Stadt Essen and the Düsseldorf Chamber of Commerce and Industry for their help, advice and constructive criticism. Our thanks are also due to David Duckworth, Member of the Institute of Export, London, Frau Sabine Quandt, Graduate of the Sparkasse Academy, Wuppertal and Herr Thomas Dünnwald, Qualified Freight Forwarder, Düsseldorf, for giving us valuable expert information.

Birgit Abegg, Michael Benford

Contents

Unit 1

Layouts

Layouts

Business Letters

British Layout

Block form / open punctuation. This is the most common form of layout.

Green Wrap Ltd 21 Fullwell Rd .... **1.** Letterhead with logo,
Preston PN2 5AJ   postcode (UK), telephone,
England   fax and e-mail numbers
Tel. +44 (0)17 72 5 62 23   and Internet address
Fax +44 (0)17 72 5 62 25
E-mail: Johnson@greenwrap.co.uk
http://www.greenwrap.co.uk

• (One free line – optional)
MB/TT .... **2.** Reference initials
10 September .. .. **3.** Date
• (one free line)
URGENT .... **4.** Special marking
•
Messrs Smith & Co
12604 Prince Street
Buda, TX 78610 .... **5.** Inside address. "TX"
USA   stands for "Texas" and
•   78610 is the ZIP code.
For the attention of Mr Lewis, Despatch Section .... **6.** Attention line
•
Dear Mr Lewis .... **7.** Salutation
•
Your Order of 3 September .. for Packaging Material .... **8.** Subject line
•
Many thanks for the above-mentioned order, which will ... **9.** Body of the letter.
be processed by our Despatch Department within the   The first word has a
next ten days.   capital letter.
•
We trust the goods will arrive punctually and in good
condition and look forward to the pleasure of serving
you again in the near future.
•
Yours sincerely .... **10.** Complimentary close
GreenWrap Ltd   with the signature, name
•   (followed by preferred title
Margaret Brown   in brackets in the case of
•   a woman) and position of
Margaret Brown (Ms)   the signatory clearly written
Managing Director
•
•
Enc .... **11.** Enclosure
•
•
cc: T. Johnson, Sales Manager .... **12.** Carbon copy for
                                                      Mr T. Johnson

[handwritten note: wichtigste Wörter groß / unter- streichen]

Fig. 1

English is the most widely-used language in business communication in the world. As it is used in so many different countries, it is impossible to lay down firm rules about the way a letter, fax, e-mail or memo should be set out.

For this reason only the most frequently found formats used in written business communication are reproduced here.

Notes on **Fig. 1**

1. The letterhead
There is no set layout for the letterhead and most companies use specially designed pre-printed stationery.

In a UK address the counties are often abbreviated, e.g. "Beds" for "Bedford-shire", "Hants" for "Hampshire". See Glossary, page 273 for a complete list. In an American address a two-letter abbreviation is normally used for the states, e.g. "CA" for "California" or "NY" for New York State. See Glossary, page 285/286 for a complete list.

The "+" sign before the telephone and fax numbers in **Fig. 1** on page 6 means that someone telephoning the company from abroad should first dial the appropriate international access code.

2. Reference / Reference Initials
The initials of the signatory – "MB" (Margaret Brown) – are normally given first. "TT" stands for her secretary (e.g. Triona Taylor). It could also be written "tt".

Other references (e.g. file / department / branch / subsidiary reference) can be given separately or included with the initials, e.g. f42/camdep or MB/TT/f42.a.

If the reference given by the recipient in previous correspondence is to be quoted, this can be done as follows:
Your ref.   LT/gg
Our ref.   MB/TT

See also **Fig. 3** (American layout).

3. The date
Here it is best to write the month out as a word to avoid confusion because in North America dates are written in the order "month-day-year", whereas the European order is frequently "day-month-year". An all-figure date such as 10-9-2001 would mean October 9, 2001 to a North American and 10 September 2001 to many Europeans. Similarly, a date written 2001-10-9 could mean either October 9 or 10 September 2001.

It is no longer necessary to write 1st (1st), 2nd (2nd), 3rd (3rd), 4th (4th), 21st (21st) etc. The letter writer is, however, free to use this form if desired.

Examples:

28 December 1999	December 28, 1999	December 28th 1999
28th December 1999	December 28 1999	December 28th, 1999

4. Special markings

These are displayed above the address to enable them to be read in the window of a window envelope. For further details see Glossary, page 286.

5. The inside address

This is the recipient's full postal address. If the recipient is a person (not a company) the most commonly used titles are as follows:

Title	Example	Meaning
Miss	Miss Ann Jones	The lady (or girl) is unmarried.
Mrs	Mrs Ann Jones	The lady is married.
Ms	Ms Ann Jones	It is impossible to say whether the lady (or girl) is married or unmarried.
Mr	Mr Alfred Freemantle	It is impossible to say whether the man is married or unmarried.
Messrs	Messrs Brown and Johnson	"Messrs" is the plural of "Mr".

The house number and street name are written after the recipient. In an American address the "suite number" (apartment number) follows the house number and street name. This is followed by the name of the city, town or village (in capital letters in the UK) on the next line. After this the postcode (UK) or the abbreviation for the state (e.g. "TX" for Texas) and the ZIP code (USA) are written. In Britain the Royal Mail asks for the postcode to be written in capital letters on a separate line after the city, town or village. In the USA the city, the abbreviation for the state and the ZIP code are usually written on the same line.

For letters abroad the name of the country must also be included.

Examples:

UK
Designer Mode Ltd
41 Victoria Parade
BRIGHTON
BR7 5TH
England

USA
Data Incorporated
3090 Powers Ferry Road, Suite 120
Atlanta, GA 30339
U.S.A.

6. Attention line

If the name of the person whose job it is to deal with the letter is known, it can be included here. Attention lines are usually written in one of the following ways:

For the attention of Ms Wilson, Sales Department

or
Attention: Ms Wilson, Sales Department

or
Attn. Ms Wilson, Sales Department

The attention line can also be capitalised or underlined.

7. The salutation

The salutation is linked with the name of the recipient in the inside address (cf 5) and the complimentary close (cf 10).

In British English the main thing to consider is whether the writer uses the recipient's name or not. If the recipient's name is used (e.g. Dear Mr Brown), the complimentary close is "Yours sincerely". If the recipient's name is unknown, a more formal, polite but impersonal form is used (e.g. Dear Sir, Dear Sir or Madam, Dear Sir / Madam) and the complimentary close is "Yours faithfully".

In a friendly letter between business associates "With best regards" or "With best wishes" can precede the complimentary close.

In American business correspondence there is normally a colon or comma after the salutation and a comma after the complimentary close (AE: complimentary closing). The salutation "Ladies and Gentlemen:" or "Gentlemen and Ladies:" has now replaced the older term "Gentlemen:". In many cases it is, however, advisable to find out the name of the person who is to deal with the letter (e.g. by calling the company) and then address it to that person. In the *simplified letter style* the salutation is left out altogether and the letter begins with the subject line.

8. Subject line

This is an optional feature and is intended to show the reader at a glance what the letter is about. In the UK it is usually after the salutation (as in **Fig. 1**, page 6) but in the USA it is placed *before* it (see **Fig. 3**, page 12). The subject line is normally written in bold type, capitalised or underlined to make it stand out. If the subject line is not completely capitalised the important words are written with a capital letter, e.g.:

Your Offer dated 25 June ..

Enquiry about Article No. 408-T

Representative's Collection of Trade Samples

American forms:
As the subject line is normally at the very beginning of the letter *before* the salutation, it is not necessary to underline it or type it in capital letters or bold type.
- Your Offer dated June 25, ..
- It can be preceded by "Re:" or "RE:" , "Subj:" or "Subject:".
- Re: Your Offer dated June 25, ..
- Subject: Your Offer dated June 25, ..

9. The body of the letter
The body of the letter always starts with a capital letter. The paragraphs are best separated by a free line and it is not necessary to indent at the beginning of each new paragraph.

10. The complimentary close
The closing part of the letter consists of 4 or 5 lines, the first of which is the complimentary close. The link between the complimentary close and the salutation is shown in the tables in the Book of Tables (*Satzbausteine*). The closing part of a letter is put together as follows:
- the complimentary close line (i. e. "Yours faithfully", "Yours sincerely" etc.)
- the name of the firm sending the letter (optional)
- the signature
- the signatory's name, clearly written and, if the writer is a woman, her preferred title (Miss, Mrs or Ms) in brackets after her name
- the signatory's position in the company.

Several free lines should be left for the signature to be added later (see **Figs. 1**, page 6 and **3**, page 12).
  If the signatory signs on behalf of another person, e. g. a secretary signs on behalf of his / her boss, it is customary to write "pp." before the other person's name (meaning *per procurationem*, "for and on behalf of"), e. g.

Carol Smith
pp. Marion Flood

11. Enclosures
It is normally enough to indicate that there is an enclosure (Enc) or enclosures (Encs) with the letter. If details of the enclosures are to be included, this can be done as follows:

	Or
Enc	Enc:
1 Cheque	1 Cheque
Encs	Encs:
2 Order Forms	2 Order Forms

12. Carbon copies

The abbreviation "cc:" is still used to mean that a copy of the letter is to be sent to the person or persons named. The position in the company of the person or persons to receive a copy is also included, e.g.:

cc: Ms Jane Stevens, Personnel Manager
     Mr Harold Johnson, Accountant

Continuation Pages

Continuation pages have the page number, the date and the recipient's name blocked at the left margin at the top of the next page.

2

•

28 June ..

•

Mr James Brown

•

•

•

Text text text text text text text text text text text text text text text text text text text text text text text text text text text text text text text text text …

Fig. 2

American Layout

Green Wrap Ltd
488 East Prince Street
Reno, NV 89509
U.S.A.
Tel. +(9 16) 2 72-8 94 99
Fax +(9 16) 2 72-9 14 88
E-mail: gwinc@greenwrap.com
http://www.greenwrap.com

1. Letterhead with logo, ZIP code (Nevada), telephone, fax and e-mail numbers and Internet address

• *(one free line)*
September 20, ..

2. Date (month-day-year)

•
Carl T. Lewis, Vice-President
Smith Shipping Corp.
12604 Prince Street
Buda, TX 78610
U.S.A.

3. Inside address. with ZIP code.

•
Re: Your Order of September 3, ..

4. Subject line before the salutation

•
Dear Mr. Lewis:

5. Salutation followed by a colon

•
Many thanks for the above-mentioned order, which will be processed by our Despatch Department within the next ten days.

6. Body of the letter

•
We trust the goods will arrive punctually and in good condition and look forward to the pleasure of serving you again in the near future.

•
Sincerely,

7. Complimentary close (AE: complimentary closing) followed by a comma, the signature and the name and position of the signatory clearly written

•
Michael Brown

•
•
Michael Brown
President

•
MB:tt

8. Signatory's and typist's initials, separated by a colon

•
Enclosure: Catalog

9. Enclosure(s)

•
Copies: Trent Johnson, Sales Manager
        Alicia Montara, Export Division

10. Copies for Trent Johnson and Alicia Montara

Fig. 3

Private Letter

Heinrich-Gustav-Str. 99
69121 Heidelberg
Germany

Your ref. ESC/kw   20 January ..

Ms Kate Williams
Human Resources Officer
PowerGen Plc
90–100 Coronation Street
LANCASTER
LA1 4GH
England

Dear Ms Williams

<u>Your Advertisement on the Internet for the Post of</u>
<u>European Sales Clerk</u>

I am writing with reference to the above-mentioned
advertisement and am most interested in applying
for the post you offer.

I am currently employed as a business administration clerk at Neckarstahl AG in Heidelberg and
have held this post for five years. Even though I am
successful in my current position I would like to
work for a firm at which I would be able to put my
knowledge of English to good use.

I enclose my CV and copies of my qualifications.
Should you require a reference Frau Wiebke Pütz,
who teaches business administration theory and
English at Heidelberg Vocational Training College,
will be pleased to provide you with any information
you may need.

I look forward to hearing from you at your
earliest convenience.

Yours sincerely

Rita Räumschüssel
Rita Räumschüssel (Ms)

<u>Encs:</u>
CV
Certificates

Notes:

1. The sender's address is written in the top right-hand corner. The sender's name is *not* normally written at the top of the page.
2. The date can be written under the sender's address or above the inside address
3. "Your ref." can be included above the inside address on the same level as the date.

4. The sender's name (Rita Räumschüssel) is clearly written after the signature. A woman can add how she wishes to be addressed by adding (Miss), (Mrs) or (Ms) after her name.

Fig. 4

Fax Layout

There is no set layout for a fax (facsimile). The following example contains all the necessary information. "FAO" stands for "For the attention of" (cf "6 Attention Line" on page 9). The total number of pages is also included, because fax transmissions can be interrupted, in which case the recipient needs to know how many pages are missing.

Faxes are not always accepted as legally binding documents.

Fax cover sheet

FAO:	Ms Heike Maybaum
	Export Sales Department
	Damen-Mode GmbH
	Gelsenkirchen Germany

| Fax No: | 00 49 (2 09) 5 56 17 |

From:	Tim Wright
	Purchasing Department
	Green Wrab Ltd
	21 Fulwell Rd
	Preston
	PN2 5AJ
	England
	Tel +44 (17 72) 5 62 23
	Fax +44 (17 72) 5 62 25
	E-mail: greenwrap@greenwrap.co.uk

| Date: | 28 December .. |

| Subject: | Birmingham |

| Total Pages: | 1 |

Dear Heike

Sorry about the delay in replying. We've now got transport arranged for the equipment so there shouldn't be any hitches.

Please contact me if you have any queries.

Kind regards

Tim

Fig. 5

E-mail

Fig. 6

E-mails are written on-screen and pre-structured by the computer program used. The five boxes in which entries can be made are as follows:

Mail to :
The e-mail subscriber's e-mail address is written here. The "@" symbol ("at") is written before the name of the server (e.g. "@t-online"). Here the address is read "designermode – one word – dot – g – m – b – h at netserve – one word – dot – d – e".

Cc:
This stands for "carbon copy" (see letter layouts "12 Carbon copies"). Copies of the e-mail can be sent automatically to any number of other subscribers listed in the e-mail program's address list.

Subject:
Here the content of the e-mail should be summarised in 8–10 words. If more words are written they might not be read by the recipient before he downloads his e-mail because the viewing box in the program may not be big enough.

Attachment:
Here a file can be sent with the e-mail. This can be any type of file (graphics, text, spreadsheets etc.) supported by the server.

The message
Here the normal rules of business letter writing are used. The style of an e-mail is normally informal (short forms, first names, uncomplicated language) and there is no signature.

Memo

TO:	Mr Anthony Wheeler, European Sales Division, Birmingham
FROM:	Michaela Schulz, German Sales Division
SUBJECT:	Factory Site in Witten, North-Rhine Westphalia, Germany
DATE:	28 December ..

The site is near Witten, a town with about 100,000 inhabitants. The nearest large city is Dortmund, 15 km away. Transport links are excellent but some of the buildings are in need of repair.

I'll be faxing you a site plan and a full report in the next few days.

Fig. 7

A memo (memorandum) is a form of written business communication circulated within a company or, for example, sent to a company's agents or sales representatives. As it is for internal company use only it does not need to contain the company's address, telephone and fax numbers etc.

It should, however, contain details of who it is from, who it is addressed to and brief details of its contents in the form of a subject line and the date.

A memorandum does not normally contain a salutation or a complimentary close. It is also not usually signed.

Exercises

1. **The date**

   How would the following dates be written in a business letter?

USA	UK (European)
1. 10 / 11 / 1998	7. 9 / 8 / 2003
2. 1 / 10 / 1999	8. 7 / 9 / 2002
3. 12 / 7 / 2000	9. 5 / 2 / 2006
4. 4 / 5 / 2001	10. 21 / 6 / 2000
5. 2 / 3 / 2003	11. 10 / 11 / 2001
6. 3 / 4 / 2005	12. 2 / 1 / 2003

2. **Inside address / salutation / complimentary close**
   What would (1) the first line of the inside address (2) the salutation and (3) the complimentary close be in the following cases?

   2.1 A letter is sent to a lady called Ramona Sanchez, who is the chief executive officer of an American company. The signatory is not on first name terms with her.

   2.2 The Manager of a British bank receives a letter from someone who has had no contact with the bank before.

   2.3 A German businesswoman writes to the managing director of Sinclair plc. His name is J. Kenton.

   2.4 A German businessman writes to a partnership consisting of Mr John Drummond and Mr Alex Shaw. He has had no contact with them before.

   2.5 An American businesman writes to a German businessman called Frank Stallmann, who is the sales director at his company. They are on friendly terms.

Layout exercises

Business Letters

3. **Use Fig. 1 (British layout) as your model.**
   Thorsten Strauch, who works in the export section of Behr Glaskunst, Rotkäppchenstr. 23 in 81739 Munich, Germany, dictates a letter to his secretary, Tina Törner. The letter is to Smith & Pettit Ltd., at 21 Highbury Road, Sheffield SH1 4WW, England. Herr Strauch wants Ms Ramona Stone to receive the letter, which is about article no. 445-A. He encloses photographs with the letter. The date is 6 / 7 / 20 ..

4. **Use Fig. 3 (American layout) as your model.**
   Klaus Teymann is an environmental technology consultant at Umwelttechnik GmbH, Harpener Hellweg 78, 44805 Bochum. He sends an air mail letter to Ms Tricia O'Neil at Hudson Environmental Consulting Inc whose office is in suite 45 at 114 East 32nd Street, New York, NY 10010. He dictates the letter to his secretary Tamara Wehrheim (today's date) and tells her to include a brochure with it. The letter is about Umwelttechnik's stand at the Chicago Environmental Convention next month.

Fax

5. **Use the layout in Fig. 5 as your model and include a salutation and a complimentary close as in a business letter.**
   Tamara Terhoven, who is the European Sales Director at Haverkamp Design AG, Im Teich 24, 41258 Essen, fax (02 01) 22 88 66, tells her secretary, Michaela Förster, to send a fax (today's date) to Mr Humphrey Hill, the Export Manager at Sterling Interiors Ltd, 99 Victoria Promenade, Eastbourne EF6 9KL, England, fax +44 (13 23) 9 87 66. The fax is in reply to Humphrey Hill's recent letter (ref. HH/BK). She also tells her secretary to include 4 more pages of information with the fax. Tamara Terhoven is on friendly terms with Humphrey Hill.

E-mail

6. **Use the layout in Fig. 6 as your model.**

   You work in the European Division of a freight forwarding agency in Hamburg. You receive an e-mail from Carola Montez, who works for a firm in New York, e-mail: delmont@gnn.com. You know Carola from previous correspondence and phone calls. You now reply to this e-mail with a special offer for transport in eastern Europe. Use an American salutation and complimentary close. You send a file, called "tarif.ost" with your e-mail.

Unit 2

Enquiries

Introduction

Anfrage *Kostenvoranschlag Bitte*

<u>Enquiries</u> can be general or specific. A general enquiry may simply be a <u>request</u> for information on a product or service, a quotation, <u>estimate</u> or a credit reference (see Unit 12). A specific enquiry is a request for more detailed information on a particular product or service.

IHK

Botschaften Common sources of companies' addresses are <u>chambers of commerce</u>, banks, <u>embassies</u>, consulates, trade fairs and <u>exhibitions</u>, advertisements in newspapers, *Ausstellung* magazines, trade journals, the Internet, commercial directories, business partners and companies specialising in addresses.

Sometimes governments or local government authorities (municipalities) put contracts out to tender (see Example on page 25). This means companies are invited to submit quotations (tenders). The company with the best tender is then given the contract.

When writing an enquiry use the letter plan to structure your letter, fax or e-mail.

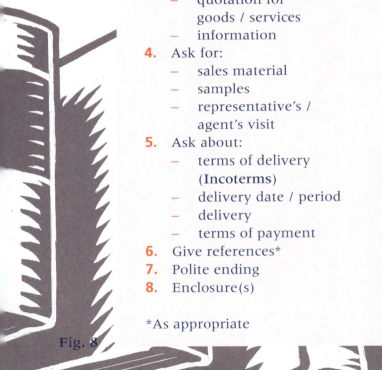

Enquiries

1. Source of address
2. Description of your company
   - reason for enquiry
3. Say what you require:
   - quotation for goods / services
   - information
4. Ask for:
   - sales material
   - samples
   - representative's / agent's visit
5. Ask about:
   - terms of delivery (**Incoterms**)
   - delivery date / period
   - delivery
   - terms of payment
6. Give references*
7. Polite ending
8. Enclosure(s)

*As appropriate

Fig. 8

Sources of address

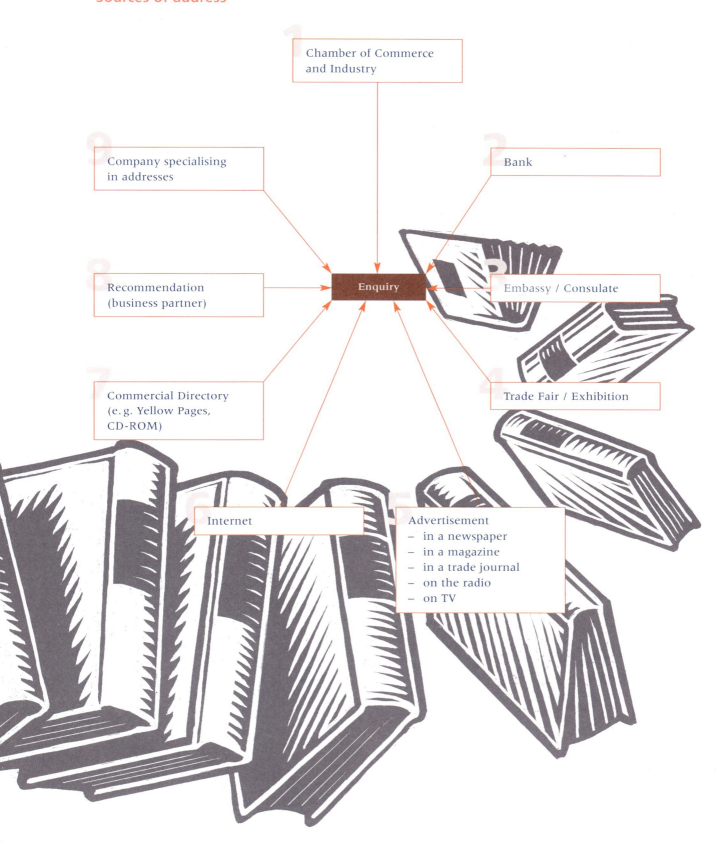

1. Chamber of Commerce and Industry
2. Bank
3. Embassy / Consulate
4. Trade Fair / Exhibition
5. Advertisement
   – in a newspaper
   – in a magazine
   – in a trade journal
   – on the radio
   – on TV
6. Internet
7. Commercial Directory (e.g. Yellow Pages, CD-ROM)
8. Recommendation (business partner)
9. Company specialising in addresses

Enquiry

Specimen Letters

1. General enquiry

DS/RB
21 October ..

Schneider Haushaltswaren GmbH
Bahnhofstr. 98
45277 Essen
Germany

Dear Sir / Madam

402/A Microwave Oven

We recently visited your stand at the Lifestyle Fair in Birmingham and were most impressed by the above-mentioned microwave oven.

As a leading importer of household appliances, with excellent business contacts throughout Britain, we feel that this product will sell well here.

Please send us an illustrated colour brochure, your current export price list and details of your discounts for quantity, cash, early payment and initial orders. Please also state your terms of delivery and payment, indicating delivery times.

Should you require references, the Midland Bank in Oxford will be pleased to provide you with any information you may desire.

We look forward to hearing from you soon.

Yours faithfully
Household Appliances Ltd

Doris Soames
Doris Soames
Purchasing Director

Household Appliances Ltd

13 London Road, Oxford OX2 7XY, England
Tel. +44 (1865) 90 45 33, Fax +44 (1865) 90 45 00,
E-mail: household.ltd@linkall.co.uk

2. General enquiry

From:	Ursula Klein	To:	Mr Chiou Fang Yeh
	Head Buyer		Export Sales Manager
	Neumoden GmbH		Ziang Kong Garments Co. Ltd.
	Düsseldorf		Taipei
	Germany		Taiwan
Fax No.:	+49 (2 11) 89 75 44	Fax No.:	+8 86 (2) 3 92 90 44
Our ref.:	UK/TT	Your ref.:	
Date:	2 February ..	Total pages:	1

Dear Mr Chiou Fang Yeh

<u>Request for offer for "Summer Vogue Fashions"</u>

We have seen your advertisement in the latest edition of "The Rag Trade" and note with interest that your range includes articles for which there is great demand here at present.

Our company is a major distributor of women's fashion clothes based in Düsseldorf, Germany. We supply retailers all over the European Union with quality goods and are now most interested in establishing new links with manufacturers of high-quality products at reasonable prices.

As our stocks of summer lines are now running low, we would be grateful if you would send us an offer for your "Summer Vogue Fashions" garments including a current illustrated colour catalogue, samples, patterns, an export price list including the usual discounts and details of your terms of payment and delivery.

Should you require references on our company, they can be obtained from the Dresdner Bank or Kaufhof AG in Düsseldorf, with whom we have worked closely for many years.

If your offer meets our requirements we will be pleased to place a trial order with you.

We hope to hear from you shortly.

Yours sincerely

Ursula Klein

3. General enquiry to an American supplier

November 1, ..

Gerald J. Thornton, President
Montana Timber Structures Corp.
Corvallis, MO 59828
U.S.A.

Re: Your Advertisement for House Construction Kits
     in the "HomeBuilder" of September 23, ..

Dear Mr. Thornton:

We have seen the above-mentioned advertisement and would be most grateful
if you would let us have further information on the following points:
a)   What wood is used to construct American-style wooden frame houses?
     Is it locally grown or imported into the US? Our company would not accept
     wood from tropical rain forests.
b)   What varnishes are used? As a result of strict environmental regulations
     here we would need a complete break-down of any or all the chemicals
     used to treat all building materials.
c)   What are your terms of delivery and delivery periods? Would you be
     prepared to ship to a German port (e.g. CIF Hamburg)?
d)   Would you be able to send personnel over from Montana to build a model
     frame house to show to our customers?
Please quote us your most favourable export prices including all discounts and
let us have full details of your terms of payment.

Many thanks in advance for your attention to our enquiry.

Sincerely,

Thomas Hermann
Thomas Hermann
Purchasing Manager

TH:FK

4. Invitation to tender

A major American corporation is opening a huge new theme park called "Never Never Land" in Bavaria. As there is a large amount of construction work to be done it places advertisements in European publications including "The Civil Engineer", a trade journal for the construction industry, inviting civil engineering companies to submit tenders for the work to be carried out.

The Civil Engineer	Classified Advertisements	January ..

Astra Theme Parks Corporation
1000 Second Avenue, Suite 485
New York, NY 10022
U.S.A.

Invitation to tender

Tenders are invited for work to be carried out to construct the "Never Never Land" theme park in Bavaria, Germany.

This is a unique project and necessitates work and workmanship performed to the highest standards. The construction phase is expected to last three years, beginning June .., and will involve an estimated 300 contractors co-ordinated by and accountable to "Theme Park Logistics Inc", who will have overall responsibility for the acceptance and punctual completion of all contract work.

Companies submitting tenders must be able to operate in an environment where English is the official language of communication in both spoken and written form.

Contractors submitting tenders must:
– be a company registered in the European Union,
– supply evidence of the successful completion of at least one similar large-scale construction project to date,
– be able to complete work contracted for in time for the opening of the theme park in May ..

Tender documents may be obtained from the above address or from our German agent, in Bavaria:

Dr. Eugen Waldmeister
TT Bauprojekt GmbH
Amalienstr. 20
80333 München
Germany

A non-refundable charge of $100 will be made for documentation.

Tenders must reach our New York Headquarters by 12.00 noon on April 30, ..

The Astra Theme Parks Corporation does not commit itself to accepting the lowest or any of the tenders submitted.

Tel: +1 (2 12) 3 55-44 08 / Fax: +1 (2 12) 3 55-44 99 / E-mail: astratheme@corp.com / http://www.astra.com

Case Study

You are Andrea Link, the Import Manager at Möbelimport Schulz GmbH, Kupfer-dreher Str. 99, 45257 Essen, tel. + (02 01) 43 45 99, fax + (02 01) 44 45 00, e-mail: moebel.schulz.essen@aol.com. Your company started off as a small business, quickly grew larger and now imports furniture of all types, which it sells to major trading partners all over Germany. At the moment it is looking for office furniture for the German market.

At the recent "Modern Office" Exhibition at the National Exhibition Centre in Birmingham, England, you saw some of the furniture made by "Office Style Manufacturing UK", Toxteth Business Park, Liverpool LO3 8LJ, tel. +44 (1 51) 89 77 75, fax +44 (1 51) 89 77 44, e-mail: office.style@firmnet.uk. You also talked to Eileen Conway, Office Style's Export Sales Manager. Having now also looked at the company's web site on the Internet you decide to contact them and ask for further information.

Activity

Using the "**Enquiries** Letter Plan" on page 20, the "**Enquiries** Standard Expressions" table and the Phraseology section (in *Satzbausteine*), write Andrea's letter / fax / e-mail to Office Style Manufacturing UK.

Fill in the "Enquiry Form" provided on Office Style's web site below to write your e-mail. Add further details as appropriate.

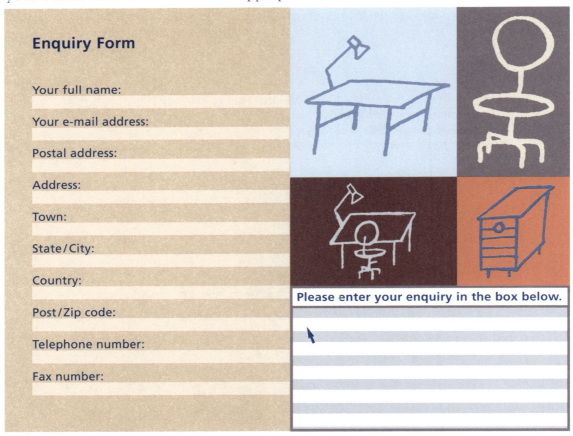

Enquiry Form

Your full name:

Your e-mail address:

Postal address:

Address:

Town:

State / City:

Country:

Post / Zip code:

Telephone number:

Fax number:

Please enter your enquiry in the box below.

Language

Use the "**Enquiries** Standard Expressions" table to find the words missing below.

1. **Verbs + nouns**
    Which verbs go with the following nouns?
    a. "Please ▨▨ us your lowest price."
    b. "If your services ▨▨ our requirements …"
    c. "If your goods ▨▨ our customers' expectations …"
    d. "If your products ▨▨ our approval …"

2. **Verbs + prepositions / particles**
    Which prepositions / particles go with the following verbs?
    a. to refer someone ▨▨ a company
    b. to pass an address ▨▨ a company (2 words)
    c. to name someone ▨▨ a reference
    d. to act ▨▨ an agent
    e. to quote a customer ▨▨ a product
    f. "We have no more steel" – "We have run ▨▨ steel" (2 words)
    g. "We must point ▨▨ that …"
    h. to correspond ▨▨
    i. to supply a customer ▨▨ a product
    j. to provide a customer ▨▨ a product
    k. to visit – to call ▨▨

3. **Nouns + prepositions / prepositions + nouns / adjectives + prepositions**
    a. an agent ▨▨
    b. a quotation ▨▨
    c. an offer ▨▨ (not "of")
    d. demand ▨▨
    e. interest ▨▨
    f. information ▨▨
    g. ▨▨ the Ideal Home Exhibition
    h. ▨▨ the Internet
    i. ▨▨ demand
    j. ▨▨ the moment
    k. ▨▨ a sale-or-return basis
    l. ▨▨ approval
    m. ▨▨ 30 June (i. e. "no later than 30 June")
    n. ▨▨ 3 weeks (i. e. "in no later than 3 weeks' time")
    o. ▨▨ our premises
    p. ▨▨ stock
    q. ▨▨ receipt of the goods
    r. "We are now low ▨▨ materials"
    s. "We are out ▨▨ soft drinks"

4. **Adjectives / adjectival phrases + nouns**
   a. Which adjective describing services means "You can be sure that we will come and do the work"?
   b. Which adjective means "on time"?
   c. Give 2 adjectives to mean a "big" company.
   d. Give 2 adjectives to mean "big" demand.
   e. Give 2 adjectives (hyphenated) to mean "of the best quality".
   f. Give 2 adjectives to mean a "big" order
   g. your whole range – your ▓▓ range
   h. "Please let us have all the details you have of …" – "Please let us have ▓▓ details of …"
   i. Give an expression to mean "up-to-date"
   j. a first order – an ▓▓ order
   k. a special discount for a new product – an ▓▓ offer discount
   l. your lowest prices – your most ▓▓ prices
   m. Give 2 adjectives to describe packing.

1 Listening

Marianne Baumann works for Topshop Fashion KG in Düsseldorf. She notices an interesting advertisement in a trade journal, so she calls a number in Taiwan to ask for further details.

Listen to the dialogue and answer the following questions.

Questions
1. What trade journal has the Taiwan Trading Company placed an advertisement in?
2. What is Topshop looking for?
3. How does the Taiwan Trading Company know what to manufacture for the customer?
4. How many units does Topshop want to buy?
5. What are Chiou Fang Yeh's two offers?
6. When can they guarantee to deliver the order?
7. What are the Taiwan Trading Company's terms of payment?

Activity
Write a summary of the dialogue in German to be given to your boss, Herr Scheider, the Purchasing Manager.

Telephone Role Play

Rolle A

Sie sind Bianca (Elmar) Schmidt und arbeiten für Junge Kleidermoden GmbH, Wielandstr. 98, 50968 Köln, Tel. +49 (2 21) 89 10 34. Rufen Sie die Firma Leisurewear Ltd. in Dublin, Irland, an und berücksichtigen Sie dabei folgende Punkte:

- Sie haben den Prospekt von Leisurewear Ltd. auf Anfrage vom British Council in Köln bekommen
- Sie interessieren sich insbesondere für junge Freizeitmode
- Bitte um umgehende Zusendung des Gesamtkatalogs
- Gleichzeitig benötigen Sie die Preise mit Nachlässen für Großbestellungen
- Können Richtpreise (*an indication of the prices*) gegeben werden?
- Ab welchen Mengen gibt es Großhandelsrabatte?
- Lieferfristen?
- Können Sie Muster bekommen?
- Sie möchten die Zusendung des Hauptkatalogs abwarten und lassen dann von sich hören.

Role B

You are Susan (Jeremy) Saunders and work in the Sales Department of Leisurewear Ltd. in Dublin. When Bianca (Elmar) Schmidt phones, you take the call. Include the following points in your conversation:

- You ask Bianca (Elmar) Schmidt where they got your company's name from
- You have such a wide variety of products that you think it would be better to send the company's complete catalogue
- You have an ex works price list in euros
- FOB prices would be approx. 10 % more
- A quantity discount (10 %) is granted on orders for more than 1,000 euros, 20 % as from 2,000 euros

Delivery:

- for orders up to for 100 articles 4 weeks
- for orders for 1,000 articles 8 weeks
- for orders for more than 1,000 articles 12 weeks
- patterns and samples can be sent at any time.

Aufgaben

1.

Name	Eigener Name	–
Position	Einkaufsleiter/in	–
Firma	Hoffmann AG	Jeremy Boulster Ltd
Anschrift	Münsterwalder Straße 11–15, 12651 Berlin, Germany	P.O. Box 110593, London W1M 7DA, England
Fax	+49 (30) 5 49 61 03	+44 (1 71) 23 90
E-Mail	hoffmann.ag@aol.com	boulster.ltd@firmnet.co.uk

Geschäftsfall:
Die Firma Hoffmann AG hat von der IHK London den Namen der britischen Firma Jeremy Boulster Ltd erhalten, die sich auf die Lieferung von Sherry spezialisiert hat.

Aufgabe:
Schicken Sie als Einkaufsleiter/in von Hoffmann der Boulster Ltd eine Anfrage und berücksichtigen Sie dabei folgende Punkte:
– Vorstellung Ihres Unternehmens (langjährig bei deutschen Kunden eingeführt)
– Interesse besonders an dem Sherry „Old England" zum Einkaufspreis von 2,50 £ pro Flasche. Ab welchen Mengen gibt es Sondernachlässe?
– Welche Lieferzeit hat Boulster?
– Kann der Sherry bei Abnahme von mindestens 30 Kisten à 12 Flaschen auch frei Haus geliefert werden?
– Zahlungsbedingungen?
– Referenzen können auf Wunsch gestellt werden.

2.

Name	Eigener Name	–
Position	Einkaufsleiter/in	The Export Director
Firma	Textilimport GmbH	Woolware Inc
Anschrift	Postfach 395860, 90776 Fürth, Germany	1480 Granville St., Vancouver, BC, Canada V6C 1T2
Fax	+49 (9 11) 20 78 19	+1 (6 04) 2 30-38 04
E-Mail	textilimport.gmbh@t-online.de	woolware.inc@linkall.com

Geschäftsfall:
Die deutsche Firma Textilimport GmbH hat in einem Prospekt Wollwaren der kanadischen Firma Woolware Inc gesehen. Sie interessiert sich für deren Produkte.

Aufgabe:

Schreiben Sie als Importleiter/in der Textilimport GmbH eine allgemeine Anfrage an den Exportleiter der Woolware Inc. unter Berücksichtigung folgender Punkte:

–   Vorstellung Ihres Unternehmens (Importeur von Damen-, Herren- und Kinder-Strickwaren aus aller Welt; großer Kundenstamm in der EU)
–   Bitte um Übersendung eines umfassenden Katalogs mit Angabe von Großhandelspreisen
–   Generelle Lieferzeiten? Zahlungsbedingungen?
–   Lagerbestand (wie schnell kann in dringenden Fällen eine „last minute order" erteilt werden?)
–   Referenzen auf Wunsch.

3.

Name	Cindy (Jeremy) Patterson	–
Position	(pp.) Franz Böttcher Einkaufsleiter	–
Firma	Radewald Photographisches Zubehör, GmbH & Co. KG	Japanese City Office
Anschrift	Beethovenstraße 93, 24943 Flensburg, Germany	5th floor, Yoyogi 2-chome, Shibuya-ku, Tokyo 151, Japan
Fax	+49 (461) 4 09 17 83	+81 (3) 45 85-59 94
E-Mail	radewald.photo@t-online.de	jap.city.office@nipponweb.com

Geschäftsfall:

Die japanische Firma Japanese City Office in Tokio stellt Kameras und Videorecorder her und hat weltweit in Zeitungen dafür geworben.

Aufgabe:

Sie sind Cindy (Jeremy) Patterson und arbeiten für den deutschen Importeur Radewald Photographisches Zubehör in Flensburg. Schreiben Sie im Auftrag Ihres Importleiters Franz Böttcher eine Anfrage an die japanische Firma und fragen Sie u. a. nach folgenden Einzelheiten:

–   Sie sind zunächst nur an einem allgemeinen Angebot der gesamten Produktpalette des japanischen Unternehmens interessiert
–   Wo können die Kameras und Videorecorder in Europa getestet werden? Referenzen?
–   Hat die japanische Firma schon eine Kontaktadresse in Deutschland?
–   Wie und wo kann man Kontakt aufnehmen?
–   Wird ein Vertreter der Firma in absehbarer Zeit nach Deutschland kommen?
–   Preise und Prospektmaterial werden erbeten.

4.

Name	Gaby (Richard) Brauchmüller	–
Position	Sachbearbeiter/in Einkauf	–
Firma	Kosmetikfirma Marschall & Höpfner KG	Cosmetics Ltd
Anschrift	Postfach 70 30 89, 70523 Stuttgart, Germany	28 Merivale Road, London SW15 2NW, England
Fax	+49 (7 11) 23 90 81	+44 (1 71) 5 49 82 70
E-Mail	marschall.hoepfner.kg@linkall.de	cosmetics.ltd@tradelink.com.uk

Geschäftsfall:

Sie sind Gaby (Richard) Brauchmüller und arbeiten im Einkauf der deutschen Kosmetikfirma Marschall & Höpfner KG in Stuttgart. Sie haben in der Illustrierten *Health and Bodycare* einen Artikel über das neue, besonders hautfreundliche Parfum „Juliette" gelesen, das von der britischen Firma Cosmetics Ltd vertrieben wird.

Aufgabe:

Ihr Chef bittet Sie, eine diesbezügliche Anfrage an den britischen Hersteller zu richten. Sie sollen dabei folgende Punkte berücksichtigen:

– In welchen Mengen und Verpackungen ist das Parfüm erhältlich?
– Gibt es Photos oder Prospekte von Geschenkpackungen?
– Preise? Mengenrabatte?
– Hat man bereits erste Erfahrungen über Kundenreaktionen? Ggf. welche?
– Werden Verkaufsförderungskampagnen (*sales promotion campaigns*) finanziell unterstützt? Wenn ja, auf welche Weise?
– Bitte um Zusendung von detailliertem Prospektmaterial.

Offers Unit 3

Introduction

When writing an offer use the letter plan to structure your letter, fax or e-mail. If you are writing in reply to an enquiry (solicited offer) you will need most or all 12 parts. If you are writing a sales letter to a company (unsolicited offer) leave out part 1 (Reference to enquiry).

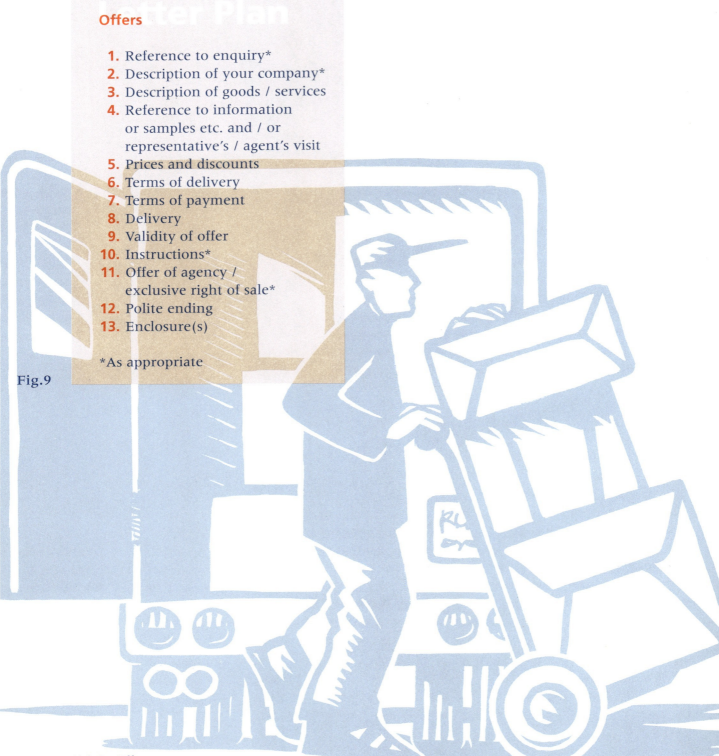

Letter Plan

Offers

1. Reference to enquiry*
2. Description of your company*
3. Description of goods / services
4. Reference to information or samples etc. and / or representative's / agent's visit
5. Prices and discounts
6. Terms of delivery
7. Terms of payment
8. Delivery
9. Validity of offer
10. Instructions*
11. Offer of agency / exclusive right of sale*
12. Polite ending
13. Enclosure(s)

*As appropriate

Fig.9

Specimen Letters

1. General offer in reply to a fax (solicited offer)

Stecker Süßwaren
Deutschland GmbH
Ringstr. 88
012607 Dresden
Germany
Tel +49 (3 51) 7 68 34
Fax +49 (3 51) 7 68 34

Your ref. MS/hh
Our ref. HvJ/sva
20 November ..

Ms Miranda Sweeney
Purchasing Director
Sweetmate Ltd
8 Coppergate
YORK
YO1 1NR
England

Dear Ms Sweeney

Your Fax Enquiry dated 19 November .. regarding Confectionery

Many thanks for the above-mentioned enquiry, in which you ask for information on our entire range of confectionery products.

We are a well-established supplier of all types of confectionery with an extensive sales network and an excellent reputation both at home and abroad. Please refer to the enclosed export price list for details of our rates. Our prices are quoted CIF UK port, and are inclusive of packing. Our usual terms of payment are 10 days 2 %, 30 days net, subject to favourable references and deliveries can be made from stock.

We very much hope that our offer is to your liking and look forward to doing business with you.

Yours sincerely
Stecker Süßwaren Deutschland GmbH

Henrietta von Jauch

Henrietta von Jauch
European Sales Director

Enc:
1 Export price list

2. Specific offer for wine (solicited offer)

Your ref. JM/MM
Our ref. IK/HT
June 10, ..

Mr. John Massecar, Head Buyer
Famous Wines and Liquors Inc
Western Boulevard
San Antonio, TX 75261
U.S.A.

Dear Mr. Massecar:

We were delighted to receive your enquiry of 2 June .. about Mariahof Spätlese –
the latest addition to our range of fine wines. As a major producer in the Mosel
region with extensive business contacts throughout the European Union and
beyond we have been producing a choice selection of top-grade wines for the
past 75 years. We enclose a leaflet on Mariahof Spätlese together with sales
literature on the rest of our range of products. We will be pleased to supply you
with samples if requested. We also offer advertising material free of charge to
help customers introduce our products to the local market.

The current wholesale price for a case of 12 × 0.7 l bottles of Mariahof Spätlese
is 60 euros, excluding taxes. New customers are granted a discount of 20%
on initial orders exceeding 20 cases or worth more than 1,000 euros. Please
refer to the enclosed export price list for further details regarding the rest of
our products.

Our prices are quoted FOB German port. Special quotations are available on
request.

Our terms are cash with order or 10 days 2%, 30 days net on receipt of our
invoice subject to favourable references. Deliveries can be made within 7 days
after receipt of order while stocks last.

This offer is valid for 30 days and we would ask you to quote the article
numbers of the wines required when placing an order. Please do not hesitate
to contact us if you require further details. We look forward to receiving
your order.

Sincerely yours,

Ingo Kornharpen

Ingo Kornharpen
Sales Manager

Enclosures

3. Fax reply to an enquiry (solicited offer)

From:	Astrid Michelbach	To:	Ms Loretta Marx
	Sole Proprietor		Purchasing Manager
	Schmuck Manufaktur OHG		Universal Gifts and
	Gelsenkirchen		Jewellery Ltd
	Germany		Plymouth, UK
Fax:	+44 (2 09) 49 29 94	Fax:	+44 (17 52) 82 34 50
Our ref.:	Mi/38	Your ref.:	LM/tt
Date:	26 June ..	Total pages:	1

Dear Loretta

Many thanks for your telephone enquiry of 20 June regarding our new "Highlight" line of accessories for evening wear.

I'm sending you some samples by separate post together with some leaflets on most of the range.

Please refer to the price list with the samples for all details including shipping arrangements, discounts and terms of delivery.

Our terms of payment would be CWO for a trial order, these terms to be reviewed in three months' time if you do regular business with us.

Deliveries can be made from stock, subject to availability.

There has been heavy demand for this article recently so we recommend you place your order soon while stocks last.

Please remember to quote the article nos. so we can process it as quickly as possible.

We look forward to doing business with you.

Yours sincerely

Astrid Michelbach

4. Sales letter (unsolicited offer)

MM/HJ
10 April ..

Mr Thomas Hughes
Managing Director
Cryer Craft Furniture Ltd
48 Farriers Lane
HARROGATE
HA3 9IJ
England

Dear Mr Hughes

As a fast-growing freight forwarding company with depots all over the European mainland we will soon be opening a freight forwarding service in your area. Our company provides a reliable and comprehensive 24-hour delivery service at rock-bottom prices for all types of goods.

We are sending you enclosed our latest catalogue containing details of our entire range of services. Our Northern England representative, Mr Arthur Pickles, will be pleased to call by and draw up a profile of your company's freight forwarding needs if requested. He will be telephoning you in the next few days.

Please refer to the enclosed export price list for details of our rates. All prices are quoted exclusive of packing, import duty, and duties of any nature but inclusive of airport taxes. Substantial discounts are granted on regular orders as are trade discounts for business customers. Special quotations for desk-to-desk, special messenger or rush deliveries are, of course, available on request. Our usual terms of payment are 7 days net by transfer to our account at a British bank. UK deliveries can be made within 24 hours after receipt of goods at a British depot. For Continental (EU) deliveries please refer to the enclosed sales literature. This offer is without engagement and subject to confirmation.

We look forward to doing business with you in the near future and feel sure you will be favourably impressed by our prompt and professional service.

Yours sincerely
Cargo International GmbH

Michaela Mai

Michaela Mai
Freight Logistics Co-ordinator UK

Encs

5. Tender

Our ref: Sch.47
April 10, ..

Astra Theme Parks Corporation
1000 Second Avenue, Suite 485
New York, NY 10022
U.S.A.

**Tender for Construction of Sub-aqua Zoo in "Never Never Land"
Theme Park, Bavaria, Germany**

Ladies and Gentlemen:

Our company has studied the documentation provided detailing work
specifications, materials, completion schedules and costing for the
construction of the sub-aqua zoo and has pleasure in enclosing its tender.

For your information we also include illustrated documentation on
previous similar projects undertaken by us on behalf of other companies
in Europe and North America and a list of our major clients over the
past five years.

Any of the clients listed will be pleased to provide you with a reference,
as will our bank, the Dresdner Bank in Bremen.

We hope that our tender will prove acceptable to you and look forward
to hearing from you in the near future.

Sincerely yours,

Walter Schleutke

Walter Schleutke
Managing Director

8 Enclosures:
1 tender
1 list of clients
6 brochures

Case Study

Martina Hensch is the European Sales Director at Designer Mode GmbH, Bahnhofstr. 110, 45128 Essen, fax +49 (2 01) 99 87 69. Her company markets clothes for young people in boutiques all over Germany and the rest of Europe. Designer Mode advertises in all the well-known European newspapers, has a stand at all the major trade fairs and puts on presentations at fashion shows all over Europe.

The company also has a home page with an e-mail address on the Internet and when Martina checks the company's latest e-mails she finds enquiries from countries all over Europe, including the one shown from TopFit Ltd.

Martina now puts together an offer to be sent to all the firms that have enquired about Designer Mode's clothes. She sends some information as printed matter by separate post and decides to have Maxine van Ahlen, Designer Mode's agent in England, call on TopFit in the next few days.

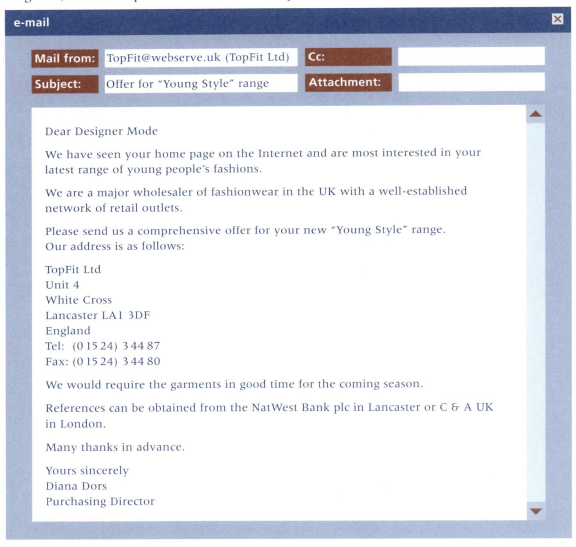

e-mail

Mail from: TopFit@webserve.uk (TopFit Ltd)   **Cc:**

Subject: Offer for "Young Style" range   **Attachment:**

Dear Designer Mode

We have seen your home page on the Internet and are most interested in your latest range of young people's fashions.

We are a major wholesaler of fashionwear in the UK with a well-established network of retail outlets.

Please send us a comprehensive offer for your new "Young Style" range.
Our address is as follows:

TopFit Ltd
Unit 4
White Cross
Lancaster LA1 3DF
England
Tel: (0 15 24) 3 44 87
Fax: (0 15 24) 3 44 80

We would require the garments in good time for the coming season.

References can be obtained from the NatWest Bank plc in Lancaster or C & A UK in London.

Many thanks in advance.

Yours sincerely
Diana Dors
Purchasing Director

Activity

Using the "**Offers** Letter Plan" on page 34, the "**Offers** Standard Expressions" table and Phraseology section, write Martina's letter / fax / e-mail to TopFit Ltd. Add further details as appropriate.

Language

Use the "**Offers** Standard Expressions" table to find the words missing below.

1. Verbs + nouns
   Which verbs go with the following nouns?
   a. to ▩ an order (i. e. to order something)
   b. to ▩ an order (i. e. to work on an order)
   c. to send goods – to ▩ goods
   d. to ▩ a discount
   e. to ▩ the catalogue number
   f. to ▩ your expectations
   g. to ▩ an appointment

2. Verbs + prepositions / particles
   Which prepositions / particles go with the following verbs?
   a. to enquire ▩
   b. to refer ▩
   c. to provide someone ▩ something

3. Nouns + prepositions / prepositions + nouns / adjectives + prepositions
   a. your stand ▩ the trade fair
   b. information ▩ our products
   c. a retailer ▩ household appliances
   d. an agent ▩ household appliances
   e. a query ▩
   f. ▩ a competitive price
   g. ▩ separate cover
   h. ▩ the same post
   i. ▩ separate post
   j. You will hear from us ▩ the end of the month (not "at").
   k. You will hear from us ▩ the next few days (not "in").
   l. The price is 50 euros ▩ unit.
   m. All prices are exclusive ▩ VAT.
   n. ▩ your information
   o. demand ▩ a product
   p. eligible ▩ credit terms

4. Adjectives / adjectival phrases + nouns
   a. Give 3 adjectives to describe a manufacturer positively
      (Some are hyphenated).
   b. a ▨ range of goods
   c. What 2 adjectives can be used to mean "the best" goods?
   d. Give 2 adjectives (one is hyphenated) used to mean low prices.
   e. a large order – a ▨ order
   f. a test order – a ▨ order
   g. "There is strong competition" – "Competition is ▨ "

5. Delivery
   a. Give two expressions to mean "straight away".
   b. Which expression means: "Your catalogue will not be posted to you
      in the same envelope."?

6. Further points
   a. ▨ printed matter
   b. The garments cost 50 euros ▨.
   c. "If the goods are not sold" – "▨ the goods being unsold". (2 words)
   d. Give 2 other words to mean "in another country".
   e. "If your references are favourable" – "▨ your references being favourable".
      (2 words)
   f. "We buy goods in large quantities and sell them to trade customers in large
      quantities." – "We ▨ goods."
   g. "We buy goods in large quantities and sell them to the customers who come
      into our shops." – "We ▨ goods."
   h. "Our advertising materials cost nothing – they are ▨ ". (3 words)

Background information

Discounts

Activity

What discounts could be granted in the following situations?
 1. The customer pays for the goods when ordering them.
 2. The customer places an order for a completely new product.
 3. A customer places his first order for a product.
 4. A customer pays within a week of receiving the goods.
 5. A customer orders a large amount.
 6. A dealer buys goods from another dealer.
 7. A manufacturer puts a new product on the market.
 8. A wholesaler wants to encourage a retailer to place a trial order.
 9. A producer wants to make his customers place larger orders.
10. One business sells a new product to another business for the first time.

Incoterms® 2010

The Incoterms® (International Commercial Terms) define the rights and obligations of the buyer and the seller as regards transport and insurance. They also indicate when the responsibility for the goods is passed on from the seller to the buyer (passing of risk). They are regularly revised by the International Chamber of Commerce in Paris.

The last revision of the Incoterms® took place in 2010. There are now 11 clauses, of which 7 (1–7 below) can be used for all kinds of transport and 4 (8–11 below) only apply to transport by sea or inland waterways. Each Incoterm® consists of 3 capital letters (an abbreviation of the English version) and must be followed by either a place or point. They distinguish between the *place of delivery*, where the risk of loss or damage passes from the seller to the buyer, and the place of destination, which is the place or port to which the carriage has been paid for by the seller. For the clauses CPT, CIP, CFR and CIF, the place of destination differs from the place of delivery.

1. EXW (ex works)
The seller makes the goods available at his premises.

2. FCA (free carrier)
The seller pays the transport costs and bears the risk until the goods have been delivered into the custody of the first carrier.

3. CPT (carriage paid to …)
The seller pays the transport costs up to the named destination. He bears the risk until the goods have been delivered into the custody of the first carrier.

4. CIP (carriage and insurance paid to …)
The seller pays the transport costs, including transport insurance, up to the named destination. He bears the risk until the goods have been delivered into the custody of the first carrier.

INCOTERMS® 2010

RULES FOR ANY MODE OR MODES OF TRANSPORT

	SELLER	LOADING	CONTRACT OF CARRIAGE	EXPORT CLEARANCE	PORT OF SHIPMENT TERMINAL / PLACE
EXW – EX WORKS (named place of delivery)		BUYER	BUYER	BUYER	
FCA – FREE CARRIER (named place of delivery)		SELLER	BUYER	SELLER	
CPT – CARRIAGE PAID TO (named place of delivery)		SELLER	SELLER	SELLER	
CIP – COST AND INSURANCE PAID TO (named place of delivery)		SELLER	SELLER	SELLER	
DAP – DELIVERED AT PLACE (named place of destination)		SELLER	SELLER	SELLER	
DAT – DELIVERED AT TERMINAL (named terminal at port or place of destination)		SELLER	SELLER	SELLER	
DDP – DELIVERED DUTY PAID (named place of destination)		SELLER	SELLER	SELLER	

RULES FOR SEA AND INLAND WATERWAY TRANSPORT

	SELLER	LOADING	CONTRACT OF CARRIAGE	EXPORT CLEARANCE	PORT OF SHIPMENT
FAS – FREE ALONGSIDE SHIP (named port of shipment)		SELLER	BUYER	SELLER	
FOB – FREE ON BOARD (named port of shipment)		SELLER	BUYER	SELLER	
CFR – COST AND FREIGHT (named port of destination)		SELLER	SELLER	SELLER	
CIF – COST INSURANCE FREIGHT (named port of destination)		SELLER	SELLER	SELLER	

COSTS
RISKS

5. DAP (delivered at place)
The seller makes the goods available ready to be unloaded at the named place of destination. He bears the risk until the goods have reached this place, before they are unloaded.

6. DAT (delivered at terminal)
The seller makes the goods available unloaded at a named terminal, which can be any place, e.g. a quay, warehouse, container depot, etc.)

7. DDP (delivery duty paid)
The seller pays all costs, including customs duty, and bears the risk until the goods have been delivered to the buyer.

8. FAS (free alongside ship)
The seller pays the transport costs up to the port of shipment. He bears the risk until the goods have been delivered alongside the ship.

< MAIN CARRIAGE >	PORT OF DESTINATION / TERMINAL / PLACE	IMPORT CLEARANCE	UNLOADING	BUYER
		BUYER	BUYER	
		BUYER	BUYER	
		BUYER	BUYER	
		BUYER	BUYER	
		BUYER	BUYER	
		BUYER	SELLER	
		SELLER	BUYER	

< MAIN CARRIAGE >	PORT OF DESTINATION	IMPORT CLEARANCE	UNLOADING	BUYER
		BUYER	BUYER	
		BUYER	BUYER	
		BUYER	BUYER	
		BUYER	BUYER	

9. FOB (free on board)
The seller pays the transport costs up to the port of shipment. He bears the risk until the goods have been loaded on board the vessel at the port of shipment.

10. CFR (cost and freight)
The seller pays the transport costs up to the port of destination. He bears the risk until the goods have been loaded on board the vessel at the port of shipment.

11. CIF (cost, insurance, freight)
The seller pays the transport costs, including marine insurance, up to the port of destination. He bears the risk until the goods have been loaded on board the vessel at the port of shipment.

Activities

Look at the diagram on pages 44 and 45 and the definitions to answer these questions.

1. Risk

Which Incoterms® are meant in the following cases? There is sometimes more than one answer.

The seller bears the risk until:

a. the goods have arrived at the named terminal of destination and are unloaded
b. the goods have arrived at the named place of destination where they must be unloaded by the buyer
c. the goods have been delivered alongside the ship in the port of shipment
d. the goods have been delivered into the custody of the carrier
e. the goods have been delivered to the buyer's premises
f. the goods have been loaded on board the ship in the port of shipment
g. the goods are made available at the seller's premises

2. Transport (freight) costs

Which Incoterms® are meant in the following cases? There is sometimes more than one answer.

The seller pays freight costs until:

a. the goods have arrived at the port of shipment
b. the goods have been delivered into the custody of the carrier
c. the goods arrive at the named terminal of destination and are unloaded
d. the goods arrive at the named place of destination ready to be unloaded
e. the goods have arrived at the port of destination
f. the goods arrive at the named destination
g. the goods arrive at the buyer's premises

3. Recommend suitable Incoterms® and state an appropriate destination in the following cases. Give reasons for your choice.

a. A German exporter has to send goods to the USA by ship but is only prepared to pay for goods to be sent to a German port and no further.
b. A German manufacturer is not prepared to pay any transport or delivery costs at all.
c. A European exporter has a contract for goods to be sent to Marseille/France but he only wants to deliver and unload them at a terminal named by the buyer.
d. A German exporter with a contract to supply goods by ship to Ireland is prepared to accept the transport costs and bear the risk up to a continental port of shipment (e.g. Brest in France) and after that will pay for the transportation of the goods to an Irish port. He is not prepared to accept the costs of having them insured for the sea voyage.
e. A German company is prepared to accept all costs for a consignment of goods to be delivered to a company in Taiwan, but expects the customer to collect and unload the goods at the Airport in Taipei.
f. A German company flies goods to Toronto Airport in Canada. It is only prepared to bear the risk in Germany but pays for transportation of the consignment, excluding insurance all the way to Canada.

g. A German company sells goods to a Moroccan customer in Tangier. The Moroccan customer requires the German supplier to have the goods sent by ship, bear all risks and pay all costs, including unloading costs, at the port of Tangier, where the customer will clear them through customs at the terminal in Tangier.

h. A German manufacturer in Essen decides that he will only pay transport costs and bear the risks for a consignment of goods to France until the goods have been collected by the local depot of the Deutsche Bahn AG.

i. An American customer wants his German supplier to ship the goods to the port of Norfolk, Virginia, via Hamburg. He requires the German company to pay for transportation to the USA and arrange for the goods to be insured during the sea trip.

j. A New Zealand company requires a German company to supply a consignment of goods to its works in Wellington, New Zealand, and bear all the costs and the risks involved.

k. A Russian company has a contract with a German company which provides for delivery of a consignment of goods to the Russian port of St. Petersburg. The German supplier has to bear all costs and risks until the goods have reached the port but does not have to unload the goods or pay Russian customs duties on them.

l. A Scottish company buys goods from a German supplier. The contract provides for the goods to be sent to Edinburgh by multi-modal transport at the German company's expense. The German company only bears the risk until the goods have been collected by a local freight forwarder but pays for the consignment to be insured all the way to Edinburgh.

Listening

2   First read the questions with this exercise then listen to the following two dialogues between a German company called Hammer Heimwerkerbedarf in Essen and an overseas supplier.

After the first dialogue answer the questions for offer 1 by Paisley Electronics Ltd, Belfast, Northern Ireland. After the second dialogue answer the same questions for Datatech Incorporated, USA.

Questions

1. Product name / number
2. Power supply
3. Terms of delivery
4. Normal trade price
5. Terms of payment
6. Quantity discount
7. Final price per unit (in euros) for the quantity required
8. Delivery

Now listen again and do the following:

1. Compare the two Incoterms here from the point of view of Hammer Heimwerkerbedarf in Essen.
2. Explain which of the two offers you would accept and why.

Activity

Write Silke's summary of the two dialogues in German for her boss, Frau Köhnen, the Head of Purchasing.

Telephone Role Play

Rolle A

Sie sind Lucy (Michael) Kemper und arbeiten für die Firma Ambrosius-Speisen GmbH in München, Tel. +49 (89) 18 76 49, Fax +49 (89) 18 76 00. Ihr Chef bittet Sie, die Firma Seafood Ltd. in Southend-on-Sea in folgender Angelegenheit anzurufen:

- Sie haben eine Anzeige von Seafood Ltd in der Zeitung gelesen
- Besonders interessieren Sie die Angebote für geräucherten irischen Lachs (*smoked Irish salmon*)
- Wie groß sind die jeweiligen Großhandelspackungen?
- Liefer- und Zahlungsbedingungen?
- Kann frei Haus (Lager München) geliefert werden?
- Ist optimale Kühlung garantiert?
- Mengenrabatte? Großhandelsrabatte?

Role B

You work in the Export Section at Seafood Ltd, 99 Hornby Road, Southend-on-Sea SS9 8GH, England, tel. +44 (17 02) 45 07, fax +44 (17 02) 4 50 00. When a prospective German customer rings give her / him the following information:

- Ask what part of Germany she / he is phoning from
- Say your Irish salmon is the best on the market and very cheap at the moment – only 5 euros 50 per kilo.
- It's sold in 10 or 20 kg boxes
- Cash with order for new customers. Terms are reviewed if regular orders are placed
- Delivery can be made franco to the customer's premises
- Refrigeration is guaranteed by Fastfish Ltd freight forwarders in Dover
- Quantity discount (10 %) granted for orders for more than 500 kg
- All prices quoted are trade prices.

Aufgaben

1.

Name	Helmut Tannerbauer	Messrs Johnson & Remington
Position	Firmeninhaber	–
Firma	Weinbau Tannerbauer OHG	–
Anschrift	Weinbergallee 90–92, 67435 Neustadt an der Weinstraße	30 Blackhill Road, Manchester MA4 1HQ, England
Fax	+49 (63 21) 4 48 79	+44 (161) 3 32 89 45
E-Mail	tannerbauer.ohg@aol.com	john.rem@firmnet.co.uk

Geschäftsfall:
Messrs. Johnson & Remington in England importieren seit vielen Jahren Weine aus Deutschland. In der englischen Fachzeitschrift *The Decanter* hat der deutsche Weinhändler und Firmeninhaber, Helmut Tannerbauer, ein entsprechendes Gesuch der britischen Firma gelesen.

Aufgabe:
Richten Sie an Johnson & Remington ein Angebot Ihres Pfälzer Weines (*wine from the Palatinate*) unter Berücksichtigung folgender Punkte:
– Bezug auf Anzeige
– Kurzbeschreibung Ihrer Firma
– Beschreibung Ihres Produkts
– Beifügung des Prospekts und der Preisliste
– Nachlass für Großhändler 25 %
– Sofortige Lieferung möglich
– Zahlung: innerhalb von 8 Tagen mit 3 % Skonto
– Gültigkeit des Angebots: 3 Monate
– Dringende Bestellung erwünscht, da Angebot nur gültig, solange der Vorrat reicht
– Höfliche Schlussformel.

2.

Name	Eigener Name	Ms Trina Partridge
Position	Verkaufsleiter/in	Head Buyer
Firma	Liberty Mode GmbH	TopFit Ltd
Anschrift	Hattinger Str. 46, 45128 Essen	48 Eaton Place, London N8 8WR, England
Fax	+49 (2 01) 94 42 38	+44 (1 81) 3 40-28 76
E-Mail	liberty.mode@t-online.de	topfit.ltd@firmnet.co.uk

Geschäftsfall:

Ihre Firma, Liberty Mode GmbH in Essen, ist Hersteller von Damen- und Herren-moden (*ladies' and men's wear*) der mittleren Preisklasse. Sie möchte jetzt ihr Sommerlager räumen, um für die Herbst- und Winterkollektion Platz zu machen.

Aufgabe:

Verfassen Sie ein Rundschreiben (*Circular*) in Form eines Serienbriefes mit persönlicher Anrede und/oder einer E-Mail an Ihre britischen Stammkunden (Anrede: Dear <<Name>> (siehe o. a. Beispiel) bzw. "Dear Customer" bei E-Mail) und berücksichtigen Sie dabei die folgenden Angaben:
- Grund Ihres unverlangten Angebots
- Bezugnahme auf gute Kundschaft
- Ausverkauf des Sommerlagers zu Nachlässen von 10 – 50 %
- Originalpreisliste liegt bei, Preise abzüglich o. a. Nachlass, aber zuzügl. MwSt
- Angebot ist gültig, bis Lagerbestände geräumt sind
- Lieferung innerhalb von 14 Tagen frei Haus oder Abholung
- Bitte um Nachricht so bald wie möglich, da Liefermenge begrenzt ist
- Höfliche Schlussformel.

3.

Name	Annemarie (Thorsten) Strauch	Ms. Jennifer Bartholomew
Position	Sachbearbeiter/in Export	Vice President
Firma	Gebr. Lothar Hansen KG	Gifts & Presents Inc.
Anschrift	Zeppelinstr. 9, 51373 Limburg an der Lahn	205 Chesapeake Park Plaza, Baltimore, MD 21220, U.S.A.
Fax	+49 (64 31) 7 76 52	+1 (4 10) 6 82-04 95
E-Mail	lothar.hansen.kg@allfirm.de	gifts.presents@gnn.net

Geschäftsfall:

Sie sind Annemarie (Thorsten) Strauch, Sachbearbeiter(in) in der Exportabteilung bei Gebr. Lothar Hansen KG in Limburg an der Lahn. Sie stellen Geschenkartikel

für den Export her und hatten kürzlich in einer internationalen Zeitschrift
The Herald eine Annonce aufgegeben. Auf diese Annonce meldet sich telefonisch
die amerikanische Fa. Gifts & Presents Inc. in Maryland, USA, mit der Bitte um
ein kurzgefasstes Angebot.

Aufgabe:
Verfassen Sie dieses Angebot mit folgenden Einzelheiten:
- Dank für erhaltene telefonische Anfrage
- Zusendung mehrerer Muster, Prospekte und einer Preisliste mit getrennter Post
- Lieferbedingungen und Nachlässe sind aus Unterlagen ersichtlich
- Zahlungsbedingungen: Zahlung bei Auftragserteilung für Erstauftrag
  minus 3% Skonto, bei regelmäßigen Aufträgen Änderung möglich
- Lieferung ab Lager
- Bitte um Angabe der einzelnen Positionen bei Auftragserteilung
- Hoffnung auf baldigen Probeauftrag.

4.

Name	Eigener Name	Ms Margaret Partridge
Position	Exportleiter/in	Purchasing Director
Firma	Elmar Sträther GmbH	Jeremy Thunderbird
		Household Linen Ltd
Anschrift	Postfach 50 30 19,	34 Elmgrove Avenue, Lancaster,
	46244 Bottrop	Lancashire RO2 4KM, England
Fax	+49 (2041) 9 98 76	+44 (15 24) 7 77 54
E-Mail	elmar.straether.gmbh@aol.com	j.thunder@firmnet.co.uk

Geschäftsfall:
Die Firma Elmar Sträther GmbH in Bottrop hat von dem britischen Importeur
Jeremy Thunderbird Household Linen Ltd ein Schreiben bekommen, in welchem
dieser um ein Angebot für die gesamte Palette von Wäsche bittet, welche die
deutsche Firma herstellt.

Aufgabe:
Schreiben Sie dieses verlangte Angebot wie folgt:
- Bezugnahme auf das erhaltene Fax
- Kurze Beschreibung Ihres Unternehmens
- Beschreibung Ihres Sortiments (Tischdecken = *tablecloths*, Servietten = *napkins*,
  Frotteetücher = *terry towels*, Geschirrtücher = *tea-towels*)
- Bezugnahme auf beigefügte Preisliste
- Preise und Nachlässe (bei Mindestbestellung von je 50 Stück 10% auf
  Listenpreis)
- Lieferbedingung: CIF britischer Hafen

- Zahlungsbedingungen: ⅓ bei Auftragserteilung, ⅓ bei Lieferung, ⅓ 30 Tage nach Lieferung
- Gültigkeit Ihres Angebots: 4 Wochen
- Höfliche Schlussformel.

5.

Name	Eigener Name	–
Position	Exportleiter/in	–
Firma	Deutsche Sportstätten GmbH	Dubai Mobil Open Tennis Corporation
Anschrift	Postfach 23 07 81, 60437 Frankfurt / Main	Doha, Dubai, Vereinigte Arabische Emirate
Fax	+49 (69) 88 76 43	+9 71 (4) 69 39 22
E-Mail	sportstaetten.gmbh@allfirm.de	dubai.tennis.corp@adcci.com

Geschäftsfall:
Die Dubai Mobil Open Tennis Corporation in den Vereinigten Arabischen Emiraten macht eine Ausschreibung für ein neues Tennis-Center im Emirat. Sie arbeiten für die Deutsche Sportstätten GmbH in Frankfurt/Main und möchten sich an der Ausschreibung beteiligen.

Aufgabe:
Erstellen Sie ein Angebot unter Berücksichtigung folgender Punkte:
- Bezugnahme auf erhaltene Ausschreibungsunterlagen
- Kurzbeschreibung Ihres Unternehmens
- Angabe von Referenzen (Sie haben schon drei ähnliche Projekte in Ägypten, Marokko und Südfrankreich erstellt)
- Katalog Ihrer Produkte und Leistungen ist beigefügt
- Allgemeine Preisliste anbei; genaue Preise können erst nach Erhalt näherer Unterlagen errechnet werden
- Zahlung durch unwiderrufliches, bestätigtes Akkreditiv
- Bitte um nähere Einzelheiten zwecks Ausarbeitung eines detaillierten Angebots
- Bei Interesse kann ein Mitarbeiter Ihrer Firma nach Dubai kommen
- Höfliche Schlussformel.

Unit 4

Orders

Introduction

Under English law the supplier's offer is not legally binding on him until the buyer has accepted it. As soon as this is the case the seller must supply the goods offered and the buyer must accept them on the terms stated.

This means that the buyer must pay for the goods within the period specified by the supplier and also check them as soon as possible for faults. If the supplier is not informed of faults it is assumed that the goods have been accepted.

When writing an order use the letter plan to structure your letter, fax or e-mail.

Orders

1. Reference to offer (optional)
2. Details of goods* / services required
3. Price and discount(s)*
4. Terms of delivery
5. Terms of payment
6. Delivery
7. Instructions / special arrangements / qualifications (optional)
8. Polite ending
9. Enclosure(s)

*Best in tabular form if more than one item is ordered

Fig. 10

To structure an order for several items use the following table:

An order in tabular form

Quantity	Description	Article Number	List Price	Unit Price (−10 % discount)	Total Price
25 pairs	Elégance Dancing Shoes	EG501	£60.00	£54.00	£1,350.00
20	Silk Top Hats	TH4711	£50.00	£45.00	£900.00
25	Bow Ties	BT4009	£20.00	£18.00	£450.00
				Total	**£2,700.00**

Delivery to be made within 10 days after receipt of order, franco to our premises.

An order for a single item can be set out as follows:

Article:	500 × 60 watt LL 93 light bulbs
Payment:	by IMO
Delivery:	within 30 days by WorldWide Parcels Service, franco to our premises
Packing:	foam-lined cardboard boxes
Price:	$0.50 each
Total price:	$250

Before doing the case study and the exercises, first study the specimen letters included.

Specimen Letters

1. Order for confectionery (see Unit 3 "Offers", Specimen Letter 1)

Your ref. HvJ/sva
Our ref. MS/hh
28 November ..

Ms Henrietta von Jauch
European Sales Director
Stecker Süßwaren Deutschland GmbH
Ringstr. 88
012607 Dresden
Germany

Dear Ms von Jauch

<u>Order for Confectionery</u>

We have studied the catalogue and export price list sent to us on 20 November ..
and enclose our order no. 21D.

We are pleased to note that your CIF Dover prices include an initial order
discount of 5 % for new customers and are inclusive of packing. We feel sure
that this will give your products a competitive edge on the British market.

The invoice amount will be remitted by transfer to your account in Germany
on receipt of your invoice. We would request you to send us the goods as soon
as possible and within 10 days at the latest in time for the coming Christmas
season. Please confirm receipt of this order by fax or telephone and advise us as
soon as the goods have been shipped. The goods will be collected at Dover on
our behalf by South East Deliveries Ltd. We reserve the right to return the goods
carriage forward if they are delivered late.

Thank you for your prompt attention to this matter.

Yours sincerely
Sweetmate Ltd

Miranda Sweeney

Miranda Sweeney
Purchasing Director

Enc: 1 Order form

8 Coppergate, York, YO1 1NR, England,
Tel. +44 (19 04) 78 53 44, Fax +44 (19 04) 78 53 00, E-mail: sweetmate.ltd@yorklink.co.uk

2. Standard Order Form

Order no.: 409/20A
Date: 20 February ..

Schäfer u. Jost Großhandel GmbH
Sanitär-Heizung-Sauna
Erlenweg 20−26
97076 Würzburg
Germany

Please supply:

Quantity	Description	Article No.	List Price	Total
200 m²	"Lintorp" floor tiles	L-FK 9089	8.00 euros m²	1,600.00 euros
500 m²	"Segler" wall tiles	S-WK 9077	5.00 euros m²	2,500.00 euros
25x	"Dekor" washbasins	J-WB 109	100.00 euros	2,500.00 euros
			Sub-total	6,600.00 euros
			−5 % discount	−330.00 euros
			Total	**6,270.00 euros**

Terms of delivery:	DAT Dover
Payment:	By transfer to your account at the Deutsche Bank in Würzburg within 30 days after receipt of invoice
Packing:	Pallets
Delivery:	Within 30 days after receipt of order
Instructions:	Boxes to be marked "EPD/40920A/Dover/1−25/EU, "To be collected" by Inland Couriers Ltd

¹pp EP Distributors Ltd

Janet Watson
Janet Watson
Purchasing Department

1 Per pro (Per procurationem) meaning "on behalf of"

Case Study

Melanie Giese works in the purchasing department of a German company called Allwetter Sport AG (Eichenkreuzstr. 40–44, 40589 Düsseldorf, tel. +49 (2 21) 20 98-0, fax +49 (2 21) 20 98-110, e-mail: allwetter.ag@t-online.de).

Her company is now buying camping gear for the coming summer season and she sees on the Internet that a company in Nevada, USA, called Wilderness Adventure Inc. (330 California Ave., Suite 1088, Reno, NV 89509, tel. +1 (9 16) 2 72-70 97, fax +1 (9 16) 2 72-70 02, e-mail: wain@communique.net) is currently offering good-quality backpacks at competitive prices. She receives a favourable reply to her enquiry (see page 58) so she decides to place a trial order for three models.

Payment is to be made in advance by international money order (IMO) and the goods are to be shipped via WorldWide Parcels Service (see e-mail from Wilderness Adventure for details). She wants the backpacks to be delivered to her company's premises within three weeks after receipt of her order.

She decides to order 5 "Yukon Trekker" backpacks list price $89.95 each, article number PK155, 5 "Outback Enduro" backpacks, article number PK160 listed at $124.95 per backpack and 5 "Kelty Women's Andes" backpacks, article number PK157 at a list price of $144.95 each.

As she is ordering more than 10 articles her company qualifies for a 5 % quantity discount, which she includes when listing her order.

Activity

Using the "**Orders** Letter Plan" in this Unit and the Standard Expressions write Melanie's letter / fax / e-mail to Wilderness Adventure Inc. Make it friendly and informal by writing in the "I" form and using short forms (e.g. "it's", "we're" etc.).

Melanie's e-mail enquiry:

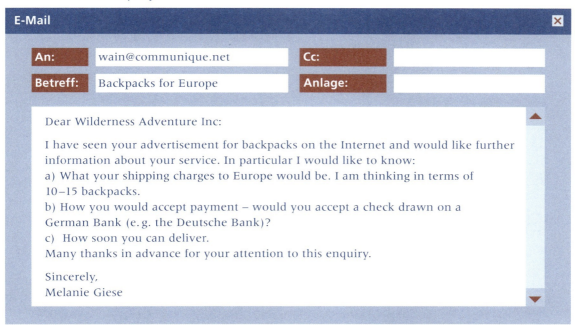

E-Mail

| **An:** | wain@communique.net | **Cc:** | |
| **Betreff:** | Backpacks for Europe | **Anlage:** | |

Dear Wilderness Adventure Inc:

I have seen your advertisement for backpacks on the Internet and would like further information about your service. In particular I would like to know:
a) What your shipping charges to Europe would be. I am thinking in terms of 10–15 backpacks.
b) How you would accept payment – would you accept a check drawn on a German Bank (e.g. the Deutsche Bank)?
c) How soon you can deliver.
Many thanks in advance for your attention to this enquiry.

Sincerely,
Melanie Giese

Wilderness Adventure Inc.'s reply:

Von:	wain@communique.net ("John D. Thomas")
Betreff:	RE: Shipping backpacks
Gesendet am:	06. Jan. .., 11:58:28 – 0600
Abgeholt am:	06. 01. .., 23:01

Dear Melanie:

We appreciate your inquiry about our products!

Wilderness Adventure would be more than happy to ship to Germany. Shipping charges on 15 backpacks would be $195.00 and delivery would be roughly 3 wks via WorldWide Parcels Service.

We accept payment by American Express, Visa, Mastercard or international money order.

Thank you very much.
John
Wilderness Adventure / 1- 6 - ..

Language

Use the "**Orders** Standard Expressions" table to find the words missing below.

1. **Verbs + nouns**
   Which verbs go with the following nouns?
   a. to ▢▢ our requirements
   b. to ▢▢ an offer (not "make")
   c. to ▢▢ an order
   d. to ▢▢ a discount (two answers)
   e. to ▢▢ the invoice amount (not "pay")
   f. to receive goods – to ▢▢ delivery of goods
   g. to supply article A instead of article B – to ▢▢ article A for article B

2. **Verbs + prepositions / particles**
   Which prepositions / particles go with the following verbs?
   a. to correspond ▢▢ our expectations
   b. to conform ▢▢ regulations
   c. to comply ▢▢ regulations
   d. to supply a customer ▢▢ goods

e. to deal [   ] an order

f. Please arrange [   ] the goods to be despatched immediately.

3. **Nouns + prepositions / prepositions + nouns / adjectives + prepositions**
   a. an offer [   ] goods
   b. an order [   ] goods
   c. immediately – [   ] return
   d. [   ] 3 weeks (not "in")
   e. no later than on 15 July – [   ] 15 July (not "on")
   f. [   ] advance
   g. [   ] your favour
   h. [   ] receipt of the goods
   i. [   ] transit
   j. [   ] board ship
   k. [   ] stock
   l. not available – [   ] stock (2 words)
   m. [   ] short supply
   n. The machines are priced [   ] £50 each.

4. **Adjectives / adjectival phrases + nouns**
   a. a first order – an [   ] order
   b. an offer for a new product – an [   ] offer
   c. in the next [   ] days

5. **Payment**
   Which abbreviations (2 or 3 letters) are used to mean the following?
   a. The customer is given the documents as soon as he has accepted a bill of exchange.
   b. The customer must pay for the goods when they are delivered to him.
   c. The customer pays for the goods when placing his order.
   d. The customer is given the documents as soon as he has paid for the goods.

6. **Packing**
   What containers are the following things normally sent in?
   a. bottles of wine
   b. coffee
   c. computers
   d. tea
   e. heavy machinery
   f. large quantities of goods

7. **Transport**
   How would the following things probably be transported or sent?
   a. flowers from one continent to another
   b. wood from South America to Europe
   c. small amounts of goods delivered by one firm to another locally

Before you listen to the dialogue, first read through the background information provided and the instructions following it.

Background information

In the following dialogue you are Melanie Schwarz and you work in the Sales Section of Mountain-Trek GmbH in Landshut, Bavaria. Your company is the European subsidiary of an American company called Mountain-Trek Inc. in California. It regularly supplies top-quality equipment to hiking and mountaineering expeditions all over the world, sometimes at extremely short notice. Today you receive an urgent phone call from a customer abroad.

Activity

Your job is to **(a)** answer the questions below and

Either:
(b) Write a short memo in English to Mr Miles Foreman, the vice president of Mountain-Trek (Europe) Inc., in which you give details of what the customer wants and ask for Mr Foreman's comments on the solution you have suggested.

Or:
(c) Write a summary in German of your telephone conversation. It is to be given to your boss, Herr Kampmann, the Sales Director.

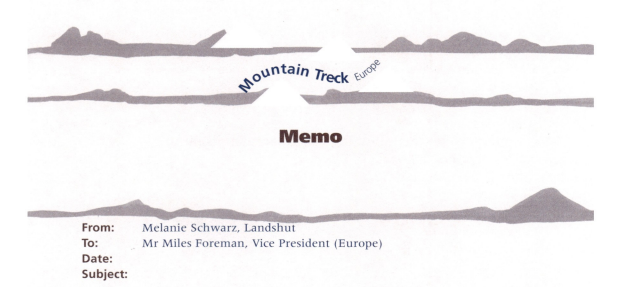

Mountain Treck Europe

Memo

From:	Melanie Schwarz, Landshut
To:	Mr Miles Foreman, Vice President (Europe)
Date:	
Subject:	

Questions

1. What is the customer's name?
2. Give the name of the customer's organisation and say what sort of activity it offers.
3. Say what the customer wants and who he wants it for.
4. How much time does the customer have?
5. Give details of Melanie's first offer and say why it is not acceptable.
6. Explain what is wrong with her second offer.
7. Say which product the customer accepts and include the price and terms of delivery first offered.
8. Explain how Melanie thinks she could get the goods to the customer without sending them as air freight and when they would arrive.
9. Say where the goods would be delivered.
10. What is the final price per item?
11. Give details of the terms of delivery and payment.
12. Say what Melanie promises to do and by when at the latest.

Telephone Role Play

Rolle A

Sie sind Angelika (Georg) Altendorff und arbeiten als Einkäufer/in für die Waren-
hauskette Peters (*Peters Department Stores*) in München, Fax: +49 (89) 58 63 08.
Rufen Sie John Callaghan in der Firma Desk Design Ltd in London an. Berücksich-
tigen Sie dabei die folgenden Punkte:
–   Der Schreibtisch Marke „Scotland" hat sich bei Ihnen so gut verkauft, dass Sie dringend nachbestellen müssen
–   Hat Callaghan 300 Stück von diesem Modell noch auf Lager? Sofort lieferbar?
–   Sie nehmen die 100 Stück sofort; bitte zum gleichen Preis und zu den gleichen Bedingungen sofort per Eilgut (*by express delivery*) absenden
–   Wie lange dauert die Nachlieferung der 200 Stück?
–   Ist 6 Wochen Lieferzeit das schnellstmögliche Angebot?
–   Sie sind mit der Lieferung von 100 Schreibtischen in 4 Wochen / Rest 2 Wochen später einverstanden
–   Gibt es bei dieser Menge einen zusätzlichen Mengenrabatt?
–   Weisen Sie auf die erfolgreich abgeschlossenen Aufträge der letzten Monate hin
–   3 % Zusatzrabatt wird dankbar angenommen.
–   Sie bitten um schriftliche Bestätigung des Angebots
–   Sie geben Ihre Fax-Nummer an.

Role B

You are John Callaghan and you work in the Export Sales Section of Desk Design
Ltd in London. Today you receive an urgent call from Angelika (Georg) Altendorff.
Include the following points in your conversation:
–   You're glad to hear how well your "Scotland" desk is selling
–   You check your stock records on the computer

- You say that you can supply 100 desks from stock immediately
- You'll send them tomorrow by express delivery
- You can deliver 200 more but it'll take 6 weeks
- You'll do your best to supply 100 in four weeks' time and the other 100 two weeks later
- You say your prices are already highly competitive
- You agree that Peters Department Stores are good customers and pay punctually.
- You agree to an exceptional quantity discount of another 3 %
- You promise to fax confirmation of all the details agreed
- Ask for the German company's fax number.

Aufgaben

1.

Name	eigener Name	Mr. Al Rogers
Position	Einkaufsleiter/in	Director of Sales
Firma	Saturn AG	Graham Brothers Inc.
Anschrift	Leuchtenbacher Kirchweg 11	24068 Venture Blvd., Encino,
	70523 Stuttgart, Germany	CA 91316, U.S.A.
Fax	+49 (7 11) 8 95 74 30	+1 (4 15) 9 04 76 83
E-Mail	saturn.ag@t-online.de	graham.bros@aol.com

Geschäftsfall:
Die Firma Graham Brothers Inc. fertigt Sicherheitsschutzhelme (*safety helmets*) und hatte einem deutschen Importeur für Fahrrhadhelme auf Wunsch ein ausführliches Angebot unterbreitet.

Aufgabe:
Bestellen Sie bei Graham Brothers folgende Artikel:
- Helm „Hurricane Race", metallic-schwarz und oliv-grün, jeweils 3.000 Stück à 25,– $; Helm „Air Wonder" 5.000 Stück schwarz à 13,50 $ und 2.000 Stück weiß à 14,00 $.
- Mengenrabatt 15 %
- Errechnen Sie den Endpreis!
- Lieferzeit: schnellstmöglich
- Verpackung: in starken Kartons à 6 Stück, auf Paletten, 40 Kartons pro Palette, im Sammelcontainer
- Lieferung: CIF Hamburg
- Zahlungsbedingung: per unwiderruflichem Akkreditiv, zu bestätigen durch eine amerikanische Bank

– (Sicherheits)garantie für die Qualität: 1 Jahr auf Material
– Bitte um Auftragsbestätigung.

2.

Name	Felicitas (Paul) Werner	–
Position	Einkaufsleiter/in	–
Firma	Adams & Partner	Cross Country Shoes Ltd
Anschrift	Reichenberger Allee 39–41	45 London Road
	24146 Kiel	Staines, Middlesex ML1 1DB
	Germany	England
Fax	+49 (4 31) 88 34 99	+44 (17 84) 89-32 51
E-Mail	adams.partner@webnet.com.de	cross.country@firmnet.co.uk

importeur

Geschäftsfall:
In der letzten Ausgabe der britischen Fachzeitschrift *Pro Sport* haben Sie eine Anzeige für Spezialschuhe der Firma Cross Country Shoes in Staines, England gesehen.

Aufgabe:
Erteilen Sie der britischen Firma folgenden Probeauftrag:
– „Sports 2000 cross-country running shoes", Stückpreis 90,– Euro, Größen 41
bis 45, je 5 Paar (*5 pairs of each whole size*); „Soccer 39 football boots", Größen 41
bis 45, Stückpreis 75,– Euro, je 10 Paar; „Indoor 64 ladies' training shoes",
Stückpreis 60,– Euro, Größen 36 bis 40, je 5 Paar.
– Bringen Sie auch einen Wiederverkäuferrabatt von 50 % in Abzug und
errechnen Sie den Endpreis!
– Zahlungsbedingungen: Zahlung bei Erhalt der Waren   cwo
– Lieferzeit: innerhalb von 14 Tagen nach Erhalt des Auftrags
– Verpackung: in Kartons, auf Euro-Paletten (*euro-pallets*)
– Garantie: 1/2 Jahr auf Material
– Bitte um Mitteilung des genauen Datums der Abholbereitschaft
(ex works-Lieferung!).

3.

Name	Dunja (Rüdiger) Mahler	–
Position	Einkäufer/in	–
Firma	Brandenburger AG	FOLIOPAC Plc
Anschrift	Breite Str. 80–84,	39 Winchester Road,
	88214 Ravensburg, Germany	Lancaster, LA3 7HJ, England
Fax	+49 (7 51) 3 25 76 54	+44 (15 24) 98 74 33
E-Mail	brandenburg.ag@webserve.de	foliopac.plc@firmnet.co.uk

Geschäftsfall:
Sie arbeiten als Einkäufer/in für die deutsche Kaufhauskette Brandenburger AG
in Ravensburg.

Aufgabe:
Bestellen Sie bei FOLIOPAC Plc folgende Artikel unter Berücksichtigung der
nachstehenden Einzelheiten:
- Notebook PC Koffer „Jennifer" 6 × 36 × 28 cm mit Zubehörtasche, Einzelpreis:
  24,30 Pfund, je 500 Stück in grau, grün und blau, Gesamtpreis: 36.450,– Pfund.
- Lieferzeit: 4 Wochen
- Lieferung: frei Haus
- Zahlung: ⅓ bei Auftragsbestätigung per Banküberweisung, ⅓ bei Lieferungs-
  erhalt, ⅓ 90 Tage nach Rechnungserhalt
- Garantie: 10 Jahre auf Materialdefekte und Herstellungsfehler
- Lieferbedingungen des Verkäufers sind gültig
- Gerichtsstand: Ravensburg (*the place of jurisdiction*)
- Bei Eignung des Koffers Aussicht auf größere Bestellungen.

Unit 5
Acknowledgements

Introduction

It is not always necessary to send an acknowledgement after goods or services have been ordered. In some cases a postcard to say that the order is being dealt with is enough.

It is, however, customary to do so
- in domestic trade if the goods cannot be supplied immediately
- in foreign trade
- if substitutes are offered
- if new terms are suggested
- if certain conditions must be fulfilled (e. g. payment)
- if the order is noted for later delivery
- if the customer has requested an acknowledgement
- if the customer is new

When writing an acknowledgement use the letter plan to structure your letter, fax or e-mail.

Acknowledgements

1. Reference to order
2. – Confirmation of order (goods / services)
   – Repetition of order (goods / services)*
   – Modification of order (goods / services)
   – Refusal of order
3. (Repetition* / modification of) price(s) and discount(s)
4. (Repetition / modification of) terms of delivery and payment
5. (Repetition / modification of) date and mode of delivery
6. Technicalities
7. Conditions to be fulfilled
8. Request for confirmation
9. Polite ending
10. Enclosure(s)

*Best in tabular form if a number of items have been ordered.

Fig. 11

The following table summarises what courses of action can be followed after an order has been placed.

Acknowledgements

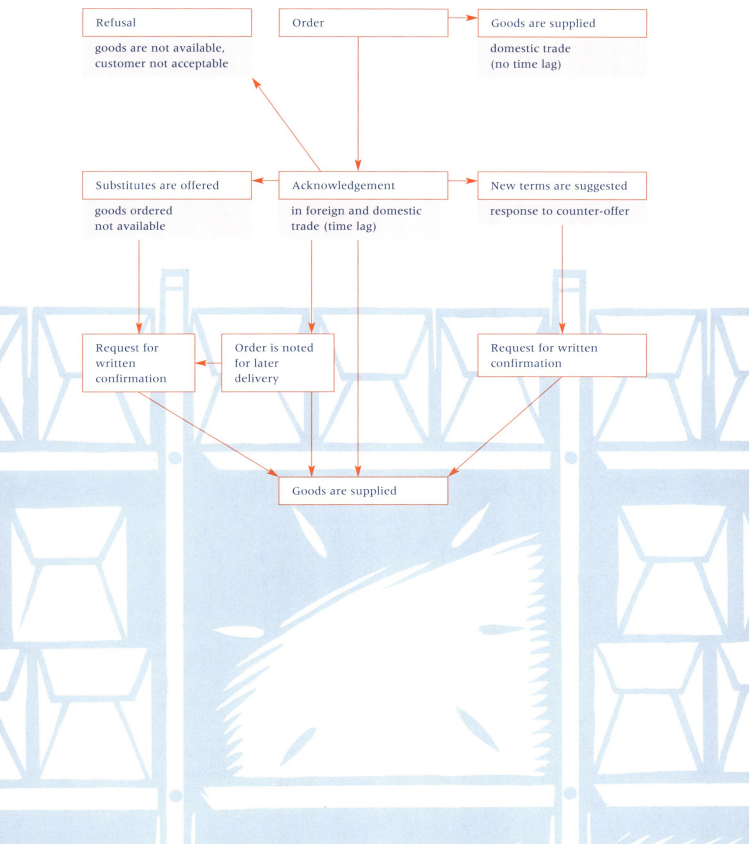

Refusal	Order	Goods are supplied
goods are not available, customer not acceptable		domestic trade (no time lag)

Substitutes are offered	Acknowledgement	New terms are suggested
goods ordered not available	in foreign and domestic trade (time lag)	response to counter-offer

Request for written confirmation	Order is noted for later delivery		Request for written confirmation

Goods are supplied

Specimen Letters

1. Letter from Schäfer u. Jost acknowledging order (see "Orders", page 56)

Erlenweg 20–26
97076 Würzburg
Germany

Our ref. tan.88
Your ref. –
25 February ..

Mrs Janet Watson
Purchasing Department
EP Distributors Ltd.
109 Stanwell Road
ASHFORD
MA2 6HH
Middlesex
England

Dear Mrs Watson

Your Order No. 409/20A dated 20 February ..

The above-mentioned order for tiles and washbasins has been passed on
to our Despatch Department and we are pleased to confirm that, as stated in
our offer, our company will grant a 5 % discount on the list prices.

As agreed, our prices include delivery CIF Dover, payment to be made by
transfer to our account at the Deutsche Bank in Würzburg within 30 days
after receipt of invoice. The goods will be delivered within 30 days and your
packing instructions will be strictly observed. Please note that this order is
subject to our General Conditions of Sale, a copy of which is enclosed. You
will be receiving our advice of despatch in the next few days.

Thank you for choosing to place your order with our company.

Yours sincerely
Schäfer u. Jost Großhandel GmbH

Elke Tannenberg
Elke Tannenberg
Export Sales

Enc

Tel.: +49 (9 31) 88 79 05
Fax: +49 (9 31) 88 79 00
E-mail: schaefer.jost@firmenet.de

2. German supplier acknowledges order

From:	Silke Harmann	To:	Ms Susan Miles
	Sales Manager		Purchasing Department
	Glas-Galerie Service GmbH		Continental Pottery Ltd
	Hamburg		Brighton
	Germany		Sussex
			England
Fax:	+49 (40) 3 21 45 99	Fax:	+44 (12 73) 76 84 00
Our ref.:	SH/TT	Your ref.:	SM/bb.3007
Date:	30 July ..	Total pages:	1

Dear Susan

<u>Your Order dated 20 July .. for Decorative Glass Lampshades</u>

We were delighted to receive your order, as listed below, which is now being attended to:

Article:	250 × SG85 glass lampshades
Payment:	by transfer to our account at Lloyds Bank, Brighton, on receipt of invoice
Delivery:	within 14 days of receipt of order, CIP Gatwick Airport
Packing:	in cardboard boxes with thick padding
Price:	2 euros per unit
Total price:	500 euros

We feel sure that the goods will meet your expectations and look forward to doing further business with you.

Best regards

Silke Harmann

3. Offer of substitutes

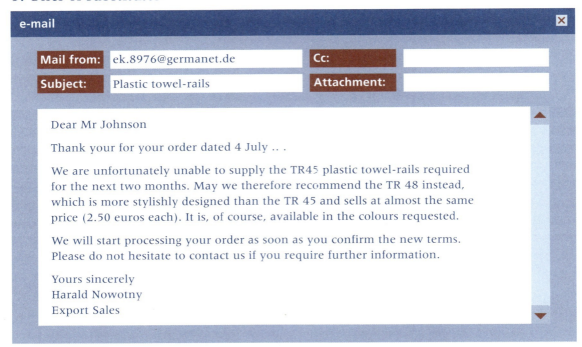

e-mail ✕

Mail from: ek.8976@germanet.de   **Cc:**

Subject: Plastic towel-rails   **Attachment:**

Dear Mr Johnson

Thank your for your order dated 4 July .. .

We are unfortunately unable to supply the TR45 plastic towel-rails required for the next two months. May we therefore recommend the TR 48 instead, which is more stylishly designed than the TR 45 and sells at almost the same price (2.50 euros each). It is, of course, available in the colours requested.

We will start processing your order as soon as you confirm the new terms. Please do not hesitate to contact us if you require further information.

Yours sincerely
Harald Nowotny
Export Sales

4. Showstar International Pty in Australia reply to Neulicht's offer of substitutes
(read after completing the case study)

Dear Gabriele

Thank you for your fax dated 27 February .., in which you suggest we purchase LS20 lasers instead of the LS 15 ordered.

We regret to inform you that the price of 80,000 euros stated is too high for our budget. We must therefore make use of Clause 4 of our Sales Agreement, which gives us the right to cancel our order within 4 weeks.

Yours sincerely
ShowStar International Pty

Sheilagh Mackenzie

Sheilagh Mackenzie
Project Manager

Case Study

Two weeks ago Neulicht GmbH in Bochum (e-mail: neu.licht@aol.com) received an order from ShowStar International, an Australian company based in Perth, to supply special laser lighting equipment for a new musical called "Goethe get your gun!" in Hamburg, due to open in 6 months' time.

The Australian company placed an order for a complete laser show including white light, colour and computer animations, delivery franco the St. Pauli Theater in Hamburg within 3 months after receipt of order. The price quoted by Neulicht in its offer a month ago was 75,000 euros including installation and testing.

Gabriele Naumann, the sales manager at Neulicht in Bochum, has to contact ShowStar International in Perth today because the Australian company faxed this morning to say it wants the laser show a month earlier. This is a problem for Neulicht because the German company has several large orders for other musicals in Europe and the lasers for ShowStar will not be available for another 10 weeks at the earliest.

The only solution is to substitute LS20 lasers for the LS15 models ordered. The new laser is better than the old one and in stock in Bochum at the moment. This would, however, make the light show 5,000 euros more expensive.

From:	*"Heaven on earth – made in Perth!"* *ShowStar International Pty*	To:
Sheilagh Mackenzie		Ms Gabriele Naumann
Project Director		Sales Manager
ShowStar International Pty		Neulicht GmbH
346 Coronation Street		Castroper Hellweg 40
Perth		44805 Bochum
Western Australia 6000		Germany

Fax No.: +61 (9) 3 22 70 06   **Fax No.:** +49 (2 34) 98 76 00
E-mail: show.star@aussienet.pw.com
Our ref.: SM/BK   **Your ref.:** GN/TT
Date: …   **Total pages:** 1

Gabriele:

Sorry to surprise you with this but we need the laser show a month earlier. There's another musical starting in Hamburg and we want to get ours up and running first!

Hope this won't cause any problems. Please get in touch if it does.

Regards

Sheilagh

Activity

Using the "**Acknowledgements** Letter Plan" in this Unit and the Standard Expressions write Gabriele's letter / fax / e-mail to ShowStar International, in which she gives details of Neulicht's new offer and asks ShowStar to confirm it.

Language

Use the "**Acknowledgements** Standard Expressions" table to find the words missing below.

1. **Verbs + nouns**
   Which verbs go with the following nouns?
   a. "Your order is being processed" – "Your order is ▩ attention"
   b. "We cannot accept your order" – "We have to ▩ your order" (2 answers)
   c. to ▩ a discount (2 answers)
   d. "We will be obliged to ▩ you a further £100 per unit."
   e. "Please ▩ the invoice amount by bank transfer"
   f. "Please ▩ our draft and return it to us"
   g. to ▩ a documentary credit
   h. to ▩ a sum of money from one account to another
   i. to ▩ your expectations
   j. to ▩ your attention to the fact that …

2. **Verbs + prepositions / particles**
   Which prepositions / particles go with the following verbs?
   a. to thank ▩
   b. to deal ▩
   c. to attend ▩
   d. to put ▩ hand
   e. to sell ▩ $100 per unit
   f. to substitute a new article ▩ an old one
   g. to qualify ▩ a discount
   h. to agree ▩ a suggestion
   i. to consent ▩
   j. to run ▩ materials (2 words)

3. **Nouns + prepositions / prepositions + nouns / adjectives + prepositions**
   a. an increase ▩ price
   b. to be entitled ▩ a discount
   c. ▩ the time being
   d. ▩ this occasion
   e. ▩ of stock
   f. ▩ stock
   g. ▩ the same price
   h. demand ▩ the goods …
   i. an order ▩
   j. ▩ the terms requested
   k. subject ▩ favourable references
   l. to make goods ▩ specifications
   m. eligible ▩
   n. to be ▩ a position to do something
   o. cut ▩ the bone

p. to increase the discount ▨ 2% to 15%

q. ▨ good time for the Car Show

r. ready ▨ despatch

s. ready ▨ collection

t. ▨ fail

u. ▨ accordance ▨ your instructions

v. ▨ your convenience

w. ▨ a loss

x. ▨ the contrary

y. ▨ respect to

4. **Adjectives / adjectival phrases + nouns**

   a. the earlier model – the ▨ model

   b. "You have not ordered enough" – "The quantity ordered is ▨"

   c. "Our prices are as low as possible" – "We have ▨ prices" (hyphenated adjective)

   d. "We must charge you $10 more per unit" – "We will be obliged to charge you a ▨ $10 per unit"

   e. in ▨ course

   f. in the ▨ future

5. **Further expressions**

   a. Give a word similar in meaning to "because".

   b. Give an expression similar in meaning to "owing to".

   c. Give an expression similar in meaning to "if".

4 Listening

1. True – False

Read through the following statements first, then listen to the recording and note on a piece of your own paper whether the statements are **True** or **False**. Make a note of the correct facts for the false statements. The first answer has been done for you.

1. Gisela Riedel works for Heatmaster Inc. in New York.
   False. She works for Lufttechnische Anlagen GmbH in Frankfurt.

2. Hank DeBona's company has ordered 100 DDV heating and cooling units.

3. The model he has ordered costs 375 euros per unit.

4. The Klarluft Z1 isn't selling well at the moment.

5. The Klarluft Z1 is out of stock.

6. Hank DeBona doesn't want to wait 5 weeks.

7. Heatmaster Inc. only wants 75 units.

8. Lufttechnische Anlagen can supply air conditioners from stock.

9. The Z1 is less expensive than the Z3.

10. There is no difference between the Z1 and the Z3 apart from the price.

11. Boston is not very far from New York.

12. The ship with the consignment of Z1s has already docked in Boston.
13. The German firm will have the Z1s sent from Boston to New York.
14. Hank DeBona accepts this suggestion immediately.
15. Gisela offers Heatmaster Inc. a 5% discount on this consignment.
16. Hank DeBona wants Gisela to post him the documents for Boston.

2. Questions

Now listen to the recording again and answer the following questions.
1. Name and description of product ordered?
2. Quantity?
3. Price?
4. Original terms of delivery?
5. Original delivery date / period?
6. New arrangements?

3. Writing

Write Lufttechnische Anlagen GmbH's letter / fax / e-mail to Heatmaster Inc. with details of the new arrangements. Use your answers to the questions above and the following information:

From: Gisela Riedel, Export Sales Manager, Lufttechnische Anlagen GmbH,
Schwedlerstr. 5, 60314 Frankfurt, fax (069) 52 20 76,
e-mail: lufttechnische.anlagen@compuserve.com
To: Mr Hank DeBona, Purchasing Director, Heatmaster Air Conditioning Inc.,
258 Grand Concourse, Bronx, NY 10451, USA, fax +1 (718) 933-1997,
e-mail: heatmaster.inc@nynet.com

Telephone Role Play

Rolle A

Sie sind Gesine (Rudolf) Jordan und arbeiten in der Verkaufsabteilung des Musik-hauses Sinfonia in Oberhausen. Ihre Telefonnummer ist: +49 (2 08) 64 93 10. Rufen Sie die Firma Templeton Music Ltd. in Oxford an und berücksichtigen Sie dabei folgende Punkte:

- Sie danken für den Auftrag von Templeton, der sich auf 20 Querflöten (*flutes*) bezieht.
- Da Templeton die Bestätigung telefonisch wünschte, tun Sie dies hiermit
- Normalerweise brauchen Sie einschließlich Versand mindestens 4 Wochen Lieferzeit
- Sie können die Instrumente per Luftexpressfracht senden, das kostet aber mehr
- Sie werden alles versuchen, die Instrumente in 14 Tagen abzuschicken
- Bei einer so illustren (*prestigious*) Gala-Veranstaltung (*gala performance*) wollen Sie dem Kunden so weit wie möglich entgegenkommen. Sie versuchen, die Lieferzeit auf 10 Tage zu kürzen
- Sie nehmen sofort Kontakt mit Ihrer zuständigen Abteilung auf
- Sobald Sie Bescheid haben, melden Sie sich.

Role B

You are Pia (Derrick) Charleston and work in the Purchasing Department of Templeton Music Ltd in Oxford. When Gesine (Rudolf) Jordan phones from Germany you take the call.

Include the following points in your conversation:

- You thank her / him for dealing with your order so quickly
- You explain that the Oxford Symphony Orchestra urgently needs the instruments for a gala performance to be attended by a member of the Royal Family
- The gala performance is in 3 weeks' time so delivery in 4 weeks is out of the question
- You are prepared to pay the extra costs of delivery by express air freight
- Delivery in 14 days' time is still too late
- You ask Sinfonia to have the instruments in Oxford within the next 10 days to enable the orchestra to rehearse with them
- You repeat what an important event this will be for the orchestra
- You thank the German company for its prompt attention to your order
- You request confirmation of the new delivery date by fax on +44 (18 65) 61 18 36.

Aufgaben

1.

Name	eigener Name	–
Position	Geschäftsführer	–
Firma	Gebrüder Johnen KG	Griffith & Co.
Anschrift	Rosenheimer Str. 90–100,	21–27 Church St.,
	81667 München	Oxford OX9 5HH, England
Fax	+49 (89) 9 98 55 70	+44 (18 65) 3 42 67
E-Mail	gebrueder.johnen@t-online.de	griffith.co@firmlink.co.uk

Geschäftsfall:
Die Firma Griffith & Co. hat bei Ihnen Diktiergeräte bestellt.

Aufgabe:
Schreiben Sie die entsprechende Auftragsbestätigung und berücksichtigen Sie dabei folgende Punkte:
— Auftrag über 25 Diktiergeräte (*dictaphones*)
— Geräte sind heute wunschgemäß per Bahn nach Hook van Holland (*the Hook of Holland*) abgeschickt worden (4 große Kisten)
— Weitertransport per Fähre über Harwich (GB) und mit British Rail nach Oxford
— Die ebenfalls bestellten PCs sind erst in ca. 2 Monaten lieferbar (sehr viele Vorbestellungen)
— Ähnliche, bessere Geräte können sofort ab Lager geliefert werden, aber gegen Aufpreis (10 %)
— Broschüre liegt bei
— Bitte um Anweisungen
— Rechnung für Diktiergeräte ist beigefügt
— Begleichung innerhalb 30 Tagen
— 3 % Skonto für Zahlung innerhalb 10 Tagen nach Rechnungserhalt.

2.

Name	eigener Name	–
Position	Exportleiter/in	–
Firma	Bremer & Brückner GmbH	World Trade Imports Ltd.
Anschrift	Efeuweg 110,	280 Cecil Street,
	38104 Braunschweig,	# 16–01 PIL Building,
	Germany	Singapore 069540, Singapore
Fax	+49 (5 31) 40 80 66	+65 (3 37) 40 90
E-Mail	bremer.brueckner@aol.com	world.trade@asianet.com

Geschäftsfall:

Sie haben von der indonesischen Firma einen Auftrag über eine Werkzeugmaschine vom Typ LY 3000 im Wert von 75.000 Euro erhalten. Die Lieferzeit soll – entgegen dem Angebot, das 5 Monate vorsah – jedoch nur 3 Monate betragen.

Aufgabe:

Schreiben Sie der World Trade Imports Ltd. eine Auftragsbestätigung unter Berücksichtigung der folgenden Einzelheiten:
– Dank für erhaltenen Auftrag
– Bestätigung des Preises und der Lieferbedingungen (CIF Singapur) sowie der Zahlungsweise (per unwiderruflichem, durch eine deutsche Bank zu bestätigendem Akkreditiv)
– Sie werden Ihr Möglichstes tun, die Maschine in 3 Monaten zu liefern. Da Sie jedoch selbst von Zulieferern abhängen (Rohstofflieferung, Outsourcing eines Teils Ihrer Herstellung), kann hierfür keine Garantie übernommen werden. Die Gültigkeitsdauer des Akkreditivs muss daher mindestens 4 Monate betragen
– Bitte um Bestätigung dieser Kondition baldmöglichst.

3.

Name	eigener Name	Ms. Marcia Hunt
Position	Exportleitung	Vice President
Firma	Lübke AG	Douglas Morgan Inc.
Anschrift	Dom-Pedro-Str. 197, 80637 München, Germany	2240 Jefferson Highway, New Orleans, LA 70112, U.S.A.
Fax	+49 (89) 39 86 64	+1 (5 04) 8 32-32 27
E-Mail	luebke.ag@t-online.de	d.morgan.inc@picnet.com

Geschäftsfall:

Sie sind Hersteller von geschnitzten Holzfiguren und Kinderspielzeug und haben von Douglas Morgan Inc. einen Auftrag erhalten.

Aufgabe:

Senden Sie der amerikanischen Firma eine Auftragsbestätigung unter Berücksichtigung folgender Punkte:
– Dank für Bestellung
– Bestätigung der bestellten Positionen wie folgt:
    a) Position 3511 – Nussknacker (200 Stk.)
       Stückpreis 8 Euro
    b) Position 4792 – Holzeisenbahn (100 Stk.)
       Stückpreis 20 Euro
    c) Position 2113 – Kuckucksuhr (50 Stk.)
       Stückpreis 55 Euro
       Gesamtsumme: 6.350 Euro

- Zahlungsbedingungen: $\frac{1}{3}$ Vorauszahlung sofort
  Rest 30 Tage nach Lieferung netto ohne Abzug
- Verpackung: seemäßig in Holzkisten, alle Einzelteile einzeln, gesichert
  gegen Bruch, wasserfest
- Lieferung: FOB deutschem Nordseehafen
- Einladung auf die in Kürze stattfindende Spielzeugmesse in Nürnberg
  (wenn gewünscht, wird Unterbringung usw. besorgt).

Unit 6

Delivery

Introduction

A supplier shipping goods abroad sends his customer an advice of despatch to say when the goods can be expected.

In some cases a multi-copy document is used, whereby the "top copy" is the original and is sent to the customer as the invoice; the second copy is the advice of despatch posted to the customer when the goods have been shipped; the third copy is a packing list accompanying the goods.

For further information and enclosures in connection with delivery refer to the letter plan and use it to structure your letter. fax or e-mail.

Delivery

1. Reference to goods ordered
2. Available for collection*
   Ready for despatch*
   Advice of despatch*:
   - terms of delivery
     (Incoterm)
   - mode of transport
   - name of forwarder
   - estimated time of arrival
   - details of packing /
     packaging
3. Request for packing
   instructions*
4. Reference to mode
   of payment*
   - request for payment
5. Reference to documentation
   enclosed or sent separately*
   (see table on pages 81–83)
6. Polite ending
7. Enclosure(s)

*As appropriate

Fig. 12

Shipping Documents

	Name of document	Obtained from	Number	Important features
1	Bill of lading *Konnossement* (also "inland waterways bill of lading" *Ladeschein*)	Shipping company	3 originals (for the shipping company, ship's captain and shipper) + copies	1. document of title – if "to order" negotiable by endorsement 2. contract of carriage 3. receipt for the goods 4. clean (goods are in apparent good order and condition) 5. foul / dirty / claused / unclean (goods are damaged / incomplete) 6. received-for-shipment Bs/L or on-board Bs/L (see Unit 14, Forwarding and Insurance) 7. details of the goods (description, value, quantity, weights, marks, number of packages) 8. terms of delivery 9. name and address of shipper (consignor) 10. freight paid or unpaid
2	Consignment note (road or rail transport) *Frachtbrief*	Carrier	3 originals (for the consignor, consignee and carrier) + copies	1. not a document of title 2. contract of carriage 3. receipt for the goods 4. non-negotiable 5. details of the goods (description, value, quantity, weights, marks, number of packages) 6. name and address of shipper (consignor) 7. name and address of consignee
3	Air waybill *Luftfrachtbrief*	Carrier	12-part document set (including one copy each for the consignor, consignee and carrier)	1. not a document of title 2. contract of carriage 3. receipt for the goods 4. non-negotiable 5. details of the goods (description, value, quantity, weights, marks, number of packages) 6. name and address of shipper (consignor) 7. name and address of consignee

Name of document	Obtained from	Number	Important features
4 Commercial invoice *Handelsrechnung*	Exporter / shipper	1, 2, 3 original(s) + copies	1. a request for payment 2. the sum due (unit price, total price) 3. terms of delivery 4. terms of payment 5. name of the ship / flight number if appropriate 6. details of the goods (description, value, quantity, weights, marks, number of packages) 7. name and address of shipper (consignor) 8. name and address of consignee
5 Pro-forma invoice *Proforma-Rechnung*	Exporter / shipper	1, 2, 3 original(s) + copies	1. normally a quotation – accompanies goods supplied on approval – accompanies consignment goods – used for payment in advance – used for the opening of an L/C or to obtain an import licence 2. the sum due (unit price, total price) 3. terms of delivery 4. terms of payment 5. name of the ship / flight number if appropriate 6. details of the goods (description, value, quantity, weights, marks, number of packages) 7. name and address of shipper (consignor) 8. name and address of consignee
6 Consular invoice *Konsulatsfaktura*	Importer's consulate in the exporter's / shipper's country	1 original + copies	1. a sworn and certified statement that the details in the commercial invoice are correct 2. it shows that the goods are not being sold too cheaply abroad (at "dumping prices") 3. it can also be used to assess import duty
7 Customs invoice *Zollfaktura*	Importer's customs authorities / Exporter / shipper	1 original + copies	Used for the assessment of customs duties in the importer's country

Name of document	Obtained from	Number	Important features
8 Insurance policy / certificate *Versicherungs- police / Versiche- rungsschein*	Insurance company	1 original + copies	One of the documents stipulated in a documentary credit in the case of a C or D-group Incoterm (e. g. CIF)
9 Certificate of origin *Ursprungszeugnis*	Chamber of commerce in the exporter's / shipper's country	1 original + copies	Used in connection with import restrictions and the assessment of customs duties
10 Customs declaration *Zollinhalts- erklärung*	Exporter / shipper	1 original + copies	Used for the assessment of customs duties in the importer's country
11 Packing list *Packliste*	Carrier	1 original + copies	Accompanies the goods
12 Export licence *Exportlizenz*	Exporting country's customs authorities	1 original + copies	Ensures that the goods may be exported (e. g. chemicals, nuclear material, weapons)
13 Bill of exchange (draft) *Wechsel (Tratte)*	Exporter / shipper	3 originals + copies	Must be accepted / paid by the customer

Activity

Study the "Shipping Documents" table and then say which of the four statements (a–d) are correct. There is only **one** right answer in each case.

1. a. A "to order" bill of lading cannot be sold to someone else.
   b. A "to order" bill of lading has already been sold to someone else.
   c. A "to order" bill of lading can be sold to someone else.
   d. A "to order" bill of lading has to be sold to someone else.

2. a. If the bill of lading is "clean" the goods are perfect in every way.
   b. If the bill of lading is "clean" the goods show no sign of damage.
   c. If the bill of lading is "foul" the goods are dirty.
   d. If the bill of lading is "dirty" the ship is dirty.

3. a. Ownership of goods cannot be transferred by selling a consignment note.
    b. Ownership of goods can be transferred by selling a consignment note.
    c. A consignment note for goods sent by rail is the same as a bill of lading for goods sent by ship.
    d. The price of the goods listed on a consignment note must be negotiated.

4. a. A B/L, a consignment note and an air waybill have one feature in common.
    b. A B/L, a consignment note and an air waybill have two features in common.
    c. A B/L, a consignment note and an air waybill have three features in common.
    d. A B/L, a consignment note and an air waybill have four features in common.

5. a. The importer always has to pay the pro-forma invoice before he can get the goods.
    b. The commercial invoice is normally used for the assessment of customs duties.
    c. A commercial invoice must be accompanied by a consular invoice.
    d. The importer's consulate in the exporter's country must sometimes certify that the commercial invoice is correct.

6. a. An insurance policy is the same as an insurance certificate.
    b. The importer's chamber of commerce issues the certificate of origin.
    c. The exporter's chamber of commerce certifies where the goods are from.
    d. The exporter's chamber of commerce issues the export licence.

7. a. Goods requiring an export licence are always dangerous.
    b. The export licence is a document accompanying the goods.
    c. An export licence is always accompanied by a customs declaration.
    d. An export licence proves that it is not illegal to export the goods.

8. a. A bill of exchange is a form of payment.
    b. Before a bill of exchange can be accepted it must be paid.
    c. Before a bill of exchange can be paid it must be endorsed.
    d. A bill of exchange is a form of invoice.

Specimen Letters

1. Seller notifies buyer that goods are ready for despatch

Champion Sportswear

95 Bromwich Road
Birmingham
BR6 7HH
England

Your ref. kp.49A
Our ref. TS/BK
20 January ..

Mr Konrad Peters
General Manager
Heckenhauer Sport- und Freizeitbedarf
Uhlandstr. 80
72764 Reutlingen
Germany

Dear Mr Peters

Your Purchase Order No. 907A of 1 January .. for Waxed Cotton Jackets

This is to advise you that the articles ordered, as per the above-mentioned Purchase Order, are now ready for despatch. Each jacket is separately packed in a strong plastic bag, clearly labelled to show both the model and size.

As agreed, we will instruct our forwarders, FastFreight Ltd, to deliver the consignment franco to your premises by road via the Channel Tunnel, as soon as we have received your remittance for 3,500 euros (see enclosed invoice).

We hope that you will be pleased with the high quality of our products and would be pleased to receive further orders.

Yours sincerely
Champion Sportswear

Terry Spinks
Terry Spinks
Export Department

Enc:
Commerical Invoice

Tel. +44 (1 21) 57 78 34
Fax +44 (1 21) 57 78 30
Website: http://www.champion.co.uk
E-mail: champion@champion.co.uk

2. Heymanns Kühlgerätebau confirms delivery of home draught beer units

Our ref. hey.92-B
Your ref. –
15 June ..

Hyde Bros Catering Ltd
49 Tippletree Road
IPSWICH
SU5 9KK
England

Attn. Mr Martin Wallis, Imports

Dear Mr Wallis

Shipment of 100 Home Draught Units as per your Order dated 27 May ..

We are pleased to confirm that the above-mentioned units have now been sent to you as a part container load. They will be shipped by cross-Channel ferry from the Hook of Holland to Felixstowe and then taken by road to your premises.

Delivery will be made by Eurotrans GmbH and the goods are expected to reach your warehouse by the end of the month. The Home Draught Units have been packed in sturdy, non-returnable, foam-lined boxes with the usual marks.

Schaumstoff

We have instructed our correspondent bank, the Midland Bank in Ipswich, to release the documents to you on payment of our draft for the outstanding balance of 15,500 euros.

We trust that the goods will arrive punctually and in good condition and look forward to the pleasure of serving you again.

Yours sincerely
Heymanns Kühlgerätebau

Johannes Heymann

Johannes Heymann
Managing Director

3. Advice of Despatch

sheet

Woosey and Hawkes Ltd,
Manufacturers of the Finest Brass Instruments,
99 Tetherington Road, London EC2 9AH, England
Tel. +44 (171) 8 97 44 35, Fax +44 (171) 8 97 44 80
E-mail: woosey.hawkes@firmlink.co.uk

FAO:	Mr Harald Rottkamp
	Purchasing Department
	Musikhaus Berger
	Hauptstr. 99
	73730 Euskirchen
	Germany
Fax No:	+49 (22 51) 88 97 65
From:	Rita King
	Export Sales Department
Date:	30 September ..
Subject:	Advice of Despatch: Order No. 998C for 25 Trombones
	dated 15 August ..
Total Pages:	1

Dear Mr Rottkamp

We are now able to confirm that the instruments ordered have been collected by our forwarding agents, CargoShip Ltd, and will be despatched to you CIP Cologne-Bonn Airport on Lufthansa Flight No. LH 8095 on 7 October. The instruments have been packed in sturdy cases with thick padding to guard against knocks.

The shipping documents stipulated in the documentary credit (air waybill, commercial invoice, packing list, insurance certificate) have now been handed over to our bankers and payment has been duly received.

We trust the consignment will arrive safely and on schedule and look forward to the pleasure of serving you again.

Yours sincerely

Rita King

Case Study

Michael Schreiner is the export sales manager at Entech Umwelttechnik GmbH in Düsseldorf. His company has received an order from Mr Richard Tang, the plant manager at the Taiwan Metal Company Ltd, for six portable "Stripanlage SA1" decontamination units. The details of the transaction as agreed in the contract of sale are as follows:

Mode of transport:	ship
Port of shipment:	Hamburg
Port of destination:	Kaohsiung in Taiwan
Name of ship:	MS "Angela"
Departure date:	end of the month (give exact date)
ETA:	2 weeks after departure (give approximate date)
Terms:	CIF Kaohsiung
Total price:	6,000 euros
Payment:	irrevocable and confirmed documentary letter of credit
Documents already given to the Dresdner Bank in Düsseldorf:	full set of clean on-board bills of lading, commercial invoice in triplicate, insurance certificate, certificate of origin

Activity

Using the "**Delivery** Letter Plan" in this Unit and the Standard Expressions write Michael Schreiner's Advice of Despatch as a letter, fax or e-mail to the Taiwanese company.

From: Entech Umwelttechnik GmbH, Potsdamer Str. 44, 40599 Düsseldorf, fax +49 (2 11) 56 48 99, e-mail: entech.recycling@compuserve.com

To: Taiwan Metal Company Ltd, P.O. Box 21–83, Taichung, Taiwan, fax +8 86 (4) 2 81 24 23, e-mail: taiwan.metal@tainet.com

Language

Use the "**Delivery** Standard Expressions" table to find the words missing below.

1. **Verbs + nouns**
    Which verbs go with the following nouns?
    a. to ▨ delivery of the goods
    b. to ▨ sail
    c. to ▨ a refund (to ask for)
    d   "Please ▨ and ▨ our draft." (i.e. "put your name on it and send it back")
    e. "Our correspondent bank will ▨ the documents as soon as you have paid."
    f. to ▨ the sum due (not "to transfer" or "to send")

2. **Verbs + prepositions / particles**
    Which prepositions / particles go with the following verbs?
    a. to pick ▨ (to collect)
    b. to get ▨ touch
    c. to guard ▨
    d. to draw ▨ you for 5,000 euros
    e. to apply ▨ an import licence
    f. "Pallets are charged ▨ 10 euros each."
    g. to credit money ▨ an account

3. **Nouns + prepositions / prepositions + nouns / adjectives + prepositions**
    a. ▨ office hours (i.e. "when the office is open")
    b. 24 hours ▨ advance
    c. "The goods have been loaded ▨ MV "Victoria." (2 words)
    d. "The ship is ▨ to set sail on Monday."
    e. ▨ all probability
    f. ▨ cost
    g. ▨ the contrary
    h. "We have no objection ▨ the goods being packed …"
    i. a cheque ▨ $1,000
    j. a banker's draft ▨ $1,000
    k. a remittance ▨ $1,000
    l. a bill of exchange ▨ $1,000
    m. ▨ settlement of
    n. ▨ our favour
    o. ▨ payment of the draft (i.e. "when you have paid the draft")
    p. ▨ acceptance of the draft (i.e. "when you have accepted the draft")
    q. ▨ accordance ▨ (1 word in each gap)
    r. ▨ your satisfaction

4. **Adjectives / adjectival phrases + nouns**
   a. in the next ▨▨ days
   b. Match the words in box A with the words in the box B:

1	air-tight	6	metal	a	crates	f	steel
2	canvas	7	silver	b	tins	g	paper
3	cardboard	8	stainless	c	bands	h	paper
4	corrugated	9	sturdy	d	bags	i	rubber
5	foam	10	wire	e	wool	j	boxes

5. **Further points**
   a. Name 3 different types of freight.
   b. Letters sent by plane are sent by ▨▨ (2 words)
   c. Letters sent overland are sent by ▨▨ (2 words)
   d. *not a whole* container load – a ▨▨ container load
   e. Cargoes such as coal, coke, wood are known as ▨▨ cargoes

5 **Listening**

In the following dialogue you will hear Britta Stein in Tyrol, Austria, speaking to John Ryan at a Canadian company in Toronto.

Britta works in the Equipment Department of Outdoor Sports (Europe) GmbH, a Canadian-owned company which is planning a big event in Austria soon.

Instructions

First read the questions. Next listen to the dialogue and make notes in answer to the questions.

Questions
Equipment:
1. Name of Canadian company?
2. Order number?
3. Wet suits: sizes and quantity?
4. Rafts: quantity?
5. Paddles: quantity?
6. Life-jackets: quantity?
7. Helmets: sizes and quantity?

Delivery:
8. Zurich Airport: Incoterm and delivery period with other cargo? Extra charge?
9. Munich Airport: Incoterm and delivery period?

Finally, as Britta Stein,

Either:

(a) Write a memo in English to the Chief Executive Officer of Outdoor Sports (Europe) GmbH, Ms Jennifer Klein, who is Canadian and is in charge of all the company's rafting centres in Europe.

Include the following points in your memo:
1. Why do Outdoor Sports GmbH in Austria need the sports equipment?
2. When do Outdoor Sports GmbH in Austria need the sports equipment?
3. What is the name of the company they have ordered it from?
4. Explain what choices are open to Outdoor Sports GmbH as regards shipment of the goods.
5. Recommend how the goods should be delivered and give reasons for your choice.

Or:

(b) Write a summary in German of your telephone conversation. It is to be given to Frau Ortner, the Purchasing Director.

Telephone Role Play

Rolle A
Sie sind Lucy (Michael) Kemper und arbeiten für die Firma Ambrosia-Speisen GmbH in München, Tel. +49 (89) 18 76 49, Fax +49 (89) 18 76 00. Ihr Chef bittet Sie, die Firma Seafood Ltd in Southend-on-Sea in folgender Angelegenheit anzurufen:

- Sie haben vor 8 Tagen per Fax 10 Seiten geräucherten irischen Lachs (*10 pieces of smoked Irish salmon*) bestellt
- Die Auftrags-Nr. war LU/KW 395, das Fax datiert vom … (vor 8 Tagen)
- Wo ist die Sendung? Sie sollte heute Morgen da sein
- Wer hat die Ware transportiert?
- Sie haben die Ware sonst immer vom Spediteur Fastfish Ltd bekommen, der sehr zuverlässig war. Warum ist diesmal gewechselt worden?

–   Sie können die Ware nur abnehmen, wenn Sie im Laufe des heutigen Tages oder spätestens morgen früh ankommt, da Sie sie für ein Dinner morgen abend brauchen
–   Betonen Sie nochmals, wie dringend die Sache ist
–   Wenn die Ware nicht pünktlich ankommt, müssen Sie außerdem die Annahme verweigern, weil dann
    a)   die Lieferzeit überschritten ist und
    b)   die Lebensmittel nicht mehr frisch genug sind.

Role B

You are Lucy (Peter) Evans and you work for Seafood Ltd in Southend-on-Sea.
When Lucy (Michael) Kemper phones, you take the call.
Include the following points in your conversation:
–   Order number?
–   This order has been dealt with. It left your premises on the evening of …
    (i. e. 2 days ago)
–   Your forwarding agent this time was Food Express Ltd in Bournemouth
–   Fastfish Ltd had no lorry available 2 days ago, so you used a different forwarder
–   You understand the urgency of the situation
–   You will contact Food Express Ltd immediately
–   Promise to phone or fax as soon as you find anything out
–   Ask for the German firm's fax number
–   Ask to be told if the goods arrive in the meantime
–   Apologize for the delay and say you think the fish will still arrive in time.

Aufgaben

1.

Name	eigener Name	Ms Fiona MacNamara
Position	Versandleiter/in	Purchasing Director
Firma	Schulenburg KG	Jonston & Farmer Ltd
Anschrift	Gutenbergstr. 99,	P.O. Box 200, Harold Hill,
	75206 Keltern, Germany	Romford, Essex RM3 8UX, UK
Fax	+49 (72 36) 88 12 40	+44 (3 70) 8 62 19 88
E-Mail	schulenberg.kg@netlink.de	jonston.farmer@firmnet.co.uk

Geschäftsfall:
Sie haben von der Jonston & Farmer Ltd am … einen Auftrag über verschiedene Kristallwaren (*crystal glass items*) erhalten, der von Ihnen am … (4 Tage später) bestätigt wurde.

Aufgabe:

Verfassen Sie mit Datum vom ... (14 Tage später) die Versandanzeige per Brief /
Fax / E-Mail unter Berücksichtigung der folgenden Einzelheiten:

- Ware wurde dem Spediteur, der Firma Expressgut Schmidt KG, heute
  übergeben
- Voraussichtliches Ankunftsdatum beim Kunden: in 3 Tagen
- Waren wurden in mit Schaumstoff aufgefüllte Kartons verpackt
- Jeweils 12 Kartons wurden in einen Umkarton (*outer box*) gepackt und mit
  Stahlband umwickelt (*with steel strapping*)
- Markierung der Kisten mit Kundenanschrift, wie gewünscht
- Rechnung wird mit separater Post geschickt.

2.

Name	eigener Name	–
Position	Exportleiter/in	–
Firma	Messinstrumente König	Maini Precision Products Ltd
Anschrift	Belpstr. 109, 3001 Bern, Schweiz	51 Residency Road, Bangalore 560080, India
Fax	+41 (31) 3 97 86 54	+91 (80) 4 56 32
E-Mail	m.i.koenig@firmennetz.de	maini.precison@asiaweb.com

Geschäftsfall:

Sie haben aus Indien einen Auftrag über ein Messgerät (*measuring device*) Typ RT
005 zum Preis von 12.500,00 Schweizer Franken erhalten.

Aufgabe:

Schicken Sie die Versandanzeige an Maini unter Berücksichtigung der folgenden
Punkte:

- Transportart: Luftfracht
- Abflughafen: Zürich
- Ankunftsflughafen: Bangalore
- Flug: Mit Swissair 709 bis Delhi, dann Weiterflug mit Air India 367
  bis Bangalore
- Abflug: 9. ... (Monat angeben) 18.05 Uhr
- Ankunft: 12. ... (des selben Monats) 8.00 Uhr
- Preis: 12.500,00 Schweizer Franken
- Lieferung: FCA Zürich
- Zahlung: mit unwiderruflichem, bestätigtem Dokumentenakkreditiv
- Importlizenz: Nr. 8563975
- Dokumente (Luftfrachtbrief 4-fach, Handelsfaktura 3-fach, Ursprungszeugnis)
  werden der Bank übergeben.

3.

Name	Patricia (Lars) Angerer	–
Position	Verkaufssachbearbeiter/in	–
Firma	Maschinenfabrik Rolf Zeidler AG	Hong Kong Machinery Ltd
Anschrift	Gold-Zack-Str. 11, 40822 Mettmann, Germany	Suite 9–11, 18/F Kinwick Centre, 48 Hollywood Road, Central, Hong Kong, China
Fax	+49 (21 04) 87 86 54	+8 53 (9 80) 3 42 55
E-Mail	pangerer.zeidler.ag@aol.com	hk.machinery@chinaweb.com

Geschäftsfall:

Sie haben einen Auftrag über eine Kunststoffspritzgussmaschine (*plastic injection moulding machine*) im Wert von 42.500,00 Euro erhalten.

Aufgabe:

Teilen Sie der Hong Kong Machinery Ltd per Brief mit, dass die Maschine heute Morgen an Bord der MS „Seagull" verschifft worden ist. Weitere Einzelheiten:

- Auslaufhafen: Rotterdam
- Bestimmungshafen: Hong Kong
- Ankunftsdatum: 2 Wochen (ab heute!)
- Lieferbedingung: CIF Hong Kong
- Zahlung: per unwiderruflichem, bestätigtem Dokumentenakkreditiv, eröffnet bei der Hong Kong Central Bank und bestätigt von der Deutsche Bank AG, Düsseldorf.
- Dokumente (reines Bordkonnossement 3-fach, Konsulatsfaktura 4-fach, Handelsfaktura 4-fach, Ursprungszeugnis, Versicherungspolice Nr. 63 085, Ersatzteilliste) wurden der Bank übergeben.

Unit 7

Payment

Introduction

Letters about payment are normally brief unless there is a discrepancy or error to be dealt with. In many such cases the easiest solution is a debit or credit note, which is taken into account when the next invoice or statement is paid.

Whereas in Britain, North America and a number of European countries domestic payments are often made by cheque, bill of exchange, bank transfer (particularly popular in Germany) or COD (cash on delivery), this is not always possible in foreign trade. Refer to the tables on pages 103 and 104 for details of "Methods of payment in foreign trade" and "Terms of payment in international trade" respectively.

When writing about payment use the letter plans to structure your letter, fax or e-mail.

Payment

A. Buyer

1. Acknowledgement of receipt of goods / performance of services
   – reference to goods
   – reference to invoice / bill / statement
2. Reference to mode of payment (see diagram)
3. Reference to discrepancies / errors / amendments*
4. Polite ending
5. Enclosure(s)

*As appropriate

Fig. 13

Payment

B. Seller

1. Reference to invoice / bill / statement*
2. Acknowledgement of receipt of payment or part-payment*
3. Reference to receipt for payment*
4. Reference to discrepancies / errors / amendments*
5. Polite ending
6. Enclosure(s)

*As appropriate

Fig. 14

Specimen Letters

1. Seller requests payment for water filter systems

**Aqua Pure
Water Filter Systems Ltd**

The Summit Centre
Harwood Road
EASTBOURNE
SU5 7JJ
England

Tel. +44 (19 32) 66 05 88
Fax +44 (19 32) 66 05 00
E-mail: aqua.pure@firmnet.co.uk
Website: www.aquapure.co.uk

Our ref. PM/BK
Your ref. kon/99
01 June ..

Mr Heribert Konrad
Purchasing Department
Astra Haustechnik GmbH
Gartenstr. 77
44149 Dortmund
Germany

Dear Mr Konrad

Invoice No. AP-WF for £4,279.85 in respect of 2,000 × Aqua Pure Water Filters

We enclose the above-mentioned invoice for goods supplied against your order
no. 906/kon/99 dated 14 May .. for settlement. We would ask you to remit
the invoice amount to our account no. 7339928 at Lloyds Bank in Eastbourne,
branch code 30-92-86, quoting the invoice number.

Please note that if payment is made within 10 days you may deduct the usual
discount of 3 % from the invoice amount.

We also enclose a brochure on the new generation of active-carbon water filters
for your information.

Thank you for choosing to place your order with Aqua Pure.

Yours sincerely
Aqua Pure Water Filter Systems Ltd

Piers Mountjoy
Piers Mountjoy.
Export Sales Director

Encs

2. German company pays for goods received

Our ref. Wosz/88.tw
Your ref. DJ/bk
2 March ..

Severn Potteries Ltd
95 Clifton Road
BRISTOL
BP4 8JK
England

For the attention of Ms Daphne Jones, Export Sales

Dear Ms Jones

Your Invoice No. EW7/HJG for £5,425.50 of 15 February ..

We have now taken delivery of the consignment of 200 earthenware bowls as per our order no. 88.tw/200 dated 30 January .. . The goods have been checked and we are pleased to confirm that they are as stipulated in our order.

We have therefore instructed our bank to remit the invoice amount to you by SWIFT as agreed. Please contact us should you not receive our remittance within the next few days.

Yours sincerely
Tonwaren Hilpert GmbH

Davina Wosz

Davina Wosz
Purchasing Department

3. German buyer returns an incorrect statement

Our ref. schu.19–5
Your ref. MM/ht
8 November ..

Morgan's Manufacturing Ltd
28 Moss Side Road
MANCHESTER
MC4 9KL
England

Dear Sir / Madam

Your Statement No. 30C for £5,250 dated 30 September .. for Industrial Cleaning Equipment

We have received the above-mentioned statement for the last quarter.

Having checked it against our own records we must draw your attention to the fact that the goods you have charged us for do not tally with those supplied. You have charged us for Item 5 of the statement twice (see enclosure). In addition to this, you have charged us for packing which has now been returned to you.

We have therefore been overcharged by £347.00 in all.

We are returning your statement and would request you to amend it. As soon as we have received your corrected statement we will have your account at the Midland Bank credited accordingly.

Yours faithfully
Köhler Haushaltswaren GmbH

Jacqueline Schulz

Jacqueline Schulz
Accounts Department

Enc.
1 Statement

Case Study

A. Buyer

Marita Schneider works in the Import Section at Megaware Handelsgesellschaft mbH in Berlin (address: 12203 Berlin, Moltkestr. 10–12, fax (0 30) 5 33-87 97, e-mail: megaware.gmbh@telnet.de). Her company wholesales household goods to department stores all over Germany and has just taken delivery of a consignment of crockery (ref. 98DS-TS) from Stafford Tableware Ltd, Long Man Business Park, Stoke-on-Trent, Staffordshire ST3 7AA, England, fax +44 (17 82) 58 97 53, e-mail: stafford.tableware@firmweb.com.uk.

When the goods were checked it was found that the invoice received was incorrect. The following discrepancies were noted:

	Megaware's order	Stafford Tableware's Invoice
1	24 dinner services at £100 each	25 dinner services at £100 each
2	Credit note for £23.97 from the last invoice (no. D-20-1, dated …) to be included	not included
3	Normal rate of £5 per crate for packing (5 crates)	£10 per crate charged (5 crates)
4	Expected invoice amount £2,401.03	Invoice amount £2,550.00

Megaware calculate that they have been overcharged by £148.97 in all. For this reason they are not prepared to accept the 60-day sight draft for £2,550.00 and return it to their suppliers. They will accept a draft for the correct amount as soon as the British company has sent them an amended invoice. They are not prepared to accept another credit note.

B. Seller

Mr Humphrey Pritchard in the European Sales Section at Stafford Tableware Ltd receives the letter from Marita Schneider at Megaware and checks the invoice details. He discovers that there has been an error on his company's part as regards the number of dinner services charged for because Stafford Tableware normally supply dinner services in crates containing 5 services; so 25 and not 24 were charged for by mistake, although only 24 services were supplied.

He notes that his company also omitted to include the credit note referred to when making up Megaware's invoice.

As regards the packing, however, there has not been an error because this particular dinner service must be packed in specially sturdy boxes because it is very fragile. The charge for these reinforced boxes is £10 each. He works out the correct invoice amount to be £2,426.03 so he sends Megaware an amended invoice and draws a new draft on the German company for this sum.

Activities

A. Buyer

Using the "**Payment** Letter Plans" in this Unit and the Standard Expressions write Marita Schneider's letter / fax / e-mail to Humphrey Pritchard at Stafford Tableware Ltd. Explain the discrepancies and ask for these mistakes to be corrected.

B. Seller

Using the "**Payment** Letter Plans" in this Unit and the Standard Expressions write Humphrey Pritchard's letter / fax / e-mail to Marita Schneider at Megaware. Give explanations and apologies as appropriate.

Language

Use both the "**Payment** Standard Expressions" tables to find the words missing below.

1. **Verbs + nouns**
    Which verbs go with the following nouns?
    a.   to check goods – to ▩ goods
    b.   to ▩ a sum of money (to send in any form – not "pay")
    c.   to pay money into a bank account – to ▩ an account with an amount of money
    d.   to settle an account – to ▩ an account
    e.   to indicate that you will pay a draft – to ▩ a draft
    f.   to pay the amount owed on a draft – to ▩ a draft
    g.   to add up all the amounts owing on a statement – to ▩ a statement
    h.   to correct an invoice – to ▩ an invoice

2. **Verbs + prepositions / particles**
    Which prepositions / particles go with the following verbs?
    a.   to check a statement ▩ our records
    b.   to tally ▩
    c.   to credit $1,000 ▩ your account
    d.   "Please draw ▩ us for the amount due."
    e.   to charge a customer ▩ goods
    f.   to debit a customer's account ▩ a sum of money
    g.   to offset a credit note ▩ the invoice amount
    h.   to take something ▩ account
    i.   to make ▩ a statement
    j.   to supply goods ▩ an order
    k.   to carry a total ▩ to next month's statement
    l.   to write a cheque – to make ▩ a cheque
    m.   to pay ▩ goods

3. Nouns + prepositions / prepositions + nouns / adjectives + prepositions

a. an invoice ___ $1,000
b. an IMO ___ $1,000
c. to remit a sum of money ___ SWIFT
d. ___ part-payment of your invoice
e. "We have balanced our account ___ you."
f. "We will honour your draft ___ maturity."
g. "We will honour your draft ___ the due date."
h. to charge someone ___ the normal rate
i. punctually – ___ time
j. "The goods will be despatched ___ receipt of your remittance."
k. a draft ___ $1,000
l. the sum ___ $1,000
m. all monies owing ___ respect of our January statement
n. ___ way of (part-)payment
o. ___ return (i. e. "straight away")
p. ___ due course
q. ___ the earliest opportunity
r. ___ your favour

4. Adjectives / adjectival phrases + nouns

a. three instalments of the same amount of money – three ___ instalments
b. an ___ error (i. e. "a mistake in adding up figures")
c. a rate for a privileged customer – a ___ rate
d. an error made by a clerk – a ___ error

5. Further points

a. Give two words for a mistake.
b. Give another word for "enclosed" (not "included").

Methods of payment in foreign trade

7 Documentary letter of credit
(Dokumentenakkreditiv)

This is the safest means of payment.

The buyer's bank is instructed to pay a sum of money to the seller's bank as long as the documents specified in the contract of sale are presented by the seller to his bank. The seller gives his bank the right documents (e. g. the B/L – bill of lading) and receives payment. His bank then sends them to the buyer's bank. The buyer is given the documents when he has paid in the manner agreed in the contract of sale.

1 Cheque
(Scheck)

The buyer sends his foreign supplier a cheque. A cheque can take up to 2 weeks or more to clear if it is not made out in the foreign supplier's currency.

2 International postal giro
(Post Office)
(Postüberweisung)

Neither the buyer nor the seller need have a post office account. The buyer pays in a sum of money at his post office, which sends it to the post office in the seller's country. A postal cheque is issued, which can be cashed or paid into a bank account

Methods of payment in foreign trade

3 International money order (Bank)
(Internationale Zahlungs-anweisung)

The customer buys this from his bank and posts it to his supplier. In the USA it can be cashed at a bank. Elsewhere it must be paid into an account.

6 Bill of exchange
(Wechsel)

The seller (drawer / payee) draws a bill of exchange on the buyer (drawee) and sends it to him. He accepts it, thereby promising to honour (pay) it on maturity, and returns it to the supplier, who can discount it with his bank, negotiate it or wait for payment on the due date.

Alternatively, the seller can instruct a bank in the buyer's country to release the shipping documents on payment or acceptance of a b/e. This is known as a documentary collection: documents against payment (D/P) or documents against acceptance (D/A).

5 Bank transfer
(Banküberweisung)

The buyer instructs his bank to transfer a sum of money to the seller's bank account abroad. In most cases payment is made using SWIFT – the Society for Worldwide Interbank Financial Tele-communication. If a bank is not in the SWIFT network a telegraphic transfer (TT) is made by tested telex (TT).

4 International banker's draft
(Bankscheck)

The buyer buys a draft from his bank which the bank has drawn upon its correspondent bank in the seller's country (or one of its branches there). The draft is to the order of the seller. The buyer then sends this draft to the seller, who can use it in the way he would a domestic cheque.

Activity

Explain how payment would be made in the following cases.

1. A German buyer wishes to transfer a large sum of money to a Canadian supplier's bank account direct.
2. A German buyer wishes to post his remittance to an American supplier so the American can cash it at his bank immediately.
3. A German supplier sells goods costing a large amount of money to a new customer abroad. The goods are to be sent by ship and the German supplier wants a guarantee that he will receive payment.
4. A German supplier sends goods to a foreign customer by ship, grants his customer 90 days credit but wishes to be paid in the near future.
5. A German supplier wishes to pay a sum of money to someone who is not able to cash a cheque at a bank but can get to a post office.
6. The German buyer's bank draws on a correspondent bank in the seller's country and this instrument of payment is posted to the seller, who can pay it into his bank account or cash it.
7. An American buyer sends a German supplier a remittance and the German supplier has to wait several weeks for the sum to be credited to his bank account.

Terms of payment in international trade

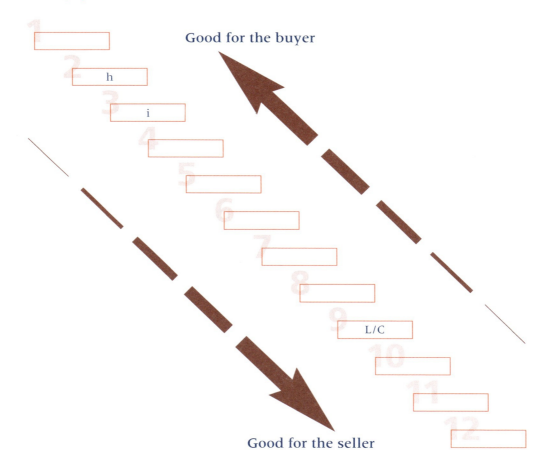

Put these terms of payment in the right boxes in the diagram.

a. CWO / payment in advance
b. L/C
c. Payment on receipt of invoice
d. D/P
e. Payment on receipt of goods
f. 30 days net
g. COD

h. Against acceptance of a b/e at 30 / 60 / 90 days after sight
i. D/A 30/60/90 days after sight / shipment
j. 2 % 14 days
k. Open account terms
l. One third with order, one third on delivery, one third within 30 days after delivery

6 Listening

Your name is Angelika Voss and you are an agent in Britain for Soda Flow GmbH in Duisburg. You recently made an offer for carbonated water systems to an English company at a trade fair in Birmingham. Today you receive a phone call from them.

Questions

1. Who calls Angelika Voss?
2. What company does he work for?
3. What is the reference number? What is the date of the offer?
4. What product is the offer for and what is the quantity?
5. What are the terms of delivery?
6. What are the terms of payment?
7. What is the price?
8. Why does the customer want to change the terms of payment?
9. What other means of payment does he suggest?
10. What further means of payment does Angelika mention?

Compare

Now compare and contrast the two documentary means of payment mentioned. Include answers to the following points in your comparison:

1. What are the exact names of the two means of payment?
2. Which means of payment guarantees payment to the exporter, if certain conditions are fulfilled? Explain what conditions are meant here.
3. At what point in the transaction does the exporter receive payment in each case?
4. Explain why Angelika Voss doesn't want to change the terms of her offer.

Activity

Write a summary of your telephone conversation in German. It is to be given to Frau Eva Berghoff, the Head of Export Sales at Soda Flow GmbH in Duisburg.

Telephone Role Play

Rolle A

Sie sind Maria (Frank) Hamanns und arbeiten in der Buchhaltung der Firma Richter & Partner GmbH in Chemnitz. Die Rechnung SR/gf 51008 vom … (vor 8 Wochen) für 18.000 Paar Strumpfhosen (*tights*) steht trotz zweimaliger Mahnung noch aus. Rufen Sie Ihren Kunden, die Firma Hampshire Garments Ltd in England, an. Berücksichtigen Sie dabei folgende Punkte:

- Sie geben die o. a. Rechnungsnummer an und fragen, warum Hampshire Garments noch nicht auf die 2 Mahnungen reagiert hat
- Welche Diskrepanz liegt vor?
- Sie werden das selbstverständlich mit Ihrer Versandabteilung klären
- Dieses Fax ist in der Buchhaltung nie angekommen. Sie werden die Verkaufsabteilung fragen
- Die Ware wurde bereits vor 8 Wochen geliefert, Zahlung sollte innerhalb von 30 Tagen erfolgen. Der Gesamtbetrag der Rechnung lautete auf 15.750 Euro. Sie erwarten dringend 10.000 Euro sofort per Banküberweisung, Rest nach Nachlieferung
- Leider müssen Sie weitere Lieferungen von der Begleichung dieser Rechnung abhängig machen
- Sie werden sich sofort um die Angelegenheit kümmern und die fehlenden Strumpfhosen per Luftexpressfracht nachliefern lassen.

Role B

You are Lydia (Bernard) Limerick. You work in the Export Department of Hampshire Garments Ltd in England. Today a German company phones to request payment for goods it has supplied your company with.
Include the following points in your conversation:

- Ask for the invoice number and check with the Accounts Department
- You find the invoice and explain that it is incorrect because the invoice your company has received is for the wrong number of goods
- You have received 14,000 pairs of "Sophia" ladies' tights, but Richter & Partner have invoiced you for 18,000 pairs. 4,000 pairs are missing
- You sent a fax 2 days after delivery (7 weeks ago) to say you had been short-shipped
- You say you'll remit the whole sum as soon as the missing tights arrive
- You finally agree to pay as the supplier wishes
- You will arrange for payment of the sum requested today or tomorrow by SWIFT
- You also ask the supplier to ensure that the 4,000 missing pairs of tights are delivered promptly, because an important customer is waiting for them.

Aufgaben

1. Seller

Name	eigener Name	–
Position	Buchhalter/in	–
Firma	Ormanns Büromaschinen GmbH	Themostocles Ltd
Anschrift	Neusser Str. 13, 80807 München, Germany	P.O. Box 1897, 1513 Nicosia, Zypern (Cyprus)
Fax	+49 (89) 7 25 45 77	+3 57 (2) 7 78 53
E-Mail	ormanns.bm@germanyweb.de	thermostocles@medlink.com

Geschäftsfall:
Sie haben am … (vor 3 Monaten) eine Sendung Büromaschinen an die Firma Themostocles Ltd geschickt. Die Rechnung belief sich auf 34.950 Euro. Der Kunde hat die 1. und 2. Teilzahlung ordnungsgemäß überwiesen, hat jedoch bei der 3. und letzten Teilzahlung in Höhe von 12.950 Euro 30% abgezogen, weil an 2 Büromaschinen Schäden aufgetreten sind, die er auf nicht ordnungsgemäße Verpackung zurückführt.

Aufgabe:
Verfassen Sie ein Schreiben an Themostocles Ltd unter Berücksichtigung der folgenden Einzelheiten:
- Verlangen Sie Fotos der beschädigten Büromaschinen und Bestätigung der Beschädigung im Frachtbrief
- In jedem Fall ist die Höhe des einbehaltenen Betrages nicht gerechtfertigt
- Sie sind bereit, einen Abzug von 10% bis zur Klärung zu gewähren
- Erbitten Sie die Zahlung der verbleibenden 20% per Banküberweisung sofort.

2. Buyer

Name	eigener Name	Mr Humphrey Singleton
Position	Buchhalter/in	Managing Director
Firma	Bauer & Döppner KG	Peter Evans Ltd
Anschrift	Fraasstr. 17, 70184 Stuttgart, Germany	62 Durham Street, London SE11 5JW, England
Fax	+49 (7 11) 90 66 54	+44 (1 71) 8 75-60 40
E-Mail	bauer.doeppner.kg@aol.com	100885.1084@capitalweb.co.uk

Geschäftsfall:
Sie sind seit einem Jahr Kunde der Peter Evans Ltd. Nachdem die Bezahlung der ersten Aufträge mit 30-Tage-Wechseln erfolgte, haben Sie die Peter Evans Ltd

gebeten, Ihnen ab sofort ein vierteljährliches Zahlungsziel einzuräumen. Hiermit war die britische Firma einverstanden. Nun haben Sie mit der Nr. 39780 von der britischen Firma eine Rechnung mit dem Datum von vorgestern erhalten, der erneut ein 30-Tage-Wechsel beilag, welcher Ihnen zum Akzept vorgelegt wird.

Aufgabe:

Verfassen Sie ein Schreiben an die Peter Evans Ltd, in welchem Sie auf die neue Vereinbarung hinweisen. Berücksichtigen Sie darüber hinaus die folgenden Einzelheiten:

- Sie schicken die Tratte unakzeptiert zurück
- Sie bitten um Zusendung eines Kontoauszugs, dessen Saldo dann vereinbarungsgemäß am Quartalsende per Überweisung beglichen wird
- Da dieses Versehen eindeutig auf das Konto von Evans geht, weisen Sie vorsichtshalber darauf hin, dass Sie keinerlei zusätzliche Kosten akzeptieren werden.

3. Buyer

Name	eigener Name	Ms. Maryellen Ryan
Position	Einkaufsleiter/in	Executive Vice President
Firma	Hagenberg & Söhne GmbH	Pacific Textiles Corporation
Anschrift	Postfach 400174,	142 Anahi Street, Honolulu,
	60399 Frankfurt, Germany	HI 96814-5935, Hawaii, USA
Fax	+49 (69) 8479-30	+1 (808) 836 2188
E-Mail	hagenberg.soehne@online.de	pacific.textiles.corp@linkall.com

Geschäftsfall:

Sie hatten bei der Pacific Textiles Corporation einen Auftrag in Höhe von 25.000,00 US$ platziert. Die vereinbarte Zahlungsart war ein unwiderrufliches und bestätigtes Akkreditiv, zu eröffnen durch eine deutsche Bank. Dies ist geschehen, die Laufzeit des Akkreditivs endet am … (in einer Woche). Sie erhalten heute ein Fax der Firma in Honolulu, in welchem diese mitteilt, dass die Ware erst am … (in 10 Tagen) in Honolulu verschifft werden kann. Aus diesem Grund bittet die Firma um eine Verlängerung der Laufzeit des Akkreditivs um 3 Wochen.

Aufgabe:

Beantworten Sie das Schreiben der Firma Pacific Textiles Corporation und teilen Sie ihr Folgendes mit:

- Sie haben Ihre Bank angewiesen, das Akkreditiv um 21 Tage, d. h. bis zum …, zu verlängern
- Die zusätzlich entstehenden Kosten sind vom Lieferanten zu tragen
- Da Sie die Ware bereits weiterverkauft haben, ist eine weitere Verlängerung nicht möglich.

4. Seller

Name	eigener Name	Mr Walter Pickles
Position	Buchhalter/in	Managing Director
Firma	Foto Seidel GmbH	Delta Photographics Ltd
Anschrift	Sep-Ruf-Weg 84,	48 Shoesmith Road, Highgate,
	81241 München	London N10 4TT, England
Fax	+49 (89) 9 98 67 54	+44 (1 81) 5 80 9 21 34
E-Mail	foto.seidel@online.de	delta.photo@firmnet.co.uk

Geschäftsfall:
Sie sind in der Buchhaltung der Fa. Foto Seidel GmbH tätig. Bei der Durchsicht Ihrer Bücher stellen Sie fest, dass das Konto der Firma Delta Photographics Ltd in London einen Schuldsaldo in Höhe von 249,78 Euro aufweist.
Diese Summe setzt sich aus mehreren Beträgen zusammen, und zwar:
–   Rechnung Nr. 0044/93A über 159 Euro vom … (vor 4 Wochen) für die Entwicklung von Bildern anlässlich der Bürofachmesse in Frankfurt. Der Rechnungsbetrag von 159 Euro beinhaltet einen Aufpreis von 75 Euro, da die Bilder postwendend entwickelt und zum Messegelände per Eilkurier (*special messenger*) gebracht wurden. Bisher sind lediglich 84 Euro für die Entwicklungsarbeiten überwiesen worden.
–   Rechnung Nr. 0044/81C über 155,78 Euro vom … (vor 10 Wochen) für eine eingehende, 3-stündige Beratung (*3 hours of in-depth consultation given to …*) der englischen Firma bezüglich Werbemaßnahmen auf der Bürofachmesse in Düsseldorf. Diese Rechnung ist nunmehr 6 Wochen überfällig.
–   3 % Skonto sind unberechtigterweise von Rechnung Nr. 0044/78D vom … (vor 7 Wochen) in Abzug gebracht worden, obwohl die Rechnung nicht fristgerecht (d. h. innerhalb 30 Tagen) beglichen wurde. Auf diesen Abzug wurde die englische Firma mit Lastschrift Nr. 41/B vom … (vor 2 Wochen) seitens der deutschen Firma aufmerksam gemacht, aber bisher ohne Erfolg.

Aufgabe:
Verfassen Sie ein Schreiben, in dem auf die oben erwähnten Punkte hingewiesen wird und Folgendes zum Ausdruck kommt:
–   Bitte um sofortige und vollständige Überweisung der überfälligen Beträge
–   Bei schleppender Zahlung in Zukunft sind Kontokorrentbedingungen nicht mehr möglich, sondern nur noch Kasse bei Auftragserteilung.

5. Buyer

Name	Melanie (Marius) Amaretto	–
Position	–	–
Firma	–	Bicycle Spare Parts and Accessories Ltd
Anschrift	Mühlbachstr. 20, 78315 Radolfzell, Germany	121 Landsdowne Road, Bedford MK40 2B7, England
Fax	–	–
E-Mail	–	–

Geschäftsfall:

Sie haben am 13. 05. bei der Bicycle Spare Parts and Accessories Ltd einen Fahr-
radanhänger (*bicycle trailer*) Marke „Light Classic" mit Alu-Felgen (*aluminium rims*)
zum Preis von 360,00 £ gekauft. Zahlungsbedingung war die Vorabsendung eines
Verrechnungsschecks. Diesen Scheck haben Sie zwar geschickt, er wird Ihnen
aber von der britischen Firma zurückgesandt mit der Mitteilung, dass der Scheck
mangels Deckung nicht eingelöst worden ist. Die zusätzlichen Kosten werden mit
12,00 £ angegeben.

Aufgabe:

Schreiben Sie an die Bicycle Spare Parts and Accessories Ltd einen Brief und führen
Sie folgende Punkte an:
– Die unzureichende Deckung ist ein Versehen Ihrerseits, das Sie zu entschuldigen bitten (Grund: Sie haben kurze Zeit vorher eine größere Überweisung
getätigt)
– Sie fügen erneut einen Verrechnungsscheck für 360,00 + 12,00 £ (Ersatz für
entstande Kosten) = 372,00 £ bei
– Bitten Sie nunmehr um möglichst schnelle Zusendung des Fahrradanhängers,
da Sie ihn für eine Urlaubsreise benötigen.

Unit 8

Delay in Delivery

Introduction

If goods are delayed the buyer normally contacts the seller in writing or by telephone to ask for an explanation and a delivery date. The seller should apologize for the delay regardless of whether he is at fault or not. It is best to apologize briefly at the beginning of the letter and then once again at the end. A mere factual explanation is not enough to promote good will between companies.

Refer to the diagrams for the different courses of action open to the buyer and the seller.

When writing about delays in delivery use the letter plans to structure your letter, fax or e-mail.

Delay in Delivery

B. Seller

1. Tell the buyer that delivery will / may be delayed*
   – reason(s)
2. Acknowledge receipt of buyer's letter
   – first (brief) apology for the delay
3. Release the buyer from the contract*
4. Explain the delay
   – refer to enclosure(s)
5. Give date for delivery or part-delivery
6. Grant a concession / concessions*
7. Second apology for the delay
8. Polite ending
9. Enclosure(s)

*As appropriate

Fig. 15

Delay in delivery (Seller)

Seller → Apologize → Explain delay → Give new delivery date

Apologize → Release buyer from the contract

Delay in Delivery

A. Buyer

1. Reference to delayed order
2. Cancellation of order*
3. Importance of prompt delivery*
4. Request for an explanation of the delay*
5. Request for delivery by a certain date*
6. Consequence(s) of (further) delay (see diagram)*
7. Polite ending

*As appropriate

Fig. 16

Delay in delivery (Buyer)

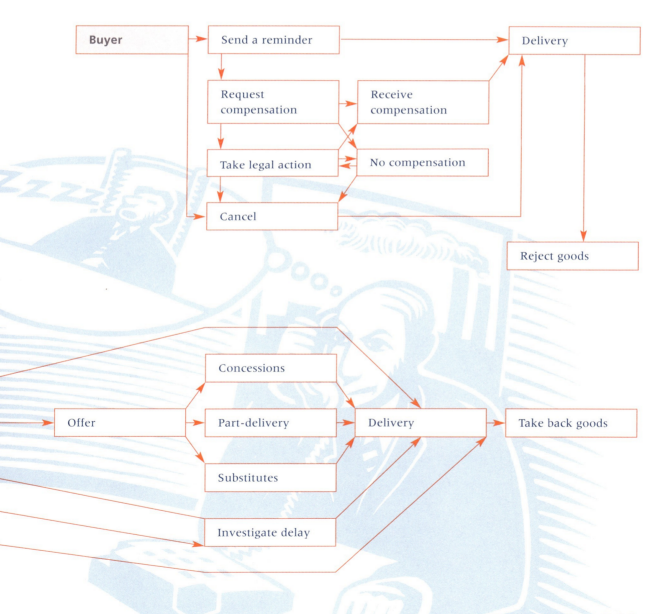

Specimen Letters

1. English company apologises for delay

Cumbria Boots Ltd

12 White Cross
Lancaster
LA1 6HH
England

TT/MT
10 April ..

Schuhhaus Seppelfrick GmbH & Co. KG
Sulzbacher Str. 50
38116 Braunschweig
Germany

For the attention of Mr Roland Bendorf, Import Section

Dear Mr Bendorf

<u>Your Order for Walking Shoes dated 2 March ..</u>

In connection with your order for 200 pairs of "Mountain High" walking shoes, we unfortunately have to tell you that, owing to circumstances entirely beyond our control, delivery of the consignment will be delayed by two weeks.

We are sincerely sorry for this delay and realise how inconvenient this must be for you. However, as a result of the insolvency of one of our suppliers, we have now had to seek an alternative source of raw materials. We have, in the meantime, been reliably informed that the shoes will be ready here in 10 days' time. Your order will be given priority and will be delivered to you by express air freight by our forwarders, Eurotrans Ltd.

Under the circumstances, we are reducing the price of this consignment by 10 %.

Please let us once again say that we sincerely regret the delay and that we will do our utmost to ensure that it does not happen again.

Yours sincerely
Cumbria Boots Ltd

Terry Tanner
Terry Tanner
Export Sales Department

E-mail: cumbria.boots@cumbria.co.uk   Tel. +44 (15 24) 4 53 22
Website: www.cumbria.co.uk   Fax +44 (15 24) 4 53 20

2. German company faxes British supplier because of delay in delivery

Wirichs Fruchtsäfte KG,
Dieselstr. 99, 46049 Oberhausen, Germany
Tel. +49 (2 08) 33 96 74, Fax +49 (2 08) 33 96 70

FAO:	Ms Sharon Waterstone
	Export Sales Dept.
	Heavytree Natural Fruit Juice Co.
	Willow Farm
	TAUNTON
	England
Fax No:	+44 (18 23) 7 92 10
From:	Brigitte Stein
	Import Section
Date:	18 February ..
Subject:	Delay in Delivery of our Order No. 997-OS dated 3 January ..
	for 5,000 1-litre Cartons of Raspberry Juice
Total Pages:	1

Dear Ms Waterstone

The 5,000 cartons of raspberry juice still haven't arrived despite your assurance that we would be able to take delivery within 5 weeks.

As some of our customers are now threatening to cancel their orders, we must be certain that the consignment will reach our premises by the end of this week at the latest.

If this deadline isn't met we'll have to cancel the order.

Please let us know by return exactly when the goods will arrive and why they have been delayed. I must also point out that any additional expense incurred by us as a result of this delay will be charged to you.

Prompt delivery of the fruit juice is all that is needed to settle this matter.

Yours sincerely

Brigitte Stein

3. German customer in Essen e-mails the American Chiaroscuro Fine Art Inc. in New York City because paintings ordered are late

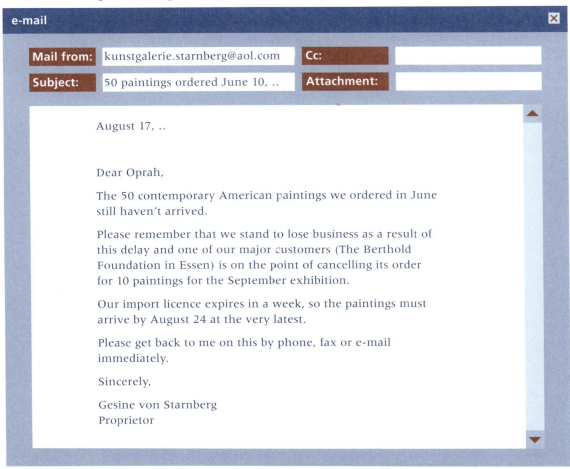

e-mail   ✕

Mail from: kunstgalerie.starnberg@aol.com   **Cc:**

Subject: 50 paintings ordered June 10, ..   **Attachment:**

August 17, ..

Dear Oprah,

The 50 contemporary American paintings we ordered in June still haven't arrived.

Please remember that we stand to lose business as a result of this delay and one of our major customers (The Berthold Foundation in Essen) is on the point of cancelling its order for 10 paintings for the September exhibition.

Our import licence expires in a week, so the paintings must arrive by August 24 at the very latest.

Please get back to me on this by phone, fax or e-mail immediately.

Sincerely,

Gesine von Starnberg
Proprietor

Case Study

A. Buyer

Margot Sareike works in the Purchasing Department of Heim & Bau GmbH, a large chain of D. I. Y. stores in Germany with its headquarters in Essen.

Ten weeks ago she ordered a consignment of 300 fabric awnings in different sizes and colours (order no. FA 98-ZW-Q dated …) from a British company called Sunflexx Ltd in Eastbourne. In addition to the awnings, 100 electric motors for the electrically operated version were also ordered.

The British company promised delivery within 8 weeks of receipt of order, CIF Rotterdam, and payment was arranged one third with order, one third on delivery and one third within 30 days after delivery.

As the awnings and motors are now two weeks overdue, Margot contacts Sunflexx and asks for an explanation of the delay and a firm delivery date for the goods. Heim & Bau need the awnings very soon because the German company has received a large number of advance orders and some of its customers have now threatened to cancel and order from another D. I. Y. store.

In her letter / fax / e-mail to Sunflexx Margot says that her company must have the goods within 10 days at the very latest, after which time she can only hope to sell the awnings at all if the price is reduced by at least 10%.

It may also still be necessary to cancel the order or part of it if Heim & Bau's customers cancel their orders within the next few days.

A. Seller

Sally Field in the European Exports Department at Sunflexx Ltd receives Margot's letter / fax / e-mail and enquires about the delay. She finds out that:

1. The fabric Heim and Bau ordered is not available for two more weeks as a result of industrial action in the textile industry. A new, more expensive acrylic fabric in the same colours can, however, be supplied immediately and would normally cost 10% more.

2. The 100 motors ordered are in stock now so they can be supplied immediately with the acrylic awnings.

As Heim & Bau are good customers Sally makes them two offers:

Offer 1
Delivery in two instalments as follows:
1. The 100 motors in stock and 150 of the more expensive acrylic awnings immediately at no extra charge, CIF Rotterdam.
2. The other 150 awnings as originally ordered in 2 weeks' time, CIP Essen.

Offer 2
Sunflexx are prepared to supply the 100 motors and 300 of the more expensive acrylic awnings immediately CIP Essen, if Heim & Bau are prepared to pay 10 % more for the acrylic awnings.

Activities
Addresses:
–   Heim & Bau GmbH, Altendorfer Str. 42, 45127 Essen,
    Fax +49 (201) 23 37 17, e-mail: Heim.und.bau@weblink.de.
–   Sunflexx Ltd, 49 West Link Road, Eastbourne, EA7 8TZ,
    Fax +44 (13 23) 60 98 77, e-mail: Sunflexx@firmnet.com.uk.

A. Buyer
Using the "**Delay in Delivery** Letter Plans" in this Unit and the Standard Expressions write Margot Sareike's letter / fax / e-mail to Sally Field at Sunflexx Ltd.

B. Seller
Using the "**Delay in Delivery** Letter Plans" in this Unit and the Standard Expressions write Sally Field's letter / fax / e-mail to Margot Sareike at Heim & Bau in Essen. Remember to make your letter / fax / e-mail apologetic.

C. Buyer
Using the "**Delay in Delivery** Letter Plans" in this Unit and the Standard Expressions
Either:
Write Margot Sareike's reply to Sally Field's offer indicating which of the two offers she wishes to accept.
Or:
Write Margot Sareike's reply Sunflexx saying that her company must cancel the order. In this case she gives reasons for cancelling and requests a refund of the amount paid when placing the order.

Language

Use both the "**Delay in Delivery** Standard Expressions" tables to find the words missing below.

1. **Verbs + nouns**
   Which verbs go with the following nouns?
   a. to keep to the terms of the contract – to ▨ the terms of the contract
   b. to ▨ inconvenience (to be the reason for)
   c. to ▨ a deadline
   d. to ▨ the validity of the documentary credit (i. e. "to make longer")
   e. to ▨ the matter in the hands of our solicitors
   f. to ▨ our losses (i. e. "to get back")
   g. to ▨ compensation (i. e. "to look for")
   h. "We would ▨ your comments."
   i. "We ▨ our sincerest apologies."

2. **Verbs + prepositions / particles**
   Which prepositions / particles go with the following verbs?
   a. to keep ▨ the terms of the contract
   b. to dispose ▨ goods (i. e. "to throw away")
   c. to result ▨ losing an order
   d. to pass an explanation ▨ to our customers
   e. "The goods have been held ▨." (i. e. "delayed")
   f. "Our order has become mixed ▨ with someone else's."
   g. to sue someone ▨ damages
   h. to deduct the additional expense ▨ an invoice
   i. "This delay has come ▨ because of a misunderstanding."

3. **Nouns + prepositions / prepositions + nouns / adjectives + prepositions**
   a. ▨ schedule (i. e. "late")
   b. ▨ schedule (opposite of a., i. e. "at the time expected")
   c. ▨ time (i. e. "early enough")
   d. ▨ condition that
   e. to be ▨ breach of contract
   f. to store the goods ▨ your expense
   g. to place the goods ▨ your disposal
   h. "We have a commitment ▨ our own customers."
   i. "We are ▨ pressure."
   j. to be ▨ the point of doing something
   k. "We are ▨ a loss to understand …"
   l. to be ▨ fault
   m. ▨ transit
   n. ▨ the (very) latest
   o. ▨ fail
   p. "There is no point ▨ delivering these goods …"
   q. ▨ the original price

r.   circumstances ▆▆ our control
s.   "Please confirm ▆▆ writing."
t.   a rise ▆▆ interest rates
u.   a change ▆▆ the law

4.   **Adjectives / adjectival phrases + nouns**
   a.   a ▆▆ order (i.e. "We will not change our minds about this order")
   b.   an ▆▆ order (i.e. "an order which has not yet been carried out")
   c.   a lot of inconvenience – ▆▆ inconvenience
   d.   the first price quoted – the ▆▆ price
   e.   a small mishap – a ▆▆ mishap
   f.   "May we express our ▆▆ regret that …"
   g.   a fax which is impossible to read – an ▆▆ fax

5.   **Further points**
   a.   What different forms of industrial action are mentioned here?
   b.   What natural catastrophes are mentioned here?

7   Listening

Before you listen to the dialogue, first read through the background information provided and the instructions following it.

Background information

Your company, Astra Entertainment, is an American-owned multi-national organisation. The Director of European Operations is Zorro A. Kidd from Atlanta, Georgia. Your company is about to put on a new musical called "Goethe Go West, Baby!" and has ordered the costumes from London, England. They are, however, delayed so you phone the English supplier, ShowGear Ltd, to find out what has happened.

Instructions

Either:

(a) Write a memo in English to Zorro A. Kidd to include the following points:
1.   The exact nature of the problem.
2.   Details of ShowGear's two offers regarding the goods (price, delivery, etc.)
3.   Your recommendation as regards what Astra Entertainment should do, with a brief explanation of your reasons.
4.   How soon you need Mr Kidd's answer.

Or:

(b) Write a summary in German of your telephone conversation. It is to be given to your Head of Department, Frau Hildebrandt.

From: Anastasia Hildebrandt
To: Mr Zorro A. Kidd, Director of European Operations
Date: Tuesday
Subject: Costumes for "Goethe Go West, Baby!"

Telephone Role Play

Rolle A

Sie sind Natascha (Dietmar) Rüsch und arbeiten im Büro der deutschen Theaterbühne AG in Offenbach, Telefon: +49 (69) 33 11 50, Fax: +49 (69) 33 11 45. Sie hatten bei der britischen Firma Foster Fashion Ltd in Henley historische Shakespeare-Kostüme für eine in Kürze stattfindende Aufführung bestellt. Diese sind noch nicht angekommen. Rufen Sie Foster Fashion Ltd an und berücksichtigen Sie dabei folgende Punkte:

- Beziehen Sie sich auf Ihren Auftrag Nr. 1195 vom … (vor einem Monat)
- Sie finden den Lieferverzug unglaublich. Der Liefertermin war fest für den … (vor 4 Tagen) versprochen. Ihre 1. Vorstellung (*performance*) ist in 10 Tagen
- Sie müssen die Kostüme allerspätestens für die Generalprobe (*dress rehearsal*) in 8 Tagen haben, sonst gibt es einen Eklat (*a catastrophe*)
- Sie werden die Kostüme nicht mehr abnehmen, wenn sie nicht in 7 Tagen da sind
- Eigentlich brauchen Sie die Kostüme morgen, falls sie nicht hundertprozentig passen und noch geändert (*altered*) werden müssen – ist das möglich?
- Sie werden die Kostüme morgen selbst am Frankfurter Flughafen abholen und bitten um Bekanntgabe der Flug-Nr. und Ankunftszeit
- Sie hoffen, dass alles noch klappt!

Role B

You are Angela (Richard) Macauley at Foster Fashion Ltd in Henley. Today you receive a call from Natascha (Dietmar) Rüsch in Offenbach about some costumes. Include the following points in your conversation:

- You ask for the order number and date and also what costumes they were

- You check it on your computer – the order is being dealt with and is almost ready
- You apologize for the delay
- You are behind schedule because one of your suppliers delivered the material late
- You've almost finished the costumes now
- You ask the caller to hold on while you find out how soon you can deliver
- You promise to deliver tomorrow morning by express air freight from Heathrow Airport
- You'll give the caller the flight number and time of arrival by fax or phone today or tomorrow. Ask for the German company's fax and phone numbers
- You assure the caller that there will be no further delay and no catastrophes.

Aufgaben

1.

Name	Margot (Werner) Meise	Ms Jeannette Francis
Position	Einkaufsleiter/in	Export Sales Director
Firma	Dynamo Paketservice GmbH	Jennifer Green Ltd
Anschrift	Am Brunnen 11, 45133 Essen, Germany	15 Ashburn Gardens, London SW7 4DG, UK
Fax	+49 (2 01) 96 75 43	+44 (1 71) 8 50-39 61
E-Mail	dynamo.paket@firmenshuttle.de.	jen.green@compulink.co.uk.

Geschäftsfall:
Vor 4 Wochen haben Sie bei der Jennifer Green Ltd mehrere Büroartikel und Softwarepakete bestellt. Lieferzeit: 3 Wochen, Zahlung: $1/3$ bei Auftragserteilung, $1/3$ bei Lieferung, $1/3$ 60 Tage nach Rechnung. Die Ware ist bisher noch nicht eingetroffen.

Aufgabe:
Schreiben Sie einen Beschwerdebrief unter Berücksichtigung folgender Punkte:
- Bezug auf den o. a. Auftrag
- Bestellte Waren werden dringend benötigt, da sonst Kundenaufträge unerledigt bleiben
- Bitte um Erklärung der Verspätung
- Setzen Sie eine Frist (höchstens 2 Wochen!)
- Sollte Lieferung bis dahin nicht erfolgt sein, behalten Sie sich weitere Schritte vor.

2.

Name	eigener Name	Mr Andrew McDuffy
Position	Hoteldirektor/in	Export Sales Director
Firma	Hotel Palladium Palace	Scottish Fish Exports Ltd
Anschrift	Saarstr. 130, 12161 Berlin, Germany	Eaglesham Road, East Kilbridge, Glasgow G75 8EA, Scotland
Fax	+49 (30) 4 37 89 65	+44 (1 41) 8 96-86 75
E-Mail	–	–

Geschäftsfall:
Sie hatten bei der Scottish Fish Exports Ltd 60 Seiten feinsten geräucherten Lachs (*pieces of finest smoked salmon*) für einen Empfang morgen in Ihrem Hotel bestellt. Die Ware sollte spätestens am … (vor 4 Tagen) geliefert werden. Heute ist die Ware trotz zweimaliger Anrufe, in denen die Lieferung angemahnt wurde, nicht eingetroffen.

Aufgabe:
Faxen Sie einen Brief (mit Sondervermerk "**Faxed and Posted**") an die Scottish Fish Exports Ltd mit folgendem Inhalt:
–   Aufgrund der Dringlichkeit der Lieferung haben Sie keine andere Wahl als
    a)   den Auftrag mit sofortiger Wirkung zu stornieren,
    b)   die Ware kurzfristig anderswo zu beschaffen und
    c)   die Kosten, die den Preis der bestellten Ware übersteigen, dem Lieferanten in Rechnung zu stellen
–   Sie können nicht länger warten, weil ein Teil der Esswaren für den morgigen Empfang, der vormittags stattfindet, bereits heute abend vorbereitet werden muss
–   Falls die Ware noch eintrifft, muss sie bis auf weitere Anweisung des Lieferanten zur Verfügung gehalten werden
–   Fragen Sie, was damit geschehen soll
–   Bedauern Sie den Vorfall, aber Sie haben leider keine andere Wahl.

3.

Name	eigener Name	–
Position	Exportleiter/in	–
Firma	Werber GmbH	Sun Hung Kai International Ltd
Anschrift	Kemnader Str. 33, 58456 Witten, Germany	Rajdamnern Avenue, Bangkok 10200, Thailand
Fax	+49 (23 02) 43 57 22	+66 (2) 4 73 10 56
E-Mail	werber.gmbh@online.com.de	sun.hung.kai@thailink.com

Geschäftsfall:

Ihre Firma hatte von der Sun Hung Kai International Ltd einen Auftrag über medizinische Instrumente erhalten. Es sollten 10.000 Stück Einwegbestecke für Transfusionen (*single-use transfusion sets*) geliefert werden. Liefertermin: in 8 Tagen.

Aufgabe:

Kündigen Sie der Sun Hung Kai Ltd. per Brief / Fax / E-Mail einen Lieferverzug an. Legen Sie folgende Gründe dar:
–   Das Herstellungsverfahren für die Einwegbestecke wurde kurzfristig geändert
–   Hierdurch wird eine größere Reinheit der Bestecke garantiert
–   Durch die Umstellung der Maschinen ergibt sich ein Lieferverzug von ca. 3 Wochen
–   Neuer Liefertermin: in 4 Wochen
–   Argumentieren Sie damit, dass die Änderung für den Kunden von Vorteil ist
–   Bitte um Verständnis und um Verlängerung des Akkreditivs um 6 Wochen
–   Alle anderen Bedingungen des Auftrags bleiben unverändert.

4.

Name	Gwendolyn (Albert) Wallis	Ms Marsha Simons
Position	Verkaufssachbearbeiter/in	Purchasing Division
Firma	König & Stiller Maschinenfabrik AG	Stuart Chancellor Ltd
Anschrift	Bahnhofstr. 64, 40489 Düsseldorf, Germany	P.O. Box 253011, St. Albans, Herts. SA3 1AD, England
Fax	+49 (2 11) 76 84 55	+44 (17 27) 32 65 44
E-Mail	koenig.und.stiller@firmenlink.de	scl@complink.co.uk

Geschäftsfall:

Die Stuart Chancellor Ltd hatte bei Ihnen vor einem Monat 20 Hebebühnen (*car lifts*) vom Typ A 690 bestellt. Lieferzeit: 4 Wochen.

Aufgabe:

Schreiben Sie einen Brief / ein Fax / eine E-Mail an die Stuart Chancellor Ltd folgenden Inhalts:

- Zu Ihrem Bedauern müssen Sie dem Kunden mitteilen, dass die Lieferung sich um ca. 2 Wochen verzögern wird
- Grund: Streik in einer Ihrer Zulieferfirmen
- Die Teile, die dort gefertigt werden, sind so schnell von keiner anderen Firma erhältlich
- Frage, ob alle Hebebühnen mit einem Transport 14 Tage später versandt werden können
- Alternative: 5 Hebebühnen könnten ggf. 1 Woche vorher versandt werden
- Die dadurch entstehenden Mehrkosten des Transports würden selbstverständlich von Ihnen übernommen
- Nochmalige Entschuldigung Ihrerseits, aber Hinweis auf höhere Gewalt.

5.

Name	eigener Name	Dr Henry Plumb
Position	Verkaufssachbearbeiter/in	Chief Executive Officer
Firma	Modeschmuck Design Sturm KG	Power & Bell plc
Anschrift	Richard-Zimmermann-Str. 18, 07747 Jena	80 Wigmore Street, London W1H9AB, UK
Fax	+49 (36 41) 6 74 53	+44 (1 71) 4 36-98 60
E-Mail	mode.sturm@t-online.de	power.and.bell@citylink.co.uk

Geschäftsfall:

Sie haben von der Power & Bell plc einen Auftrag über 1.500 Quarz-Armbanduhren (*quartz wristwatches*) für Damen, Marke „Cynthia", und 200 Quarz-Armbanduhren für Damen, Marke „Jeanette", zum Gesamtpreis von 25.000,00 Euro erhalten. In Ihrer Auftragsbestätigung hatten Sie der britischen Firma versprochen, innerhalb der nächsten 8 Tage zu liefern. Aufgrund der unerwartet hohen Nachfrage sind Sie jedoch nicht mehr in der Lage, diese Lieferfrist einzuhalten.

Aufgabe:

Schicken Sie der Power & Bell plc einen Brief, in dem Sie u. a. die folgenden Punkte zum Ausdruck bringen:

- Grund für Lieferverzug
- Die 200 Damenuhren „Jeanette" sind sofort lieferbar
- Da Sie die große Menge der „Cynthia"-Uhren nicht auf Lager haben, sondern nur 500 Stück, könnten Sie diese 500 sofort schicken.
- Die verbleibenden 1.000 Uhren müssten Sie sofort beim Hersteller bestellen
- Sie haben mit diesem bereits Kontakt aufgenommen und erfahren, dass die Uhren in 14 Tagen lieferbar sind
- Dies bedeutet also eine Lieferzeit für die 1.000 „Cynthia" von 3 Wochen

- Bitte um Fax-Nachricht, ob die Power & Bell plc zustimmt
- Sie stehen jederzeit für weitere Fragen zur Verfügung
- Ihr Gesamtprogramm geht dem Kunden mit getrennter Post zu.

6.

Name	eigener Name	Ms Maria Gomez
Position	Geschäftsführer/in	President
Firma	Petersen GmbH	Canadian Investment Projects Inc.
Anschrift	Schwanallee 35, 35037 Marburg, Germany	Suite 608, 1240 May Street, Toronto, Canada M5R 2 A7
Fax	+49 (64 21) 8 56 49	+1 (4 16) 9 22 87 02
E-Mail	petersen.gmbh@weblink.com.de	caninvest.@tazo.com

Geschäftsfall:

Ihre Firma hatte bei der Canadian Investment Projects Inc. vor 10 Wochen eine Marktstudie zur Investitionsbewertung (*investment appraisal*) verschiedener kanadischer Regionen in Auftrag gegeben. Die Studie sollte in spätestens 6 Wochen fertig sein und 20.500,00 CDN$ kosten. Eine Anzahlung von 20 % hat Ihre Firma bereits geleistet, aber die Studie ist bis zum heutigen Tag immer noch nicht eingetroffen.

Aufgabe:

Schreiben Sie eine Beschwerde bezüglich des Lieferverzugs an die kanadische Firma und berücksichtigen Sie dabei folgende Punkte:
- Bezug auf erteilten Auftrag
- Hinweis auf Dringlichkeit der Studie (mehrere Ihrer Kunden haben wegen Investitionen in Kanada bereits nachgefragt)
- Hinweis auf Ihr Fax vor 10 Tagen, auf das Sie keine Antwort erhalten haben
- Wenn die Studie bis Mitte nächsten Monats nicht da ist, ist sie für Sie wertlos und Sie werden die geleistete Anzahlung gerichtlich einfordern
- Falls andere Gründe vorliegen, bestehen Sie auf Darlegung derselben.

Unit 9

Complaints

Introduction

If goods or services are unsatisfactory the buyer should contact the seller immediately.

The seller should always express regret that the buyer is dissatisfied, investigate the matter and then offer an explanation. If appropriate, he should apologize and suggest a solution (see **Fig. 19**).

Complaints should be expressed and dealt with politely and factually in order to promote goodwill between companies. In many cases it is advisable to give the buyer the benefit of the doubt so as not to endanger future business relations.

When making or responding to a complaint use the letter plans to structure your letter, fax or e-mail.

Making a Complaint

A. Buyer

1. Confirm receipt of the goods / performance of services
2. Say what is wrong
   – refer to / enclose proof*
3. Ask for an explanation
4. Consequences for the buyer's company
5. Return the goods to the seller*
6. Request the seller to take appropriate action*
7. Polite ending
8. Enclosure(s)*

*As appropriate

Fig. 17

Dealing with a Complaint

B. Seller

1. Acknowledge receipt of the buyer's letter immediately
2. Say you are sorry that the buyer is dissatisfied
3. Say that the matter will be / is being / has been dealt with
4. Ask for more time to investigate the complaint*
5. Request proof*
6. Explain*
7. Apologise*
8. Explain that you are
   – not at fault
   – partly at fault
   – at fault*
9. Suggest a solution*
10. Suggest arbitration*
11. Polite ending
12. Enclosure(s)

*As appropriate

Fig. 18

Complflaints

□ Buyer

□ Seller

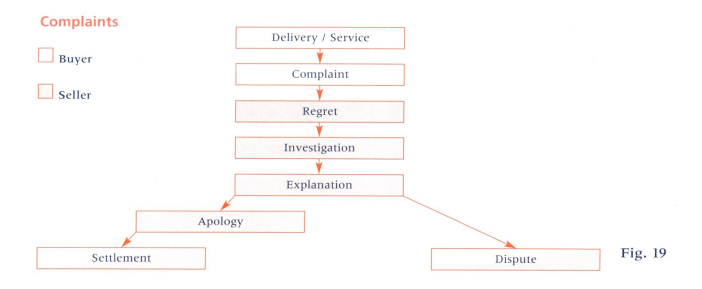

Delivery / Service → Complaint → Regret → Investigation → Explanation → Apology → Settlement / Dispute

Fig. 19

The buyer

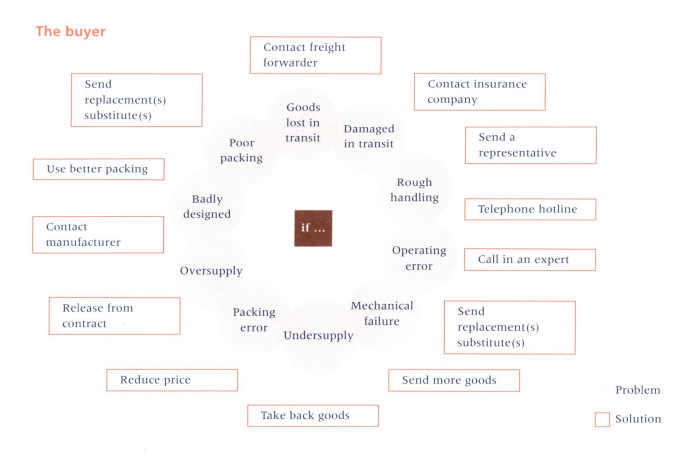

Contact freight forwarder

Send replacement(s) substitute(s)

Contact insurance company

Goods lost in transit

Damaged in transit

Send a representative

Poor packing

Use better packing

Rough handling

Badly designed

Telephone hotline

if ...

Contact manufacturer

Operating error

Call in an expert

Oversupply

Release from contract

Packing error

Mechanical failure

Send replacement(s) substitute(s)

Undersupply

Reduce price

Send more goods

Take back goods

Problem

□ Solution

Activity

Using the diagram above make 10 sentences using the word "if".

Example: "If the goods are damaged in transit you contact the freight forwarder."

You may also find it helpful to begin your sentences with:

"If there is ..."   "If the goods have been ..."   "If the problem is ..."

Specimen Letters

1. Complaint from an English company about touring cycles

Tel. +44 (171) 2 22 98 45 Fax +44 (171) 2 22 98 00 E-mail: ferris.wheel@ferriswheel.co.uk Website: www.ferriswheel.co.uk		Ferris Wheel Cycle Stores Ltd 400 Commercial Road London EC2 9JK England

Ferris Wheel Cycle Stores Ltd

HB/MT
10 May ..

Ms Marita Henkel
Managing Director
Henkel Fahrradbau GmbH
Industriestr. 52
44577 Castrop-Rauxel
Germany

Dear Ms Henkel

Our Order No. RB-007-D dated 3 March .. for 500 26" and 28" Touring Cycles

The above-mentioned goods were delivered to us today and on opening
the container we found that 25 cycles were badly scratched and consequently
unsaleable. This is most likely because they were poorly packed and roughly
handled in transit. We enclose photographs of the damage for your information.

Needless to say we cannot sell these goods at the price agreed and will only
consider keeping them if a reduction in price of 25 % is granted on the damaged
items.

We look forward to receiving your comments on this matter in the very near
future.

Yours sincerely

Henry Butcher

Henry Butcher
Purchasing Director

Encs

2. Henkel Fahrradbau's reply to the complaint from the English company about touring cycles

Henkel Fahrradbau GmbH,
Industriestr. 52, 44577 Castrop-Rauxel, Germany
Tel. +49 (23 05) 9 98 76, Fax +49 (23 05) 9 98 75
E-Mail: henkel.fahrrad@firmenetz.de

FAO: Mr Henry Butcher
Purchasing Manager
Ferris Wheel Cycle Stores Ltd
London EC2
England
Fax No: +44 (1 71) 2 22 98 00
From: Marita Henkel
Managing Director
Date: 14 May ..
Subject: Your letter dated 10 May .. regarding Order No. RB-007-D
dated 3 March .. for 500 26" and 28" Touring Cycles
Total Pages: 1

Dear Mr Butcher

We have just received your letter in connection with the above-mentioned order and are dismayed to hear that some of the cycles arrived scratched. We are now looking into the matter and have contacted the freight forwarding company which transported the goods. It will take us some time to find out how the damage could have happened and we would very much appreciate it if you would let us have a few more days to make enquiries.

Judging by your description of the damage and the photographs supplied, however, it would seem that this problem has come about because of rough handling rather than poor packing. We believe that such damage can only have been caused after the goods left our premises and are now waiting for the freight forwarder's report.

We do, of course, very much regret that this should have happened at all and are sure that the matter will be settled to the satisfaction of all parties concerned.

We will be contacting you in the very near future.

Yours sincerely

Marita Henkel

3. German supplier assures Saudi Arabian customer that equipment will be repaired

e-mail

Mail from: krone.aufzugbau@t-online.de

Cc:

Subject: Lifts in Kingdom Center, Riyadh

Attachment:

4 July ..

Dear Mr Al-Dabbagh

Many thanks for your message this morning regarding the lifts in the Kingdom Center in Riyadh.

We are sorry to hear that they are not performing as expected but would add that you instructed our technicians to operate them a week before installation was fully completed.

However, as a gesture of our goodwill and at the cost of materials only, we are sending out Mr Georg Nowak, the Head of our Maintenance Team, who is in Bahrain at present, to re-adjust the machinery. He will be arriving in Riyadh next Monday with a team of technicians.

Might we also point out that you can call our service hotline to obtain expert advice on problems of a technical nature 24 hours a day.

We hope our suggestion meets your approval and look forward to doing further business with you in the future.

Yours sincerely

Thorsten Fiege
Customer Services

Case Study

A. Buyer

Charlotte Christiansen works in the purchasing department at Zeitgeist Antik Forum in Cologne. At the request of a German customer, an up-market fashion boutique in Düsseldorf called Mode-Trends GmbH, her company recently ordered some antique furniture from a British supplier, Farmer's Furniture Bazaar, in Tunbridge Wells, England. Farmer's representative, Mr Tony Laird, visited Zeitgeist Antik Forum in Cologne two weeks ago and showed Charlotte photographs of a pair of Chippendale mahogany chairs at £1,250 each. He told her they were in good condition for their age (circa 1775).

As Zeitgeist had already bought several items from the English company, they paid a deposit of £500 towards the price of the chairs and arranged to pay the balance within a week after delivery.

The chairs have now arrived in Cologne and Charlotte is disappointed with their condition. One of the chairs has a scratch down the back (rough handling?) and the upholstery on the other chair is stained in two places.

Charlotte therefore contacts the Manager of Farmer's Furniture Bazaar, Ms Sarah Plunkett, to complain. She says that her customer wants the chairs very soon so her company will have them repaired and cleaned in Germany and deduct the cost of this from the balance of £2,000 still to be paid.

B. Seller

Sarah Plunkett receives Charlotte's complaint and immediately contacts Tony Laird. He tells her that the scratch on the back is small and was certainly made at least a century ago. As it is on the back of the chair it is not easily noticeable.

He knows nothing about the upholstery stains because there were none when he saw the chairs last. They may have happened on Farmer's premises or in transit.

Sarah Plunkett contacts Zeitgeist and tells them what Tony Laird said about the scratch and the stains. As the scratch is small and at the back she says that it makes no difference to the value of the chair. As regards the stains, she says that her company is prepared to pay to have them removed by a specialist furniture restorer in Germany. She recommends Konrad Restaurierungswerkstätte in Düsseldorf.

As a gesture of her company's goodwill, she is prepared to pay 50 % of the cost of treating the scratch, if Zeitgeist so wish.

Finally, she asks Zeitgeist to settle the invoice first and send her the German furniture restorer's estimate before any work is carried out on the chairs.

Activities

Addresses:
— Zeitgeist Antik Forum, Isenburger Str. 98, 51067 Köln,
    Fax: +49 (2 21) 8 95 67, e-mail: zeitgeist.antik@firmenlink.de.
— Farmer's Furniture Bazaar, 49 The Parade, Tunbridge Wells, Kent TN7 9NK,
    England, Fax: +44 (17 32) 8 97 65, e-mail: Farmers.bazaar@telcom.co.uk.

A. Buyer

Using the "**Making and Dealing with Complaints** Letter Plans" in this Unit and the Standard Expressions write Charlotte Christiansen's letter / fax / e-mail to Sarah Plunkett at Farmer's Furniture Bazaar.

B. Seller

Using the "**Making and Dealing with Complaints** Letter Plans" in this Unit and the Standard Expressions write Sarah Plunkett's letter / fax / e-mail to Charlotte Christiansen at Zeitgeist Antik Forum in Cologne.

A disastrous desk

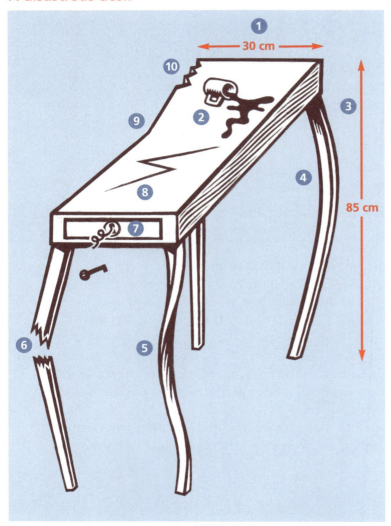

This desk is unsaleable because it has a number of defects. It's in such poor condition because it was roughly handled in transit.

It was, however, also badly designed so it's unsuitable for office use. It can't be locked properly, the wood it's made of is of inferior quality and it's the wrong width and height.

Using the list of **"Useful Expressions"** on page 135 find the right adjectives to describe what's wrong.

Useful expressions

When describing what is wrong use expressions from the table below.

Goods

General	Specific	
not up to sample	too fast	bent (*metal, plastic*)
sub-standard	too slow	broken
not up to standard	too heavy	chipped (*china*)
damaged (*serious*)	too high / low	cracked (*china, stone*)
defective (*serious*)	too light	crooked (*not straight*)
faulty (*smaller problem*)	too many	crushed (*box, container*)
imperfect (*pattern, cloth*)	too few	deformed (*irregular shape*)
inefficient (*machine, service*)	too little	dented (*metal*)
in poor condition	too noisy	discoloured
in an unsatisfactory	too wide / narrow	faded (*cloth, colours*)
condition	wrong colour	frayed (*cloth*)
unacceptable	wrong dimensions (*objects,*	illegible (*print*)
unreliable (*machine, service*)	*machines*)	inferior quality
unsaleable	wrong finish	leaky (*container for liquids*)
unsatisfactory	wrong goods	low quality
unsuitable	wrong height	noisy
unusable	wrong length	poor quality
	wrong width	out of date
	wrong material(s)	out of shape (*clothes*)
	wrong quality	perished (*rubber*)
	wrong quantity	rough (*wood, plastic, metal*)
	wrong size	rusty (*metal*)
	wrong specifications	scratched (*surface*)
	(*materials, machinery*)	smudged (*print*)
	wrong type	squashed (*box, container*)
	wrong weight	stained (*dirty mark*
	wrong measurements	*on something*)
	(*clothing*)	tarnished (*metal*)
		torn (*cloth, paper*)
		twisted (*metal, wood, plastic*)
		warped (*wood, metal, plastic*)
		wet

Services

Work	Person		
below standard	aggressive	messy	unpunctual
not up to standard	clumsy	negligent	unreliable
careless	dirty	offensive	untidy
incomplete	dishonest	off-hand	untrained
inaccurate	impatient	rude	untruthful
inexact	impolite	unavailable	
poor	incapable	uncommuni-	
poorly carried out	incompetent	cative	
sloppy	inefficient	unfriendly	
unfinished	insolent	unhelpful	
unsatisfactory	late	unprofessional	

Language

Use the "**Making and Dealing with Complaints** Standard Expressions" table to find the words missing below.

1. **Verbs + nouns**
   Which verbs go with the following nouns?
   a. to find a solution – to ▨ the matter
   b. to ▨ an edge over our competitors
   c. to ▨ payment (i. e. "to keep back")
   d. to ▨ steps
   e. to ▨ the situation (i. e. "to put right")
   f. to ▨ the damage (i. e. "to see how much damage there is")
   g. to ▨ the invoice amount (i. e. "to pay back")
   h. "The guarantee has run out" – "The guarantee has ▨"
   i. to ▨ costs (i. e. "to make no charge for costs")
   j. to ▨ an agreement (i. e. "to come to")

2. **Verbs + prepositions / particles**
   Which prepositions / particles go with the following verbs?
   a. to put ▨ service
   b. to come ▨ to our expectations
   c. to comply ▨ EU standards
   d. to be inundated ▨ complaints
   e. to get ▨ with our daily business
   f. to sue ▨ damages
   g. to find ▨ what has happened
   h. to look ▨ the matter
   i. to deal ▨ the equipment
   j. "Judging ▨ your description …"
   k. to bring the matter ▨ your attention
   l. to alert someone ▨ a problem
   m. to draw ▨ a report
   n. to pay ▨ a replacement
   o. to provide ▨ settlement by arbitration
   p. to abide ▨ a decision

3. **Nouns + prepositions / prepositions + nouns / adjectives + prepositions**
   a. not up ▨ scratch
   b. ▨ standard (i. e. "not good enough")
   c. ▨ board the plane
   d. to make enquiries ▨ the matter
   e. an explanation ▨ why this happened (2 words)
   f. your comments ▨ this matter
   g. a market ▨ goods of this quality
   h. to be liable ▨ any losses incurred
   i. ▨ your expense

j.   ▨ the next available flight
k.   dependent ▨
l.   an error ▨ our part
m. a collision ▨ the Irish Sea
n.   a collision ▨ the Danube
o.   "▨ what you say about the damage …"
p.   responsible ▨
q.   to be ▨ fault
r.   ▨ our custody

4.   **Adjectives / adjectival phrases + nouns**
a.   ▨ flooding (i. e. "flooding over a large area")
b.   ▨ humidity (i. e. "too much")
c.   ▨ handling (i. e. "careless")

5.   **Further points**
Give a word or expression to mean:
a.   goods sent in a container with another customer's goods
b.   the quality of a person's work
c.   impossible to sell
d.   a guarantee
e.   "No problems at all" – "No problems ▨"
f.   to discipline an employee

8   Listening

Before you listen to the dialogue, first read through the background information provided and the instructions following it.

Background information
In the following dialogue you are Martina Klein, the Export Sales Manager at Möbel Havemann in Essen. You recently sent a consignment of office furniture to an English company called Continental Furniture Ltd in Eastbourne, Sussex, using a haulage company called "EuroHaul". Today Continental Furniture Ltd phone you to complain.

Instructions
Your job is to (a) list the information required (see 1–8 on page 138) and

Either:
(b) Write a memo to your English agent in the south of England, Ms Pam Adams, explaining the problem and telling her what to do. Include the information listed in (a).

Or:

(c) Write a summary in German of your telephone conversation. It is to be given to the Managing Director, Dr Büdenbender.

Information required

1. Give the order number, date and the name of the person who called.
2. Give exact details of the goods supplied.
3. Say what customer Continental Furniture want the goods for.
4. Explain what is wrong with them.
5. Explain how the problem probably came about.
6. Give details of any deadlines and consequences for Möbel Havemann.
7. Say what solution the English company might be prepared to accept.
8. Explain what Pam Adams must now do.

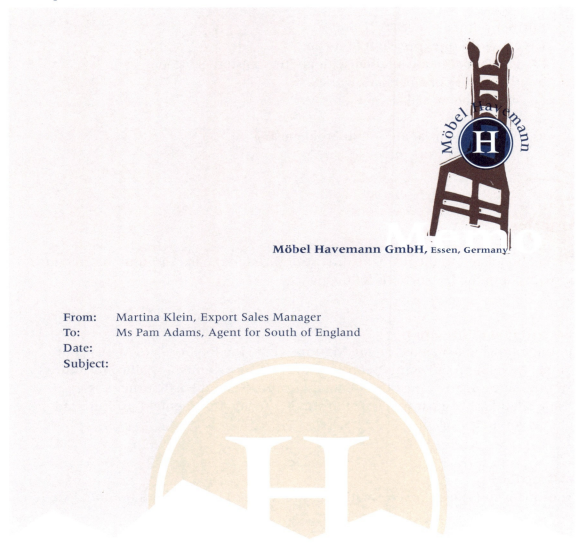

Möbel Havemann GmbH, Essen, Germany

From:	Martina Klein, Export Sales Manager
To:	Ms Pam Adams, Agent for South of England
Date:	
Subject:	

(Swivel chair = *Drehstuhl*)

Telephone Role Play

Rolle A

Sie sind Vanessa (Markus) Battenstein und arbeiten als Einkäufer/in bei der Firma Vanderjohn GmbH in Berlin (Fax: +49 (30) 58 37 04. Rufen Sie Pauline (Patrick) Shriver von der Firma Elbridge Ltd in London an und berücksichtigen Sie dabei folgende Punkte:

- Die von Elbridge geschickten 240 Teeservice (*tea sets*) sind heute in absolut unglaublichem Zustand angekommen
- In den 60 Kisten (*cases*) sind einige Teile (*pieces*) kaputtgegangen, einige fehlen ganz
- Sie werden sofort eine genaue Liste der Schäden anfertigen und diese der englischen Firma zufaxen
- Sie bitten um Angabe der Fax-Nummer
- Sie wissen nicht, wo der Schaden verursacht wurde, weil die Ware in einem Container verstaut war
- Sie werden sofort Ihre Versicherung benachrichtigen, bitten aber Pauline (Patrick) ebenfalls sofort die britische Versicherungsgesellschaft zu informieren
- Sie brauchen dringend Ersatz, da Sie sonst die Teeservice nicht verkaufen können
- Sie möchten nicht, dass Ihnen die Ersatzlieferung in Rechnung gestellt wird
- Sie wollen die Stellungnahmen der Versicherungsgesellschaften abwarten.

Role B

You are Pauline (Patrick) Shriver and work for Elbridge Ltd in London (fax: +44 (1 71) 5 80-40 16). When Vanessa (Markus) Battenstein rings you, you take the call. Include the following points in your conversation:

- Ask what happened
- You cannot understand how the damage happened – rough handling?
- You cannot understand how some items could be missing – theft?
- Ask for a detailed list of the broken and missing pieces to be faxed to you
- You give your fax number
- It was an FOB Dover delivery; where did the damage happen: in Britain or on the Continent?
- You promise to notify your insurance company
- Ask about replacements
- You'll have them sent tomorrow by air freight with an invoice
- You finally agree to wait for the insurance companies' reaction
- You apologise for the difficulties and trust the matter will be settled amicably.

Aufgaben

1.

Name	Paul (Britta) Gundlach	–
Position	Importsachbearbeiter/in	–
Firma	Otto Meyer Getränke-Import GmbH	Minerva Fruit Juices Ltd
Anschrift	Swiftstr. 85, 04159 Leipzig, Germany	P.O. Box 502987, London SW1 1HG, England
Fax	+49 (3 41) 8 76 45	+44 (1 71) 8 30-49 00
E-Mail	otto.meyer.gmbh@firmnet.de	minerva.fruit@webnet.co.uk

Geschäftsfall:
Sie hatten bei der Minerva Fruit Juices Ltd 200 Kartons à vier 5-Liter-Behälter Tomatensaft Marke „Minerva Export 3000" bestellt, die vorgestern per Lkw frei Haus geliefert wurden. Sie haben mehrere Mängel bei der Lieferung festgestellt.

Aufgabe:
Teilen Sie dies der Minerva Fruit Juices Ltd schriftlich mit. Bitte berücksichtigen Sie dabei folgende Punkte:
– Der Lkw kam mit einer Verspätung von 36 Stunden in Ihrem Lager in Leipzig an, wodurch eine Verzögerung in der Auslieferung an Ihre Kunden entstand
– Von den 200 Kartons hatten sich (offenbar durch unsachgemäße Behandlung) bei 20 Behältern die Verschlüsse gelockert, so dass bei diesen Behältern Saft ausgelaufen ist. Sie können so nicht mehr verkauft werden.
– Sie fügen eine Kopie der Bescheinigung bei, die Ihr Lagerleiter (*warehouse manager*) bei Abnahme der Kartons ausstellte, um diese Mängel festzuhalten
– Bitten Sie um Stellungnahme, was mit den nicht verwendbaren Dosen geschehen soll
– Falls der Lieferant einverstanden ist, sind Sie bereit, diese 20 Behälter mit einem Nachlass von 50 % abzunehmen
– Eine diesbezügliche Entscheidung ist aber bis morgen 12 Uhr erforderlich, da sonst der Saft nicht mehr verkäuflich ist
– Hinweis darauf, dass bei zukünftigen Lieferungen die Verschlüsse der Dosen nochmals überprüft werden
– Dringende Mahnung, demnächst pünktlich zu liefern, da sonst reibungsloser Weiterverkauf gefährdet ist.

2.

Name	eigener Name	–
Position	Exportsachbearbeiter/in	–
Firma	Deutsche Photo Gerlach KG	Jonathan & Burger plc
Anschrift	Tiefenbronner Str. 30, 75175 Pforzheim	120 Queen Victoria Street, London, EC4 V4DD, England
Fax	+49 (72 31) 85 13 59	+44 (1 71) 4 15-13 56
E-Mail	photo.gerlach@firmennetz.de.	jb.plc@busilink.co.uk

Geschäftsfall:

Die Jonathan & Burger plc hatte vor 6 Wochen bei Ihnen 10 Fotoapparate Marke „Flash 2000" und 30 Stative (*tripods*) Marke „Luxor" bestellt. Bei der Lieferung waren versehentlich die Zahlen vertauscht worden, so dass die englische Firma vor 5 Tagen 30 Photoapparate und nur 10 Stative erhielt. Jonathan & Burger plc beschwert sich daraufhin bei Ihnen und verlangt sofortige Klärung der Angelegenheit.

Aufgabe:

Verfassen Sie mit dem heutigen Datum die Antwort auf diese Beschwerde unter Berücksichtigung folgender Punkte:
– Bestätigung des Schreibens Ihres Kunden
– Ausdruck des Bedauerns über den Vorfall
– Sie haben Ihre Versandabteilung beauftragt, die Sache zu untersuchen
– Sie haben sofort veranlasst, dass die 20 fehlenden Stative per Luftfracht auf Ihre Kosten nachgeschickt werden
– Für die 20 zuviel gelieferten Fotoapparate machen Sie folgende Alternativvorschläge:
   a) Gewährung von 15 % Nachlass, falls der Kunde sie behält,
   b) Rücknahme auf Ihre Kosten
– Nochmalige Entschuldigung und Versicherung, dass bei künftigen Lieferungen sorgfältiger gearbeitet wird.

3.

Name	eigener Name	Ms. Jane Foster
Position	Einkaufsleiter/in	Export Sales Director
Firma	Design Marschall & Co.KG	Chalkman & Fryers Design Inc.
Anschrift	Bruchstr. 11–13, 34130 Kassel, Germany	82 Otis St., San Francisco, CA 94103, U.S.A.
Fax	+49 (5 61) 30 99 55	+1 (4 15) 4 31 18 88
E-Mail	design.marschall.kg@aol.com	chalkman.fryers@uslink.com

Geschäftsfall:

Sie hatten mit Auftrag L 28 PR bei der Chalkman & Fryers Design Inc. 2000 Handys (*mobile phones*) zum Gesamtpreis von 410.000,00 US$ bestellt. Die Handys sind zwar pünktlich angekommen, doch weisen sie verschiedene Mängel auf.

Aufgabe:

Schreiben Sie eine Beschwerde an Frau Foster, in der Sie folgende Punkte berücksichtigen:

– Bestätigen Sie den pünktlichen Erhalt der Sendung
– Die Handys sollten in 40 Kisten à 50 Stück verpackt werden
– Wie bereits auf den Frachtdokumenten vermerkt, fehlen von den 40 Kisten 2, also 100 Stück
– 3 der verbleibenden 38 Kisten waren von außen beschädigt (Fotos anbei), dadurch ist der Inhalt teilweise unbrauchbar (Liste der Mängel in der Anlage)
– Bei einer Prüfung stellte sich heraus, dass insgesamt 20 Handys nicht einwandfrei arbeiten
– Alle beschädigten Handys halten Sie für den Lieferanten zur Verfügung
– Fragen Sie an, ob Sie sie unfrei zurückschicken oder vor Ort auf Anweisung und Kosten des Lieferanten reparieren lassen sollen
– Weisen Sie vorsorglich darauf hin, dass Sie sich die etwaigen Schadensersatzansprüche vorbehalten, die ggf. durch verspätete Lieferung an Ihre Kunden entstehen
– Von der Zahlung des Restbetrages von 280.000,– US$, die 30 Tage nach Lieferung fällig wird, werden Sie bis zur Klärung der Angelegenheit 20 % vorläufig einbehalten
– Bitte um baldige Beseitigung der Schäden und Stellungnahme.

4.

Name	Rolf (Gabi) Neutzner	Ms Denise Johnson
Position	Exportsachbearbeiter/in	Purchasing Manager
Firma	Fitness Baumgartner GmbH	Sports Fashion Ltd
Anschrift	Postfach 10 93 28,	Talbot Place, Blackheath,
	09126 Chemnitz, Germany	London SE3 OTZ, England
Fax	+49 (3 71) 95 11 03	+44 (1 81) 3 68-87 54
E-Mail	fitness.baumgartner@t-online.de	sportfash@omnilink.co.uk

Geschäftsfall:

Vor 5 Tagen lieferten Sie an die Sports Fashion Ltd 250 Expander (*expanders*)
Marke „Schwarzenegger", die in 10 Kisten à 25 Stück verpackt waren. Ihr Kunde
teilte Ihnen gestern per Fax mit, dass eine Kiste mit 25 Expandern fehlt. Da die
Lieferbedingung frei Haus war, verlangt er von Ihnen die sofortige Klärung der
Angelegenheit und Übernahme aller Kosten.

Aufgabe:

Schreiben Sie an den Kunden unter Berücksichtigung folgender Punkte:
- Bestätigung der Faxmitteilung
- Bedauern des Vorfalls
- Sie haben bereits Ihren Spediteur informiert, der sich sofort mit dem
  zuständigen Fahrer in Verbindung setzen wird
- Sie haben ebenso die Versicherung angewiesen, Ihnen das Formular für
  die Schadensmeldung zu schicken
- Bieten Sie eine sofortige kostenlose Ersatzlieferung an, die von einer
  Proforma-Rechnung begleitet wird
- Nochmaliges Bedauern und Hoffnung auf weitere gute Zusammenarbeit.

5.

Name	Raimund (Anke) Leitner	–
Position	Einkaufsleiter/in	–
Firma	Exklusives Glas & Geschirr GmbH	Japanese China Inc
Anschrift	Morgensternstr. 30,	16-8-503, Sakuragaoka-cho,
	12207 Berlin, Germany	Shibuya-ku, Tokyo, Japan
Fax	+49 (30) 27 27 900	+81 (3) 34 56 70 31
E-Mail	exclusiv.glas.gmbh@netlink.de	japanese.china@tokyolink.com

Geschäftsfall:

Vor 4 Monaten hatten Sie bei der Japanese China Inc 50 Teeservice (*tea sets*) Marke „Japanese Rose" zum Gesamtpreis von 44.500,00 US$, Lieferung CIF Bremerhaven, bestellt. Die Sendung wurde vor einer Woche in Bremerhaven von Ihrem Spediteur in äußerlich einwandfreiem Zustand in Empfang genommen und gestern bei Ihnen abgeliefert. Beim Auspacken stellen Sie fest, dass an 8 der kostbaren Tassen der Henkel (*handle*) abgebrochen ist und 5 Untertassen gesprungen sind (*cracked*). Eine Reparatur wäre zwecklos.

Aufgabe:

Schreiben Sie eine Beschwerde an die japanische Firma und berücksichtigen Sie dabei die folgenden Punkte:

– Bestätigen Sie den Empfang der Ware
– Erklären Sie die festgestellten Mängel und weisen Sie darauf hin, dass äußerlich nichts auf solche Beschädigungen hinwies (Beweis: reines Bordkonnossement!)
– Da die Sache eilt, Bitte um sofortige kostenlose Nachlieferung von 8 Tassen und 5 Untertassen per Luftfracht mit entsprechendem Vermerk auf dem Luftfracht-brief und der Proforma-Rechnung, um erneute Zollgebühren zu vermeiden
– Wahrscheinlich ist Schaden beim Schiffstransport entstanden, daher Bitte um Benachrichtigung der Versicherung
– Fragen Sie, ob zur Klärung der Angelegenheit der Bericht eines unabhängigen Schadensgutachters angefordert werden soll
– Bitte um baldige Stellungnahme.

6.

Name	eigener Name	–
Position	Exportleiter/in	–
Firma	Düngemittel Bauer GmbH	International Fertilizer Organization
Anschrift	Müllerstr. 11–13, 13585 Berlin, Germany	130 Monipuripara Tejgaon, Dhaka 1036, Bangladesh
Fax	+49 (30) 2 89 04 05	+8 80 (2) 91 25 36
E-Mail	duengemittel.bauer@aol.com	ifo@asialink.com

Geschäftsfall:

Die International Fertilizer Organization hatte vor 10 Tagen von Ihnen 100 Säcke Spezialdünger der Marke „Spix" à 50 kg, auf Paletten in einem Container verpackt, erhalten. Beim Auspacken der Säcke wurde festgestellt, dass von den 100 ursprünglich gelieferten Säcken 10 Säcke fehlten, die offensichtlich gestohlen wurden. Die International Fertilizer Organization schickt daraufhin an Sie das polizeiliche Protokoll der Diebstahlanzeige sowie eine Schadensmeldung (*the police report on the theft and the notice of loss with the shipping company's confirmation*), welche sie bei der Reederei bestätigen ließ. Da es sich um einen CIF Dhaka-Transport handelt, bittet die International Fertilizer Organization nunmehr um Klärung des Schadensfalles mit der Versicherung und Nachlieferung der 10 fehlenden Säcke.

Aufgabe:

Richten Sie mit heutigem Datum an die Firma in Dhaka ein Schreiben unter Berücksichtigung der folgenden Punkte:

– Bestätigen Sie den Erhalt der übersandten Dokumente, die Sie jetzt an die Versicherung weitergeleitet haben
– Bedauern Sie den Vorfall
– Nach telefonischer Rücksprache mit der Versicherung braucht diese noch weitere Angaben, um den Fall zu klären
– Die Versicherung wird sich direkt mit dem Kunden in Verbindung setzen
– Sie bieten an, die fehlenden Säcke mit dem nächsten Transport per Sammelcontainer nach Bangladesh zu schicken
– Da die Bank das Akkreditiv bereits gegen Vorlage der Dokumente auf Grund des reinen Bordkonnossements bezahlt hat, werden Sie eine neue Rechnung ausstellen, die später – wenn der Schaden von der Versicherung erstattet wurde – verrechnet werden kann.

Unit 10

Delay in Payment

Introduction

As unknown or unreliable customers are required to pay before goods are shipped, delays in payment usually only occur when the customer has been given credit in some form or other (see diagram in Unit 7 "Terms of payment in international trade", page 104).

With a trusted customer non-payment may be due to an oversight, in which case an impersonal standard reminder may be enough to obtain payment.

If an impersonal standard reminder is not appropriate, one or several personalised reminders should be addressed to a senior executive of the company and marked "CONFIDENTIAL" to ensure that it is given immediate attention. In many cases legal action is taken after three reminders, the third of which is then known as the final demand.

In export trade invoices are often sold to a factor (see diagram on page 149), who buys them at a lower price than their face value but bears the risk of non-payment. In some cases collection agencies can be used to deal with overdue accounts.

All reminders and final demands should, however, whatever the circumstances, be polite in order not to endanger future business.

When writing about delays in payment use the letter plans to structure your letter, fax or e-mail.

Delay in Payment	Delay in Payment
Seller	**Buyer**
1. Refer to overdue invoice / account (copy enclosed)	1. Reference to overdue invoice / account / reminder(s)
2. Refer to previous reminder(s) (copy / copies enclosed)*	2. First apology and explanation why payment is / will be late*
3. Express surprise that this should happen*	3. Confirmation that payment has been made / will be made* / Request for concessions / a concession*
4. Request an explanation	
5. Request payment and set a deadline*	4. Hope that the concession(s) will be granted* Second apology for the delay*
6. Consequences of non-payment*	
7. Regret that a reminder is necessary*	5. Polite ending
8. Polite ending	6. Enclosure(s)
9. Enclosure(s)	
*As appropriate	*As appropriate

Fig. 20

Fig. 21

Delay in Payment

Seller's reply
1. Refer to buyer's letter / fax / e-mail
2. Grant or refuse the concession(s)
3. Polite ending

Fig. 22

Delay in payment

Del credere agent

A del credere agent sells an export company's goods to a foreign customer and agrees to pay for them if the customer cannot. He receives extra commission for taking this risk.

ECGD / Hermes

The Export Credits Guarantee Department is an organisation run by the UK government to insure export orders against commercial and political risks. "Hermes" is the German equivalent.

Safeguards

Factor

A factor buys an export company's debts. He pays the export company for the goods as soon as they are supplied to the foreign customer and charges a fee. He then collects payment from the customer.

Credit insurance company

This is a private company which insures export orders against commercial risks.

Sell the account to a collection agency

Stop all further deliveries

Take legal action

Sanctions

Cancel credit terms – L/C, CWO, D/P only

Report the company to its
– chamber of commerce
– trade mission
– diplomatic mission

Draw a sight draft on the debtor for collection through his bank

Ask the company to return the goods

Specimen Letters

1. Standard reminder (first reminder)

Nürnberg

TM/TT
15 April ..

The People's Gallery
95 Hackney Road
London
EC1 8GJ
England

Dear Sir / Madam

Account Number 980/PG/GB

According to our records, our statement of account dated 31 March has not
been settled.

The enclosed copy of the statement shows an outstanding balance of £345.95.

We would request you to remit the sum in question in the next few days.

Yours faithfully
Kunsthaus Wetzel

Tamara Mainz

Tamara Mainz
Export Sales

Enc

Herzogstr. 42   90478 Nürnberg   Germany
Tel.: +49 (9 11) 5 43 65   Fax: +49 (9 11) 5 43 00   E-Mail: kunsthaus.wenzel@t-online.de

2. Second reminder

Nürnberg

TM/TT
30 April ..

Confidential

Ms Bernice Malone
Director
The People's Gallery
95 Hackney Road
London
EC18GJ
England

Dear Ms Malone

Account Number 980/PG/GB

We refer to our first reminder of 15 April .. and once again enclose a copy of our
statement showing an outstanding balance of £345.95.

We have now been waiting for this statement to be paid for a month. As we
have received neither an explanation nor a remittance we would urgently request
you to give us your reasons for non-payment and ensure that the amount in
question is paid without delay.

Yours sincerely
Kunsthaus Wetzel

Tamara Mainz
Tamara Mainz
Export Sales

Enc

Herzogstr. 42   90478 Nürnberg   Germany
Tel.: +49 (9 11) 5 43 65   Fax: +49 (9 11) 5 43 00   E-Mail: kunsthaus.wenzel@t-online.de

3. Final demand (third reminder)

Nürnberg

TM/TT
15 May ..

Confidential

Ms Bernice Malone
Director
The People's Gallery
95 Hackney Road
London
EC18GJ
England

Dear Ms Malone

Account Number 980/PG/GB

With reference to our statement of 31 March and our two reminders of 15 and 30 April (see enclosures) we regret to inform you that the amount of £345.95 is still overdue.

As your company has neither sent us the sum due nor given any indication of why payment has not been forthcoming, we are allowing you a further 10 days, after which time we will have no choice but to take legal action against you.

We very much hope that this matter will be settled swiftly and to the satisfaction of all concerned.

Yours sincerely
Kunsthaus Wetzel

Tamara Mainz
Tamara Mainz
Export Sales

Encs

Herzogstr. 42   90478 Nürnberg   Germany
Tel.: +49 (9 11) 5 43 65   Fax: +49 (9 11) 5 43 00   E-Mail: kunsthaus.wenzel@t-online.de

Case Study

Seller

Telemobil GmbH, an electronics firm in Bochum, recently supplied 1,000 mobile phones to Kodaphone Ltd, a British wholesaler in London with whom it has been doing small amounts of business for several years now. The price agreed was 50 euros per unit, CIP London Airport. Payment was to be made one third with order, one third on delivery and one third within 30 days after delivery.

Kodaphone paid the first two instalments on schedule but payment of the final third (16,670 euros) is now more than three weeks overdue. Telemobil sent Kodaphone a first standard reminder two weeks ago and then addressed a second application to Mr Martin Shaw, the Finance Controller, a week ago but has so far received no reply. Repeated attempts to telephone Mr Shaw directly have also been unsuccessful and each time the German company was told by one of his office staff that the remittance was "on its way".

Sandra Klump, the director of the export sales department at Telemobil, is surprised that there should be such difficulties, as there has been no trouble in the past. She writes to Mr Shaw at Kodaphone again requesting an explanation of the delay and referring to previous correspondence on this matter. She also makes it clear that her company can only wait another 10 days for payment, after which time it will have to charge interest on the outstanding amount and change its terms of payment to CWO. If payment is then still outstanding Kodaphone will have to return one third of the goods supplied.

Buyer

Martin Shaw, the Finance Controller at Kodaphone Ltd, receives Sandra Klump's letter / fax / e-mail and writes back explaining that there has been industrial action by the office staff at his company. For this reason he has had to employ temporary staff to deal with the backlog of office work. It has been impossible to make payments to suppliers punctually because, among other things, the temporary office staff were unfamiliar with Kodaphone's computerised accounting system.

The dispute has now been settled and the office workers have returned to work so Martin Shaw apologises for the delay and promises to remit the amount owed by SWIFT to Telemobil's account at the Ruhrbank in Bochum within the next three days. He finishes his letter by saying he hopes that this delay will not affect future orders.

Activities

Addresses:

— Telemobil GmbH, Industriestr. 98, 47713 Bochum,
   tel. +49 (2 34) 8 75 54 24, fax +49 (2 34) 8 75 54 00,
   e-mail: telemobil.gmbh@telnet.de
— Kodaphone Ltd, 88 Victoria Avenue, Chiswick, London W4 9GJ,
   tel. +44 (1 81) 7 69-34 67, fax +44 (1 81) 7 69-34 00,
   e-mail: kodaphone.ltd@firmweb.uk.com

Seller

Using the "**Delay in Payment** Letter Plans" in this Unit and the Standard Expressions write Sandra Klump's letter / fax / e-mail to Martin Shaw at Kodaphone Ltd.

Buyer

Using the "**Delay in Payment** Letter Plans" in this Unit and the Standard Expressions write Martin Shaw's letter / fax / e-mail to Sandra Klump at Telemobil Gmbh in Bochum. Make it clear that Martin Shaw is most apologetic about the delay.

Language

A. Seller

Use the first "**Delay in Payment** Standard Expressions" table to find the words missing below.

1. Verbs + nouns
   Which verbs go with the following nouns?
   a. to ▉ your notice (i.e. "You didn't notice it")
   b. to ▉ a deadline
   c. to ▉ a sight draft on someone
   d. to ▉ legal proceedings (i.e. "to start")

2. Verbs + prepositions / particles
   Which prepositions / particles go with the following verbs?
   a. to run ▉ financial difficulties
   b. to credit 1,000 euros ▉ our account

3. Nouns + prepositions / prepositions + nouns / adjectives + prepositions
   a. an explanation ▉ why payment has not been made (2 words)
   b. ▉ arrears with payment
   c. ▉ date (i.e. "up to now")
   d. ▉ your part

4. Adjectives / adjectival phrases + nouns
   a. an ▉ balance (i.e. "unpaid")
   b. to go through a ▉ patch
   c. an ▉ solution (i.e. "friendly")

5. Further points
   a. "We have received ▉ an explanation ▉ a remittance"
   b. What official bodies can a company which is behind with its payments be reported to?

B. Buyer + C. Seller's Reply

Use the second "**Delay in Payment** Standard Expressions" table to find the words missing below.

1. Verbs + nouns
    Which verbs go with the following nouns?
    a. "Please ▨ our apologies"
    b. to ▨ the deadline by 14 days (i.e. "to make longer")
    c. to ▨ a request (i.e. "to refuse")
    d. to ▨ a debt (i.e. "to get back the money owed")

2. Verbs + prepositions / particles
    Which prepositions / particles go with the following verbs?
    a. to agree ▨ a suggestion
    b. to turn the matter ▨ to an agent for collection

3. Nouns + prepositions / prepositions + nouns / adjectives + prepositions
    a. the increase ▨ price
    b. the drop ▨ price
    c. ▨ no fault of our own
    d. ▨ two-monthly intervals
    e. ▨ the time being

4. Adjectives / adjectival phrases + nouns
    a. the ▨ price (i.e. "changing")
    b. ▨ circumstances (i.e. "unexpected")
    c. ▨ financial obligations (i.e. "urgent")

5. Further points
    a. When a firm officially registers itself bankrupt it ▨ bankruptcy. (2 words)
    b. If a firm is unable to pay it is ▨.
    c. Give 2 expressions to mean "to receive too few goods".
    d. Give an expression to mean "to receive too many goods".

9 **Listening**

Before you listen to the dialogue, first read through the background information provided and the instructions following it.

Background information

Your name is Michaela Schlohmann and you work in Essen for HG Instruments GmbH, the German subsidiary of HG Instruments Inc., an American company manufacturing hospital equipment. Today you phone a British company about payment.

Instructions

Either:

(a) Write a memo to your American boss Mr Vance, the Executive Vice President of HG Instruments Inc. Include the points covered by the questions below in your memo.

Or:

(b) Write a summary in German of your telephone conversation. It is to be given to your boss, Frau Dr. Kanis, the Managing Director.

Questions

Note: The date is May 2nd.

1. What is the name of the British company?
2. What goods have the British company ordered?
3. What is the order number and the date?
4. How much money is owing?
5. Why haven't the British company paid?
6. How long have the British company had to pay?
7. What will the French company do and when will they do it?
8. What could the British company sell straight away?
9. What does Michaela need before she can do more business with the British company?
10. What solution does Frank suggest?

Now listen to the dialogue again and answer the following questions.

1. What were the terms of payment HG Instruments GmbH first granted the British company?
2. What has the British company done to make a bad impression on HG Instruments GmbH?
3. Why might HG Instruments GmbH still want to do business with the British company?
4. In what way might HG Instruments GmbH change the new terms of payment suggested by the British company?

Telephone Role Play

Rolle A

Sie sind Sachbearbeiter/in in der Exportabteilung der Alpha Parfümerie KG in Wattenscheid.

Ihre Firma verkauft seit ca. 2 Jahren Parfüm an die Firma Designer Perfumes Ltd in Newcastle, England. Da die englische Firma regelmäßig Aufträge erteilt, sind Ihre Zahlungsbedingungen „10 Tage 2%, 30 Tage netto".

Heute rufen Sie bei der englischen Firma an, um herauszufinden, warum die Begleichung Ihrer letzten Rechung über 1.250,– Euro noch nicht vorgenommen

worden ist. Es handelt sich um Rechnungs-Nr. JG96 vom … (vor 6 Wochen).
Die Rechnung war vor 14 Tagen fällig.

- Erklären Sie Mr Peter Miller bzw. Ms Patricia Miller, worum es sich handelt
- Fragen Sie ihn / sie, ob besondere Gründe vorliegen, weswegen seine / ihre Firma nicht gezahlt hat
- Sagen Sie Ihrem Gesprächspartner zunächst einmal, dass Sie Verständnis für seine Schwierigkeiten haben
- Sagen Sie ihm, dass Sie mit Ihrem Chef wegen seiner Bitte sprechen und heute wieder anrufen werden.

Role B
You are Peter / Patricia Miller of Designer Perfumes in Newcastle, England.
A German supplier calls you to ask about an outstanding invoice:
- Answer the phone as Peter / Patricia Miller
- Ask for the order number
- Say you only have details of the goods but not the date for payment because there was a fire in your office at the beginning of … (5 weeks ago), which destroyed the company's computer system
- Say you have no computers at the moment so everything is taking a lot longer than usual
- Explain that it will take your computer firm another week to install a new system
- Ask to be allowed to pay the invoice by the end of next week
- Apologise for the delay.

Aufgaben

1.

Name	Eigener Name	(3. Mahnung: Mr Jackson,
Position	Exportleiter/in	Head Buyer)
Firma	Grabert & Neuenberger KG	Westwood Ltd
Anschrift	Richthofener Str. 110,	47 Golf Road,
	40699 Erkrath	Durham SR88 1SH, England
Fax	+49 (2 11) 77 60 97	+44 (191) 5 56 34
E-Mail	grabert.neuenberger@aol.com	westwood.ltd@fimnet.co.uk

1.1 Geschäftsfall:
Die Grabert & Neuenberger KG in Erkrath hatte vor 5 Wochen der Westwood Ltd in Durham, England, Parfümerieartikel im Wert von 3.375 Euro geschickt. Zahlungsbedingung war per Banküberweisung innerhalb von 30 Tagen abzüglich 3 % Skonto vereinbart worden. Bis zum heutigen Tag ist das Geld bei Ihrer Bank noch nicht eingetroffen.

Aufgabe:

Schicken Sie an die Westwood Ltd eine 1. Mahnung mit folgenden Angaben:

–   Bezug auf Lieferung
–   Höfliche Zahlungserinnerung
–   Beifügung der Rechnungskopie über 3.375 Euro
–   Schlussformulierung, in der Sie Hoffnung auf baldige Zahlung ausdrücken.

1.2 Geschäftsfall:

In der o. a. Angelegenheit sind weitere 2 Wochen verstrichen (insgesamt 7 Wochen), ohne dass Sie schriftlich oder mündlich etwas gehört haben.

Aufgabe:

Schicken Sie an die Westwood Ltd eine 2. Mahnung mit folgenden Angaben:

–   Erneuter Bezug auf die Lieferung und Rechnung über 3.375 Euro vom …
      (vor 7 Wochen)
–   Bitte um Erklärung des Zahlungsverzugs
–   Angebot einer Hilfeleistung, falls Schwierigkeiten aufgetreten sind
–   Fristsetzung bis zum … (in 14 Tagen)
–   Höfliche, aber etwas energischere Schlussformulierung.

1.3 Geschäftsfall:

In der o. a. Angelegenheit haben Sie inzwischen 2× mit der britischen Gesellschaft telefoniert. Das 1. Mal haben Sie mit einer Frau Panders gesprochen, die den Vorgang nicht kannte, aber zurückrufen wollte. Da dies nicht geschehen ist, haben Sie vor 3 Tagen mit Herrn Jackson, dem Leiter der Einkaufsabteilung, gesprochen, der Ihre Sendung seinerzeit entgegengenommen hatte und jetzt sofortige Zahlung zusagt. Sie haben nunmehr den … (heutiges Datum, d. h. 10 Wochen nach Verschickung der Ware), und das Geld ist immer noch nicht da.

Aufgabe:

Schreiben Sie die 3. und letzte Mahnung an Ihren Kunden und richten Sie sie an Herrn Jackson persönlich. Nehmen Sie folgende Punkte auf:

–   Bezug auf die vorhergehenden 2 Mahnungen
–   Bezug auf beide Telefonate (siehe oben)
–   Letzte Fristsetzung bis zum … (in 14 Tagen) (unweigerlich letzter Termin!)
–   Bei Nichtzahlung Androhung gerichtlicher Schritte, um fälligen Betrag zuzügl.
      Zinsen und Kosten einzuziehen
–   Höflicher, aber unmissverständlicher Schluss.

2.

Name	Eigener Name	–
Position	Leiter/in der Buchhaltung (Credit Manager)	–
Firma	Bungert KG	Lalit Granite Exports Ltd
Anschrift	Hadersbacher Str. 26, 94333 Geiselhöring	131 Residency Road, Bangalore 560 080, India
Fax	+49 (94 23) 81 76	+91 (80) 5 58 69 90
E-Mail	bungert@t-online.de	lalit.stones@indialink.com

Geschäftsfall:

Sie sind Leiter/in der Buchhaltung beim deutschen Importeur Bungert KG in Geiselhöring. Sie hatten über die Lalit Granite Exports Ltd in Bangalore, Indien, eine Sendung Granit (*granite*) erhalten. Geschäftssprache war Englisch. Die Rechnung belief sich auf 7.684,50 Euro und war in Raten von 2.500 Euro vor 6 Wochen, 2.500 Euro vor 4 Wochen, Rest vor 2 Wochen fällig. Die Sendung ist jedoch teilweise in beschädigtem Zustand angekommen, so dass Sie vor 6 Wochen und vor 4 Wochen nur jeweils 1.250 Euro überwiesen haben. Sie hatten einen Tag nach Ankunft der Ladung vor 6 Wochen eine Schadensmeldung in Höhe von (*notification of damage valued at …*) 2.500 Euro an den Lieferanten geschickt und die Restzahlung vor 2 Wochen wie vereinbart überwiesen. Trotzdem erhielten Sie gestern eine Mahnung des indischen Lieferanten, in der er die fehlenden 2.500 Euro verlangt.

Aufgabe:

Beantworten Sie die Mahnung des Lieferanten unter Berücksichtigung der folgenden Punkte:
- Bezug auf den gesamten Vorgang wie oben beschrieben
- Ihrer Meinung nach ist die Mahnung völlig unberechtigt, da Ihre Schadensmeldung ordnungsgemäß erfolgt ist
- Lieferung war frei Haus vereinbart einschließlich Transportversicherung
- Angelegenheit ist für Sie somit erledigt
- Höflicher Schlusssatz.

3.

Name	eigener Name	Ms Angela Drabble
Position	Geschäftsführer/in	Chief Accountant
Firma	Konzertagentur Meierhofer GmbH	Starcomb Ltd
Anschrift	Bayernstraße 3, 80331 München	32 Canada Square, Canary Wharf, London E14 5DL, England
Fax	+49 (89) 2 90 49 81	+44 (171) 4 81-16 16
E-Mail	meierhofer@t-online.de	starcomb@firmnet.uk

Geschäftsfall:

Sie sind Geschäftsführer/in der Konzertagentur Meierhofer GmbH. Der Sänger Peter Power, der vor 6 Wochen in Deutschland gastierte, hat seine Gage in Höhe von 20.000 £ noch nicht erhalten und schickt über seine Agentur Starcomb Ltd in London, England, eine Mahnung.

Aufgabe:

Reagieren Sie auf diese Mahnung unter Angabe folgender Punkte:
- Bezug auf Mahnung
- Entschuldigung für Verspätung in der Zahlung
- Es sind unerwartete Schwierigkeiten aufgetreten (zu wenig Nachfrage bei einigen der letzten Konzerte)
- Sie werden die Hälfte der Summe in den nächsten Tagen überweisen
- Bitte, den Rest um 3 Monate zu stunden (*delay payment for …*)
- Nochmalige Entschuldigung und Bitte um Verständnis.

4.

Name	eigener Name	Mr. Vance Banderas
Position	Leiter/in der Buchhaltung (Credit Manager)	President
Firma	Hotel Astoria Star	Freeline Inc.
Anschrift	Hunsrückstr. 60–62, 41239 Mönchengladbach, Germany	700 5th Avenue, New York, NY 10021, U.S.A.
Fax	+49 (21) 61 38 60 44	+1 (2 12) 9 35 4 09 83
E-Mail	astoriastar@t-online.de	freeline@uslink.com

Aus der Sicht des Verkäufers:

Geschäftsfall:
Herr Larry Thompson von der Freeline Inc. hatte vor 8 Wochen 3 Nächte in Ihrem Hotel übernachtet und Sie gebeten, die Rechnung an seine Firma in New York zu schicken. Sie haben vor 7 Wochen eine Rechnung über 430 Euro an die Freeline Inc. geschickt, aber bis heute keine Antwort und auch keine Überweisung erhalten.

Aufgabe:
Heute schicken Sie eine Mahnung an den Geschäftsführer der Freeline Inc. Berücksichtigen Sie dabei folgende Punkte:
– Bezug auf Besuch von Herrn Thompson
– Bezug auf Rechnung von vor 7 Wochen
– Es ist normalerweise nicht üblich, dass Gäste nicht bar bzw. per Scheck oder Kreditkarte bezahlen
– Im vorliegenden Fall haben Sie sich auf die Broschüre und die Visitenkarte, die Ihnen ausgehändigt wurden, verlassen, da die Kreditkarte von Herrn Thompson in Deutschland nicht akzeptiert wurde
– Bitte um sofortige Begleichung des Betrages
– Andernfalls müssen Sie zusätzliche Kosten erheben und ggf. den Rechtsweg einschlagen.

5.

Name	Kelly (Daniel) König	Ms Georgina Tucker
Position	Sachbearbeiter/in Einkauf	Export Sales Department
Firma	Feininger KG	Antiques Shop
Anschrift	Bachstr. 9, 40548 Düsseldorf, Germany	P.O. Box 2498, London W1A 2NX, England
Fax	+49 (2 11) 8 73-9 01	+44 (1 71) 79 00 14 56
E-Mail	feininger.kg@aol.com	antiques.shop@linkall.uk

Aus der Sicht des Käufers:

Geschäftsfall:
Vor 12 Wochen erhielten Sie vom britischen Antiques Shop mehrere Möbelstücke mit einer Rechnung in Höhe von 18.937,00 £, die in einer Summe ohne Abzug vor 4 Wochen zahlbar war. Sie können die volle Summe aber nicht aufbringen, da die Möbel noch nicht verkauft sind. Der Lieferant hat schon mehrmals die Zahlung angemahnt.

Aufgabe:
Schicken Sie mit Datum von heute ein Schreiben an den Antiques Shop und weisen Sie auf Folgendes hin:
— Bezug auf Lieferung (guter Erhalt)
— Möbel entsprechen durchaus allen Voraussetzungen
— Allerdings unerwartete Absatzschwierigkeiten
— Gründe: Arbeitslosigkeit vieler Leute, weniger Kaufkraft, Rückgang der Nachfrage
— Bitte, folgende Zahlungsweise zu akzeptieren: 1. Rate in Höhe von 8.937,00 £ in 4 Wochen ; Restzahlung von 10.000,00 £ einen Monat später
— Bitte um Verständnis
— Höfliche Schlussformulierung.

6.

Name	Eigener Name	–
Position	Exportsachbearbeiter/in	–
Firma	Richter & Cunningham GmbH	Cook plc
Anschrift	Namslaustr. 110, 13507 Berlin	14 St. Andrew's Terrace, Waterford, Ireland
Fax	+49 (30) 39 87 50	+3 53 (51) 82 09 63
E-Mail	richter.cunning@t-online.de	cook.plc@firmnet.com

Geschäftsfall:
Die Richter & Cunningham GmbH in Berlin hatte der Cook plc in Waterford, Irland, 30 Maschinen des Typs JK 9080 im Gesamtwert von 17.750 Euro geschickt. Die Zahlung sollte vor 10 Tagen erfolgen. Sie haben den … (heutiges Datum), und nach Anfrage bei Ihrer Bank stellen Sie fest, dass noch keine Überweisung erfolgt ist.

Aufgabe:
Schreiben Sie eine erste höfliche Erinnerung an die Cook plc. Berücksichtigen Sie dabei die folgenden Punkte:
– Bezug auf Auftrag vom … (vor 4 Monaten)
– Bitte um Mitteilung, ob die Sendung zufriedenstellend ausgefallen ist
– Fügen Sie eine Kopie der Rechnung bei
– Sollte sich die Überweisung mit diesem Schreiben gekreuzt haben, bitten Sie, das Erinnerungsschreiben als gegenstandslos zu betrachten
– Höflicher Schluss.

7.

Name	Beate (Rüdiger) Offenheimer	–
Position	Leiter/in der Buchhaltung (Credit Manager)	–
Firma	Maschinenfabrik Steller & Schröder GmbH	African Trading Corporation
Anschrift	Alte Bahnhofstr. 110–112, 42119 Wuppertal, Germany	P.O. Box 4897, Asmara, Eritrea
Fax	+49 (2 02) 25 72 09	+2 91 (1) 12 78 93
E-Mail	steller.schroeder@germanet.de	african.trading@africalink.com

Geschäftsfall:
Reaktion des Verkäufers auf Bitte des Käufers um Zahlungsaufschub:
Vor 3 Monaten hatte Ihre Firma der African Trading Corporation eine Maschine vom Typ ST 47 A geliefert. Da die Firma schon mehrmals bei Ihnen bestellt und pünktlich bezahlt hatte, waren Sie mit einer Vorauszahlung von 60.000 Euro, Restzahlung von 25.000 Euro nach 3 Monaten, einverstanden. Diese Restzahlung ist aber vor 14 Tagen nicht eingetroffen. Als Antwort auf Ihre Mahnung von vor einer Woche per Fax erhielten Sie gestern eine E-Mail-Nachricht der African Trading Corporation, in welcher diese wegen Zahlungsschwierigkeiten um eine Verlängerung des Zahlungsziels um weitere 3 Monate bittet.

Aufgabe:

Beantworten Sie diese E-Mail per Brief / Fax / E-Mail unter Berücksichtigung folgender Punkte:

— Bestätigung der E-Mail
— Sie haben zwar Verständnis für den Kunden, haben aber selbst Zahlungs-verpflichtungen einzuhalten
— Äußerstes Angebot: Zahlung von 15.000 Euro sofort, Restzahlung von 10.000 Euro in 2 Monaten
— Dringende Bitte um Einhaltung dieser Kondition, sonst kann Kunde nicht mehr beliefert werden
— Höflicher Schluss.

Unit 11

Agency Agreements

Introduction

When exporting goods and services suppliers can either employ their own *representatives* or reduce costs by using an *agent*. Whereas a representative receives a salary from his or her employer and *commission* on sales, an agent acts for one or more *principals* and is paid entirely on a commission basis.

Agents have an *agency agreement* with their principals, are given a *territory* and submit an *account sales* to their principals at regular intervals (usually monthly or quarterly). A *commission agent* acts *in his principal's name*, sells *for his principal's account* and *at his principal's risk*. If the commission agent assumes the risk of non-payment by one of his customers, he is known as a *del credere (commission) agent* and receives an extra *del credere commission*. A *sole agent* is an agent who has been granted the *exclusive right of sale* by his principal for a particular territory. He has the *sole agency* there.

Another type of agent is a *consignee*, who sells *consignment goods* in his own name but for his *consignor's* (principal's) account and at the consignor's risk. A consignee *indents* for goods from the consignor and returns them if they cannot be sold.

In addition to their commission, agents are also paid to *advertise* their principals' products, provide *after-sales service* and *settle disputes*.

Foreign or overseas *buying agents (purchasing agents)* receive *indents* for goods from their principals, i.e. instructions to buy certain goods on their principals' behalf. They receive commission on the goods they purchase.

A foreign *distributor* purchases goods from a foreign supplier and sells them *at a profit*. He has the exclusive right of sale for a particular territory, as stated in the *distributorship agreement*. He buys and sells in his own name, at his own risk and for his own account.

	In whose name?	On whose account?	At whose risk?	Income	German terms
Commission agent (Buying / Selling agent)	principal's	principal's	principal's	commission	*Kommissionär (Einkaufs- / Verkaufs-kommissionär) (principal = Auftraggeber)*
Del credere commission agent (Selling agent)	principal's	principal's	own risk	commission + Del credere Commission	*Delcredere-kommissionär*
Consignee	own name	consignor's (i.e. principal's)	principal's	commission	*Konsignatar* (consignor = *Konsignant*)
Distributor	own name	own account	own risk	profit margin	*Vertragshändler (Vertriebsfirma)*
Representative	principal's	principal's	principal's	salary (+ commission)	*Handlungsreisender*

A commission agent in foreign trade

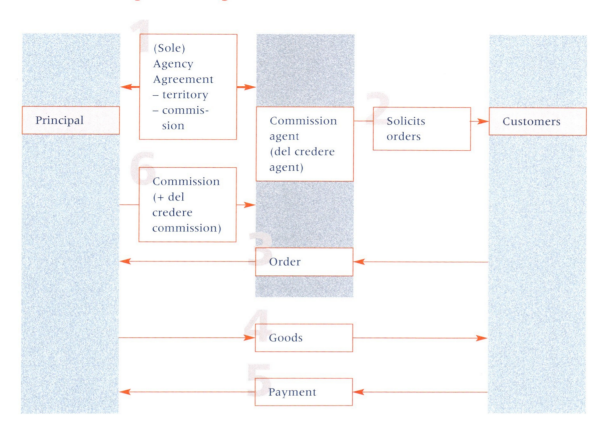

Consignee

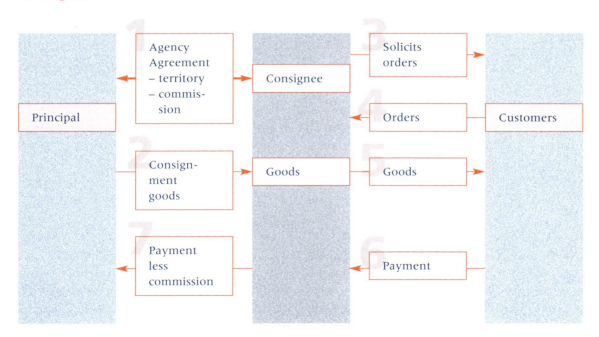

When writing about agency agreements in foreign trade use the letter plans to structure your letter, fax or e-mail.

Agent's Application for Agency

1. Source of address + application for agency
   - solicited*
   - unsolicited*
2. Description of yourself / your company
   - experience*
   - sales contacts*
   - personal qualities
   - qualifications / recommendations*
3. Interest in sole agency / del credere*
4. Reference(s)
5. Availability for interview
6. Polite ending
7. Enclosures

*As appropriate

Fig. 23

Principal's Offer of Agency

1. Reference to application for agency / Recommendation / Source of agent's address
2. Description of your company
3. Description of the sort of agent you require
4. Request for (more) information on the agent's market*
5. Request for (more) references / information*
6. Arrange an interview
7. Polite ending
8. Enclosure(s)

*As appropriate

Fig. 24

Specimen Letters

1. Application for a post as agent for a German company's products in America

September 8, ..

Paul Hughes
3702 South Fairfax Drive
Suite 1012
Arlington, Virginia 22203

Ms Regina Stoppel
Chief Executive Officer
Stoppel International GmbH
Zelt- und Leichtbauhallen
Samoastr. 6
45257 Essen
Germany

Dear Ms. Stoppel:

I recently attended the CANVAS CONVENTION in Richmond, Virginia and heard that your company is looking for an American agent to represent your interests on the East Coast.

I am no newcomer to the tent and portable buildings business, having worked as a sales representative for the Stamford Canopy Corporation in New York for five years. All in all, I can look back on more than 15 years of experience in this line.

As our American tent supplier has now closed down we are looking for a manufacturer of high-quality products. We feel that, with the right marketing mix, we will be able to establish your lines in the U.S. and boost your overall sales figures.

My company can provide you with excellent trade and bank references and I am enclosing a list of our major business partners both in the U.S. and Europe, who will be pleased to give you any information you may require.

May I call you next week to talk over terms?

Many thanks in advance for your attention to this application.

Sincerely yours,

Paul Hughes

Paul Hughes
President

Tel: (7 03) 9 08-75 41 • Fax: (703) 908-75 49
E-mail: phmarkt@aol.com
Web site: http://www.phmarketing.com

Enclosures

PH:ow

2. Stoppel International GmbH's reply to American agent's application

fax cover sheet

Stoppel International GmbH,
Zelt- und Leichtbauhallen, Samoastr. 6, 45257 Essen, Germany
Tel.: +49 (201) 33 38 42, Fax: +49 (201) 33 38 00
E-Mail: stoppel.int@t-online.de

FAO:	Mr. Paul Hughes
	President
	Paul Hughes Marketing
	Arlington, Virginia
	U.S.A.
Fax No:	+1 (703) 908-7549
From:	Ms Regina Stoppel
	CEO
Date:	September 15, ..
Subject:	Your Application for our Agency in Virginia
Total Pages:	2

Dear Mr. Hughes:

Many thanks for your letter dated 8 September .., in which you apply for the position of agent for our company in Virginia.

As a fast-growing manufacturer of tents and portable buildings for both commercial and leisure purposes, we are looking for a highly motivated person with experience and a sound knowledge of the local market. This post also pre-supposes a great degree of flexibility and initiative on the part of the agent.

Would you please therefore provide us with details of your projected sales figures and some information on potential customers in your area? Would they be private or corporate customers? We must also know whether you still represent any other companies with similar lines.

Please fill in the enclosed application form and mail it to us with your résumé and a recent passport photograph. Our Export Sales Director, Mr Konrad, will be visiting your area in the near future and would welcome the opportunity of meeting you personally. Please let us know whether you will be able to meet him.

We look forward to hearing from you in the near future.

Sincerely yours,

Regina Stoppel

3. Stoppel International approaches another prospective agent

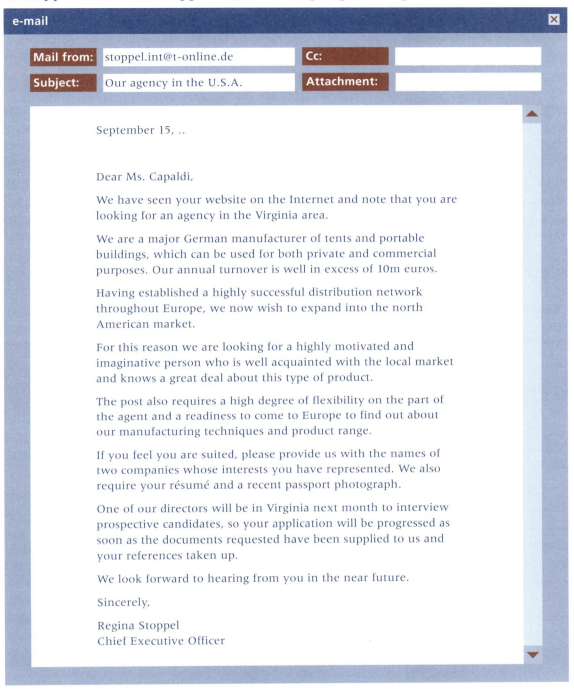

e-mail

| Mail from: | stoppel.int@t-online.de | Cc: | |
| Subject: | Our agency in the U.S.A. | Attachment: | |

September 15, ..

Dear Ms. Capaldi,

We have seen your website on the Internet and note that you are looking for an agency in the Virginia area.

We are a major German manufacturer of tents and portable buildings, which can be used for both private and commercial purposes. Our annual turnover is well in excess of 10m euros.

Having established a highly successful distribution network throughout Europe, we now wish to expand into the north American market.

For this reason we are looking for a highly motivated and imaginative person who is well acquainted with the local market and knows a great deal about this type of product.

The post also requires a high degree of flexibility on the part of the agent and a readiness to come to Europe to find out about our manufacturing techniques and product range.

If you feel you are suited, please provide us with the names of two companies whose interests you have represented. We also require your résumé and a recent passport photograph.

One of our directors will be in Virginia next month to interview prospective candidates, so your application will be progressed as soon as the documents requested have been supplied to us and your references taken up.

We look forward to hearing from you in the near future.

Sincerely,

Regina Stoppel
Chief Executive Officer

Agent's Correspondence with Principal

1. Reference to account sales
2. Explanation of good / poor sales figures*
3. Reference to customers' comments (praise / complaints)*
4. Agent's request(s) regarding goods*:
   - improved product(s)
   - new products(s)
   - lower prices
   - faster delivery
   - larger / smaller quantity of goods required
   - better packing
5. Agent's requests regarding the agency agreement:
   - more commission
   - change in territory
   - improved advertising
   - extension of the agreement
   - termination of the agreeement
6. Polite ending
7. Enclosure(s)
   (– letters / faxes / e-mails from customers)

*As appropriate

Fig. 25

Principal's Correspondence with Agent

1. Reference to account sales*
2. Praise / criticism*
3. Reference to customers' praise / criticism*
4. Principal's comments regarding goods:
   - improved product(s)
   - new products(s)
   - change(s) in price
   - delivery
   - quantity
   - packing
5. Principal's comments regarding the agency agreement:
   - change in commission rate
   - change in territory
   - change in advertising allowance
   - extension of the agreeement
   - termination of the agreeement
6. Polite ending
7. Enclosure(s)
   (– letters from customers)

*As appropriate

Fig. 26

Case Study

Principal's offer of agency

The Fontana-Gray Shoe Corporation is a rapidly expanding shoe manufacturer in Wisconsin, USA. It caters for the outdoor market – sportswear, hiking, mountaineering – and is already well represented in North America (USA, Canada), where it has recently been highly successful with its new line "Solemate Footwear". It now wishes to expand into the European market and is targeting Germany for its next sales drive.

At the Las Vegas Shoe Convention Lance D. Fontana, the president of the American company, meets a German commission agent called Erika Jung and discovers that she might be interested in representing his company in Europe. After the convention he sends her details of what his company would require from an overseas agent and invites her to submit an application. As he will be in Europe soon for the "Schuh-Premiere" Exhibition in Düsseldorf next month he would welcome an opportunity of meeting her there again personally.

When Lance writes to Erika he includes, among other things, questions about the following points:
- her company's history
- her qualifications and background
- her personnel
- her company's current sales volume
- how would she sell his products – retail, wholesale or direct marketing?
- the location of the territory / territories
- other US or foreign clients / competitors?
- references.

Agent's application for agency

Erika Jung in Cologne is a well-established commission agent in Germany who has been working the German market on behalf of a number of well-known specialist shoe manufacturers in Italy (Alzaturificio Creative, Via Costantina 20, 35020 Saonara, Italy), China and Vietnam since 1989. Her company, Erika Jung KG, of which she is the managing director, has a staff of 12 highly qualified fieldworkers operating in Germany, Austria and Switzerland and had a turnover of approx. 5m euros last year. Her main customers are retail chains selling good quality children's and adults' sports shoes and include such German household names as "Schlosswinkel GmbH & Co KG" and "Röhmer GmbH": She is not acting on behalf of any North American companies at present.

At the recent Las Vegas Shoe Convention in the USA she meets Lance D. Fontana, the president of the Fontana-Gray Shoe Corporation in Wisconsin. She finds out that they are looking for agents in Europe to market a new brand of shoe called "Solemate Footwear". She leaves her business card with them in case they want to contact her. On returning to Cologne she finds a letter / fax / e-mail waiting for her with details of the American firm's requirements of a European agent.

After looking up the firm on the Internet she decides to apply for the company's agency in Europe.

In her application she includes the fact that she obtained a degree in leather processing and shoe technology after a 3-year course at the Fachhochschule Kaiserslautern (Kaiserslautern Institute of Higher Education) in 1982. After that she worked in the Product Development Department of a major German shoe manufacturer, "Fußfest AG" in Nuremberg, for 3 years, before becoming an independent agent.

When applying she also adds that she has such reliable customers that she would be prepared to assume the del credere and would also be interested in a sole agency for the products. She includes a list of her major customers, all of whom can be contacted for references, as can her bank, the "Rheinländische Kreditbank" in Cologne.

Finally Erika says that she would be pleased to meet Lance D. Fontana in Germany the next time he is in Europe.

Activities

Addresses:

– *Commission agent:* Erika Jung KG, Graditzer Str. 10–14, 50735 Cologne, fax +49 (2 21) 67 32 44, e-mail: erika.jung.kg@globalnet.de
– *Principal:* Fontana-Gray Shoe Corporation, 100 East Seven Hills Road, P.O. Box 779, Port Washington, WI 53074-0998, fax +1 (4 14) 2 84-12 65, e-mail: fontana.gray.shoes@aol.com

A. Principal's offer of agency
Using the "**Principal's Offer of Agency** Letter Plan" in this Unit and the Standard Expressions write Lance D. Fontana's letter / fax / e-mail to Erika Jung in Cologne.

B. Agent's application for agency
Using the "**Agent's Application for Agency** Letter Plan" in this Unit and the Standard Expressions write Erika Jung's letter / fax / e-mail to Lance D. Fontana in Wisconsin, USA.

Language

Use the "**Principal's Offer of Agency**" and "**Agent's Application for Agency** Standard Expressions" table to find the words missing below.

1. Verbs + nouns
   Which verbs go with the following nouns?
   a. to ▨ an agent (i.e. "to give an agent a job")
   b. to ▨ all competitors (i.e. "to sell more than")

c. to ░░ expectations (i. e. "to be more than")
d. to ░░ your sales figures (i. e. "to increase")
e. to ░░ an appointment (i. e. "to fix a date for")
f. to ░░ expenses (i. e. "to pay back")
g. to ░░ a university (i. e. "to go to")
h. to ░░ the del credere (i. e. "to take on / accept")

2. **Verbs + prepositions / particles**
   Which prepositions / particles go with the following verbs?
   a. to apply ░░
   b. to act ░░ an agent
   c. to keep ░░ the latest trends (2 words)
   d. to open ░░ the market
   e. to take ░░ an offer (i. e. "to accept")
   f. to take ░░ references (i. e. "to contact the referees named")

3. **Nouns + prepositions / prepositions + nouns / adjectives + prepositions**
   a. to be acquainted ░░
   b. ░░ the Ideal Home Exhibition
   c. "I would have no hesitation ░░ accepting the del credere"
   d. ░░ 5 days' notice
   e. ░░ your earliest convenience
   f. to act ░░ our behalf
   g. ░░ the field of data-processing equipment
   h. ░░ the part of the agent

4. **Adjectives / adjectival phrases + nouns**
   a. "Highly" is used several times to describe adjectives. Give two examples.
   b. "Well-" is used several times in a hyphenated expression. Give two examples.
   c. Find adjectives to mean:
      – "hard-working"
      – "able to do many different things"
   d. a good knowledge – a ░░ knowledge

5. **Further points**
   a. Someone who has studied business administration at a British university gets an academic title called either a ░░ Degree or a ░░ Degree in Business Administration.
   b. A general reference addressed to no-one in particular is a ░░.
   c. A CV with no gaps is a CV without ░░.
   d. People such as doctors, lawyers and architects (i. e. people with high status jobs) are known as ░░ people.
   e. How are the three levels of income mentioned here described?
   f. People who do heavy, physical work are known as ░░ workers.
   g. A mechanic, electrician or plumber is a ░░ worker.

Before you listen to the dialogue, first read through the background information provided and the instructions following it.

Background information

In the following dialogue you are Denise Lohmann and you work in the Human Resources Department at RAP Fashion GmbH in Essen. You recently advertised for an agent in Britain in all the major British newspapers and on the Internet and have received a number of replies. Today you phone one of the applicants in London.

Instructions

Your job is to **(a)** answer the questions below and

Either:

(b) Write a memo in English to Mr Sam Hayworth, the European Sales Director at RAP Fashion. It should contain details of your telephone conversation and your recommendation, with reasons, as to whether you think the applicant is suitable or not.

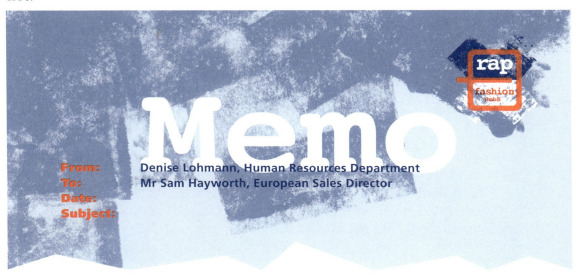

Memo

From: Denise Lohmann, Human Resources Department
To: Mr Sam Hayworth, European Sales Director
Date:
Subject:

Or:

(c) Write a summary in German of your telephone conversation to be given to Frau Schneider, the Director of Human Resources at your company.

Questions

1. What is the applicant's name?
2. Where did he see the advertisement?
3. How did he contact RAP Fashion?
4. What work experience does he have of the fashion trade?
    Two answers: **(a)** and **(b)**

5. Why did he leave his last job?
6. What is he doing now **(a)** in general, **(b)** in particular?
7. When would he be available?
8. How would he find time to work as an agent?
9. What area of England does he know well?
10. What must he do now?

Telephone Role Play

Rolle A

Sie sind Ursula (Frank) Kramer und arbeiten in Hamburg als Exklusiv-Vertreter/in (*sole agent*) für die kanadische Holzfabrik Timber Trade Inc in Vancouver, Kanada. Ihre Abrechnung (*account sales*) für letzten Monat wurde um 520 CDN\$ gekürzt. Sie rufen deshalb Ihren Chef, Herrn Gary Thompson, in Vancouver an. Berücksichtigen Sie dabei die folgenden Punkte:

– Leider zahlen die Kunden schleppend, daher wurden einige Beträge nicht pünktlich überwiesen
– Sie verstehen aber nicht, warum Ihre Provision um 520 CDN\$ gekürzt wurde
– Sie nennen die Nummer Ihrer Abrechnung 5017 Kr vom 3. dieses Monats
– Die von Herrn Thompson genannte Summe wurde inzwischen vom Kunden (Möbel Schulz in Münster) überwiesen
– Sie haben nichts gegen den Lösungsvorschlag von Herrn Thompson
– Sie bitten aber um Bestätigung, damit Sie Ihre Bücher bis Ende des laufenden Monats in Ordnung bringen können.

Role B

You are Gary Thompson, Export Manager at the Canadian company Timber Trade Inc in Vancouver, Canada. You receive a call from your German agent, Ursula (Frank) Kramer in Hamburg. Include the following points in your conversation:

– Yes, you know that some customers aren't paying punctually
– Tell her / him to put more pressure on them to pay on time
– Ask her / him to hold the line while you get her / his account sales
– You say you've found it. The sum of CDN\$1,500 is still owing – that's why there was less commission
– Say you'll check with the Accounts Department to see if the remittance has arrived. If so you'll correct your records
– You ask if the CDN\$520 can be paid next month
– Promise to send confirmation by fax.

Aufgaben

1.

Name	eigener Name	–
Position	Geschäftsführer/in	–
Firma	Musikhaus Angerfeld GmbH	Musical Instruments Ltd
Anschrift	Angerstr. 19, 45128 Essen, Germany	28 Lewisham High Street, London SE1 9QQ, England
Fax	+49 (2 01) 34 57	+44 (1 71) 3 57 88 52
E-Mail	angerfeld@aol.com	music.inst@firmlink.co.uk

Bewerbung eines Vertreters:

Geschäftsfall:
Ihre Firma verkauft in Deutschland Synthesizer und Keyboards, vornehmlich aus Amerika und Japan. Sie haben durch einen Geschäftsfreund von einem neuen japanischen Keyboard Marke Somaha AN-1X gehört, das über eine Londoner Zentrale vertrieben wird. Sie möchten für Deutschland die Alleinvertriebsrechte bekommen.

Aufgabe:
Schreiben Sie die entsprechende Bewerbung an die Firma Musical Instruments Ltd unter Berücksichtigung folgender Punkte:
– Sie sind seit ca. 10 Jahren im deutschen Musikgeschäft tätig
– Sie haben Verbindungen zu Groß- und Einzelhändlern in ganz Deutschland
– Durch internationale Kontakte halten Sie sich ständig auf dem Laufenden
– Das neue Somaha AN-1X Keyboard ist in Deutschland noch nicht bekannt
– Sie glauben, Stückzahlen von 5.000 – 10.000 im Jahr auf dem deutschen Markt absetzen zu können
– Bitte um Konditionen und baldige Antwort.

2.

Name	eigener Name	Mr Jeremy Whittacker
Position	Geschäftsführer/in	Managing Director
Firma	Heizungsbau GmbH	Whittacker Distribution Ltd
Anschrift	Limesstr. 42, 35510 Butzbach, Germany	Canada Square, London E14 7AN, England
Fax	+49 (60) 33 9 97 61	+44 (1 71) 4 57 84 20
E-Mail	heizungsbau.gmbh@firmenetz.de	whittacker.ltd@linkall.co.uk

Angebot des Prinzipals an einen Vertreter:

Geschäftsfall:
Sie stellen Heizgeräte (*heating systems*) her, die nur von zugelassenen Händlern gewartet werden dürfen. Sie suchen einen Vertriebspartner in Großbritannien, der über ein Netz von Service-Stützpunkten verfügt oder bereit ist, ein solches aufzubauen. Von der deutschen Handelskammer in London haben Sie die Adresse einer möglicherweise geeigneten Vertreterfirma erhalten.

Aufgabe:
Schreiben Sie das entsprechende Vertretungsangebot und machen Sie folgende Angaben:
–   Stellen Sie sich und Ihr Unternehmen vor
–   Beschreiben Sie, wie Sie Ihr Produkt verkaufen (über zugelassenes Händlernetz: *a network of approved dealers*)
–   Hat Whittacker Ltd ein solches Netz oder kann sie ein solches aufbauen?
–   Wenn ja, werden Sie einen entsprechenden Fragebogen schicken
–   Alle weiteren Einzelheiten (Provision, Lagerhaltung, Abrechnungsmodalitäten, usw.) müssten in einem persönlichen Gespräch geklärt werden
–   Bitte um baldige Nachricht.

3.

Name	eigener Name	Ms. Catherine Scott-Walker
Position	Vertreter/in	Executive Vice President
Firma	Bathtubs & Jacuzzis Inc.	Bathtubs & Jacuzzis Inc.
Anschrift	Bachstr. 28, 50858 Köln, Germany	P.O. Box 1580, Fourth Street, Denver, CO 30789, U.S.A.
Fax	+49 (2 21) 9 34 67 32	+1 (3 03) 8 97 65
E-Mail	btj.germany@alltalk.com	btj.inc@alltalk.com

Korrespondenz Vertreter / Prinzipal:

Geschäftsfall:
Sie sind die deutsche Vertretung des amerikanischen Herstellers Bathtubs & Jacuzzis Inc.

Aufgabe:
Schicken Sie dem amerikanischen Prinzipal Ihren 1. Quartalsbericht des laufenden Jahres unter Angabe folgender Einzelheiten:
–   Nach einem schlechten Jahresabschluss haben sich die Zeichen einer Geschäftsbelebung verstärkt (siehe beiliegende Verkaufsabrechnung)
–   Das Modell Waterstream 3000 erfreut sich besonderer Beliebtheit
–   Die Lagerbestände dieses Modells sind fast auf null gesunken

– Dringende Lieferung von 200 Stück erforderlich (Wann kann damit gerechnet werden?)
– Bitte um Kontenausgleich
– Hoffnung auf weitere gute Verkaufszahlen im laufenden Jahr.

4.

Name	eigener Name	Mr Thomas Cutter
Position	Verkaufsleiter/in	General Manager
Firma	Gronemeyer KG	Upper Crust Bakery Products
Anschrift	Lessingstr. 89, 82194 Gröbenzell, Germany	84 Abingdon Road, London W83 6AL, England
Fax	+49 (81 42) 33 76	+44 (1 81) 5 72 90 77
E-Mail	gronemeyer.kg@online.de	ucbp@allbake.co.uk

Korrespondenz Prinzipal / Vertreter:

Geschäftsfall:
Sie haben von Ihrem britischen Vertreter die monatliche Abrechnung und den Monatsbericht erhalten. Sie sind mit diesem Bericht äußerst unzufrieden.

Aufgabe:
Beantworten Sie den Bericht unter Berücksichtigung folgender Punkte:
– Bestätigung des Erhalts des Vertreterberichts
– Die Anzahl der Bestellungen ist gegenüber dem Vormonat um 30 % zurück-gegangen. Gründe?
– Ihnen ist eine direkte Beschwerde des Großhändlers Malcolm & Gordon aus Liverpool zugegangen, der sich über häufig verspätete Lieferungen beschwert
– Zweifel an der Effizienz des Vertreters (Werden Kunden oft genug besucht? Erfolgt die Verteilung der frischen Backwaren schnell genug?)
– Dringende Bitte um Verbesserung des Service
– Bei weiteren Klagen muss eine frühzeitige Beendigung des Vertretervertrages in Betracht gezogen werden.

5.

Name	eigener Name	Ms Julia Griffiths
Position	Verkaufsleiter/in	Sales Representative
Firma	Peter Bauer GmbH	–
Anschrift	Postfach 39 40 16, 99084 Erfurt, Germany	The Old Rectory, Birmingham WR10 3AG, England
Fax	+49 (3 61) 5 67 74	+44 (1 21) 9 87 65
E-Mail	peter.bauer.gmbh@eastlink.de	j.griffiths@brumtalk.co.uk

Geschäftsfall:
Sie sind Küchengerätehersteller und schreiben Ihrer britischen Vertreterin, um
ihr u. a. das neueste Produkt Ihres Hauses, den Mixer „Avantgarde" anzukündigen.

Aufgabe:
Schreiben Sie ihr einen Brief / ein Fax / eine E-Mail und berücksichtigen Sie dabei
folgende Punkte:
– Dank für letzten Abrechnungsbericht
– Drücken Sie Ihre Zufriedenheit mit dem Monatsumsatz aus
– Auf Grund der guten Geschäftsergebnisse gewähren Sie Frau Griffiths außer der
    besonderen üblichen Provision einen einmaligen Umsatzbonus von 2.500,00 £
– Ihr neuer Mixer „Avantgarde" wird nächsten Monat auf den Markt kommen
– Prospekt mit neuem Preis ist beigefügt
– Die neue Lieferung von 500 Stück für den Lagerbestand in Großbritannien wird
    in ca. 4 Wochen erfolgen
– Wenn Werbekampagne erwünscht, Bitte um Kostenvoranschlag
– Dank für gute Zusammenarbeit.

6.

Name	Henrietta (Harald) Biermann	Mr Lance Percival
Position	Vertreter/in	European Sales Director
Firma	Büroartikel-Import GmbH	Exclusive Design Ltd
Anschrift	Postfach 371178,	240 Lords Road,
	90419 Nürnberg, Germany	London N16 0QL, England
Fax	+49 (9 11) 56 49 77	+44 (1 81) 4 56 98 22
E-Mail	bueroart.import@germanet.de	exclusive.design@linkline.co.uk

Geschäftsfall:
Sie vertreiben die silbernen und versilberten Füllfederhalter (*silver and silver-plated fountain pens*) der britischen Firma Exclusive Design Ltd.

Aufgabe:
Schreiben Sie einen Vertreterbericht (heutiges Datum) an den britischen Prinzipal unter Angabe folgender Punkte:

–   Der Absatzmarkt für teure Büroartikel ist stark zurückgegangen (Gründe: Arbeitslosigkeit, wenig Kaufinteresse in der Zeit vor Ferienbeginn)
–   Ihr Hauptkunde, die deutsche Kaufhauskette Golderjahn, hat in diesem Monat keinen Auftrag erteilt (auf Nachfrage: schwache Konjunkturlage!)
–   Ihr Vorschlag: neue Verkaufskampagne im Herbst für die Vorweihnachtssaison
–   Kosten von ca. 6.000 Euro müssten aber von der Exclusive Design Ltd getragen werden
–   Versicherung, dass Sie Ihre Verkaufsanstrengungen verstärken werden, die Marktlage jedoch schwierig ist
–   Besteht die Möglichkeit, die Preise geringfügig zu senken oder Sonderrabatte für gute Kunden zu gewähren?
–   Bitte um wohlwollende Prüfung der Vorschläge.

Unit 12
Credit Enquiries

Introduction

When a customer requests credit the supplier will, in most cases, require trade references and sometimes also a bank reference. In addition, the seller may wish to use a credit reference agency (AE: credit bureau).

Credit reference agencies and credit bureaus play a major role in the granting of credit. In the USA there are more than 1,000 credit bureaus with hundreds of millions of files on virtually every adult and firm in the United States. In general, much of the information such agencies have is freely accessible to the public, e.g.:

- county court judgements (e.g. for unpaid debts)
- bankruptcy filings
- liens against property (e.g. if a property owner is unable to pay a debt)
- publicly available information on a company's business affairs, e.g. its balance sheet, profit and loss account, the names of the directors etc. (e.g. available from Companies House in the UK)

Many commercial organisations such as banks, building societies, insurance companies, credit card companies and department stores provide each other with information by pooling it (e.g. the German "Schufa" = "Schutzgemeinschaft für Allgemeine Kreditsicherung") or make it available on a regular basis to credit reference agencies. (Many companies send monthly computer tapes to credit bureaus listing all credit activity in their customers' accounts.). Using such data a profile of a person or company can be put together very quickly.

In order to comply with data protection laws, companies offering financial services usually ask their customers to sign a statement allowing financial data to be made available to other companies such as credit reference agencies.

Credit Enquiries

1. Direct / indirect reference to company for which a credit reference is required*
2. The sort of information required, e.g.
   - a snapshot report*
   - a full report*
   - buyer's reputation
   - company's director(s)
   - volume of business
   - profitability
   - payment habits
   - credit line requested
   - advisability of granting this amount of credit
   - recommended credit line
   - request for any other relevant information (e.g. from a credit reference agency)
3. Promise to treat all information confidentially and without obligation
4. Polite ending
   - offer of reciprocation
5. Enclosure(s)
   - stamped, addressed envelope / international reply coupon

*As appropriate

Fig. 25

Credit Reference

1. Direct / indirect reference to company for which a credit reference is required*
2. Information on the company / individual(s)
   - favourable impression
   - non-committal
   - unfavourable impression
3. Recommended terms of business with the company / individual in question
4. Reminder that you are only expressing an opinion*
5. Reminder that the information is confidential
6. Reminder that no responsibility will be accepted for it
7. Polite ending

*As appropriate

Fig. 26

Types of Credit Reference

Trade Reference

When taking up a credit reference it is customary to mark the enquiry "CONFIDENTIAL" (see Unit 1 "Layouts") and address it to a senior member of the company. As the information requested is highly sensitive, it is important to state that it will be treated in the strictest confidence. A company requesting information will also offer to reciprocate the favour.

Bank Reference

A supplier requiring a bank reference on a buyer normally goes through his own bank. This is so because bankers do not normally respond to enquiries from non-bankers about their clients. Bankers normally use very cautious language, which is not easily understood at first sight.

Credit Reference Agency's Report

On payment of a fee a "snapshot report" or a full report can be obtained on a company. Such reports contain a professionally compiled profile of a company covering a number of years. It normally includes information about its history, its directors, its volume of business and its payment behaviour. The company in question is also placed in a credit category, e. g. "acceptable", "caution", "warning", "serious risk", "bankruptcy". In addition, the report may contain a comparison between the company and other companies in the same field of commerce and an indication of the credit line the company in question is good for.

Points of Style

As the information requested and given is sensitive, it is best to avoid stating the name of a company when supplying information on it. Reference is thus made to "the company in question", "the company named", "the firm you refer to", "the firm referred to in your letter" or even "the company named on the enclosed slip". Expressions such as "the figure(s) you mention", "the sum mentioned in your letter" or "a credit in the sum you mention" are used when talking about the line of credit required. All this is intended to make it hard for an outsider to make sense of the information provided.

Specimen Letters

1. Unfavourable trade reference

44 Commercial Road
London EC2 2GJ
England
Tel. +44 (171) 67 53 44
Fax +44 (171) 67 53 00
E-mail: merryweather@linkall.co.uk

**Merryweather
Trading Co.**

RA/GI
6 June ..

Glashandlung Ernst GmbH
Verdistr. 22
90455 Nürnberg
Germany

Attn. Ms Angelika Neumann, Export Sales Department

Dear Ms Neumann

Credit Reference on your Customer

In answer to your enquiry of 28 May .. regarding your customer in Eastbourne we can give you the following information.

We started doing business with this company three years ago and we have gained the impression that it is not on a secure financial footing. It has come to our notice that the company has recently incurred heavy losses. In its dealings with us this company has had irregular payment habits, frequently having been up to 30 days in arrears with its payments.

In view of its poor credit record to date, we would strongly recommend that you avoid all dealings with this company on an unsecured basis.

Please note that the above details are supplied on condition that they remain strictly confidential and are made available without any obligation whatsoever on our part.

We hope the information provided will be of use to you. Please do not hesitate to get in touch with us, should any of the points mentioned above require clarification.

Yours sincerely
Merryweather Trading Co.

Rita Adam

Rita Adam
Credit Manager

2. Extract from sample Snapshot Report from the CreditLine Credit Bureau, USA

Business Snapshot Rating as of 12-31-..

SERIOUS RISK

Subject Company Inc.
100 Wall Street
New York, NY
Phone: 212 777 666

15 % of all businesses fall into this higher-risk category, which is based on seriously derogatory payment performance and/or seriously derogatory legal filings.

Based on the data currently on CreditLine's database for SUBJECT COMPANY INC., CreditLine strongly recommends further investigation of this company prior to making any credit or business decisions. Key elements on the CreditLine database that lead to this category include paying creditors on average 55 days past the invoice due date, 2 judgment filings with a total balance of $1,000, 1 tax lien with a total balance of $10,500 and a collection account with $12,000 placed for collection.

Detailed payment behavior

There are a total of 35 supplier relationships reported to CreditLine within the past 18 months. The total recent high credit for these 35 trade relationships is $214,900, with the highest single credit being for $68,500. The total current balance owed on the 35 trade relationships is $67,300, with the highest single balance due of $23,100. The account status for the total $67,300 balance due is 24 % current, 8 % is 1–30 days past due, 24 % is 31–60 days past due, 12 % is 61–90 days past due and 32 % is 91+ days past due. The average days past the invoice due date that it takes SUBJECT COMPANY INC. to pay its balance is 55 days.

3. German company takes up a trade reference

sheet

Ulrich Handelsgesellschaft mbH,
Schänzlestr. 5, 79104 Freiburg, Germany
Tel.: +49 (7 61) 77 64 53, Fax: +49 (7 61) 77 64 50
E-Mail: ulrich.handel@aol.com

FAO:	Mr Martin Jameson
	Credit Manager
	Bull Ring Art Supplies Ltd
	Birmingham
	UK
Fax No:	+44 (1 21) 70 52 34
From:	Sylvia Terhoven
	Credit Manager
Date:	15 December ..
Subject:	Credit Reference on Farmer's Furniture Bazaar, Tunbridge Wells, UK
Total Pages:	1

Dear Sir / Madam

The above-mentioned company has named you as a trade reference and, since we have not done business with them before, we would be grateful if you would let us have any relevant information you may have.

In particular, we would like to know how much business the company has done with you, its payment habits and how you assess the company's performance currently. In addition to this, we would be interested in any information you may have on the manager of the company, Ms Sarah Plunkett. As Ms Plunkett has requested an unsecured quarterly credit line of 25,000 euros, we would be most grateful if you would let us know whether you think it advisable to grant the company this much credit. Should you feel that this is excessive, what would a reasonable figure be in this case?

It goes without saying that any information supplied will be treated in the strictest confidence with no obligation on your part whatsoever. We will, of course, also be pleased to reciprocate the favour, should you require assistance of a similar nature.

Many thanks for your attention to our enquiry.

Yours faithfully

Sylvia Terhoven

Case Study

Company requesting a reference:
Biotech GmbH in Bremen (Brabantstr. 86, 28217 Bremen, fax +49 (4 21) 98 63 44, e-mail: biotech.gmbh@unilink.de)

Company supplying a reference:
Ecosafe Biological Products Ltd (Unit 90, Longdown Industrial Estate, Exeter, Devon DN6 9ZH, England, fax +44 (13 92) 43 56 44, e-mail: ecosafe@bionetwork.co.uk).

Biotech GmbH in Bremen are manufacturers and exporters of soft technology products for the health food industry with customers all over Europe. BTN Ltd, a British wholesaler of food processing equipment in East Grinstead, Sussex, England, has placed several orders with the German firm over the past six months and has so far paid on a "payment on receipt of invoice" basis. BTN now wish to deal with Biotech on a credit basis and therefore apply for open account terms with quarterly settlement. They anticipate placing orders worth approx. £50,000 per quarter.

When applying for credit BTN name two companies as references in the UK. One of them is Ecosafe Biological Products Ltd in Devon. Roswitha Harmann, the export sales manager at Biotech GmbH, therefore writes to Mr Rodney Parker, the credit manager at Ecosafe, requesting a reference on BTN to include the following details:
- the company's financial standing
- history
- directors
- volume of business done with BTN
- payment habits
- prospects
- whether it is good for a credit line of £50,000 per quarter
- any other relevant information

She also offers to reciprocate the favour for Ecosafe and promises confidentiality for any information supplied.

Ecosafe's Business Relations with BTN

Ecosafe first started dealing with BTN five years ago. At that time BTN was a partnership mainly purchasing catering equipment for factory canteens. It only placed occasional orders for organic food processing equipment and Ecosafe dealt with BTN on a "cash with order" basis.

After two years Ms Rosemary Farmer joined BTN from Barclays Bank plc, where she had been a well-respected local branch manager. Six months after arriving she had BTN incorporated as a private limited company and became its managing director. She was joined by Mr Terry Jones, a successful local solicitor as company secretary.

Since the arrival of Rosemary Farmer as managing director three years ago BTN has concentrated more on marketing organic food processing equipment (see table). The company also plans to go public next year.

Year	Type of Business Organisation	Orders placed with Ecosafe for organic food processing equipment p.a.	Collection Period (average number of days)
1	Partnership	£5,000	40
2		£4,000	42
3	Private limited	£150,000	15
4	company	£200,000	16
5		£250,000	15

Rodney Parker, Ecosafe's Credit Manager, writes the reference on BTN for the German firm. Ecosafe currently deals with BTN on open account terms with monthly settlement and a credit line of up to £75,000 per quarter.

Activities

A. Request for reference
Using the "Credit Enquiries Letter Plan" in this Unit and the Standard Expressions write Roswitha Harmann's credit enquiry in the form of a letter, fax or e-mail to Rodney Parker at Ecosafe Ltd in Exeter.

B. Credit reference
Using the "Credit Reference Letter Plan" in this Unit and the Standard Expressions write Rodney Parker's reference on BTN Ltd in the form of a letter, fax or e-mail to Roswitha Harmann at Biotech GmbH in Bremen. Include the information in the table in the reference.

Language

Use the "Credit Enquiries" and "Credit Reference Standard Expressions" tables to find the words missing below.

1. Verbs + nouns
    Which verbs go with the following nouns?
    a. to ▩ dealings with a firm
    b. to ▩ a financial obligation (i. e. "to pay the money owed")
    c. to ▩ a favour (i. e. "to do a favour for someone who did you one")
    d. to ▩ a goal (i. e. "to reach")
    e. to ▩ an impression (i. e. "to get")
    f. to ▩ difficulties (i. e. "to have")
    g. to ▩ responsibility for something

2. Verbs + prepositions / particles
    Which prepositions / particles go with the following verbs?
    a. to act ▩ a referee
    b. "Please advise us ▩ to whether …"
    c. to take ▩ more business than it can handle
    d. "It has come ▩ our notice that …"
    e. to rely ▩ someone to do something
    f. to default ▩ its payments
    g. "The company is good ▩ your figures."

3. Nouns + prepositions / prepositions + nouns / adjectives + prepositions
    a. to keep your head ▩ water
    b. ▩ the Internet
    c. ▩ schedule (i. e. "not late")
    d. to be ▩ arrears
    e. "This company spends ▩ its means" (i. e. "more than it can afford")
    f. to have difficulty ▩ handling a credit line of $10,000
    g. "We have no hesitation ▩ suggesting … "
    h. ▩ view of
    i. ▩ the time being
    j. ▩ different circumstances
    k. to bear ▩ mind
    l. to take ▩ consideration
    m. a claim ▩ objectivity
    n. ▩ condition that
    o. ▩ the assumption that …

4. Adjectives / adjectival phrases + nouns
    a. A company which is known to be honest and trustworthy is ▩.
    b. "We have ▩ reason to believe that …"
    c. on a ▩ financial footing (i. e. "stable")
    d. bad, e. g. *bad* payment record

5. Further points
    a. amount of business – ▩ of business
    b. How reliably does the firm pay? – What are its payment ▩?
    c. "This company is selling just enough goods to cover its costs" –
        "It's just ▩" (2 words)
    d. a credit ▩ of $10,000 (i. e. "limit")
    e. "It goes without ▩ that any information given will remain confidential."
    f. with no liability at all – with no liability ▩
    g. well managed – well ▩
    h. "The firm has a good ▩ record" (i. e. "a record of good performances
        in the past")
    i. to ▩ bankrupt (i. e. "to become")
    j. almost
    k. hardly

You are Alexandra Reimann and you work in the Export Sales Section of a new and rapidly expanding German furniture company called Bio-Stil KG in Bremen.

You have now received a large order from a British importer and, as you wish to know whether the British firm will be able to pay for its order, you phone a credit reference agency in Britain for information.

Listen to the dialogue and answer the questions below.

Questions

1. What is the name of the credit reference agency?
2. What is the name of the person Alexandra speaks to?
3. What sort of information can't John Danvers give Alexandra over the phone?
4. What sort of company does Alexandra want a credit reference on?
5. Where is information on such companies stored in the UK?
6. What are "secured charges"?
7. What are the two sorts of company profiles mentioned?
8. Give two examples of the type of information contained in a company profile.
9. What is a CCJ?
10. What is the credit reference agency's Internet address?

Now listen again and answer the following questions:

11. What information is available from Companies House?
12. Complete the list of facts about a company which can be contained in a company profile (question no. 8 above). There are 12 facts in all.

Telephone Role Play

Rolle A

Sie sind Diana (Elmar) Stein und arbeiten bei der Firma Automaten Weber GmbH in Düsseldorf (Fax: +49 (2 11) 8 97 78, E-Mail: weber.gmbh@aol.com). Ihre Firma hat von der Belvedere Brothers Ltd in Bristol einen Auftrag im Wert von 12.250 Euro erhalten. Sie haben über die Firma keinerlei Informationen. Rufen Sie die Ihnen bekannte CreditLink Ltd in London an. Ihre Gesprächspartnerin ist Ruth (Jeremy) Brown-Findlay. Berücksichtigen Sie die folgenden Punkte:
- Sie haben lange keine Kreditauskunft mehr aus GB benötigt
- Machen Sie die nötigen Angaben zu dem soeben von Belvedere Brothers Ltd erhaltenen Auftrag
- Was kann Ruth (Jeremy) über die Firma sagen?
- Erbitten Sie eine kurze schriftliche Auskunft, so detailliert wie möglich, als Fax oder E-Mail
- Danken Sie für prompte Erledigung. Sie werden die Gebühr für die Auskunft per Kreditkarte zahlen.

Role B

You are Ruth (Jeremy) Brown-Findlay and work for the CreditLink Ltd in London.
You receive a call from Diana (Elmar) Stein of Automaten Weber GmbH in Düsseldorf. Include the following points when answering it:
-   You are pleased to hear from Ruth (Jeremy) again
-   You can't say much over the phone but you'll check your records
-   You have the following information on file:
    -   it's a private limited company
    -   it sells vending machines in GB
    -   the Managing Director is Charles Belvedere
    -   the Company Secretary is his brother John Belvedere
    -   the company's address is 45 Watershed Road, Bristol
    -   the rest of the information is out of date
-   You offer a snapshot reference with information on
    -   the company's performance over the last four years
    -   its payment habits
    -   a comparison with similar companies in the same line
    -   a recommended credit limit
-   Promise to send the information by fax or e-mail by return
-   Ask for the caller's fax number and e-mail address
-   Ask how she / he would like to pay
-   Tell her / him to get back to you if there are any queries.

Aufgaben

1.

Name	eigener Name	–
Position	Leiter/in der Kreditabteilung	–
Firma	Morgenstern GmbH	Messrs Bradley & Pitt
Anschrift	Kaiserstraße 7, 3100 Bern, Schweiz	95 Donleavy Street, Belfast BT 4 JX, UK
Fax	+41 (31) 12 32-3 57	+44 (12 32) 24 51 00
E-Mail	morgenstern.gmbh@swissnet.ch	brad.pitt@irishweb.co.uk

Bitte um Auskunft:

Geschäftsfall:
Sie haben von der Sean O'Connors Ltd einen Auftrag über eine Fräsmaschine (*milling machine*) des Typs LOT 473 im Wert von 47.715 Euro erhalten. Die Firma möchte in 3 Raten (1. Rate in Höhe von 15.000 Euro bei Lieferung, 2. Rate

ebenfalls in Höhe von 15.000 Euro bei Inbetriebnahme (*when put into operation*), Rest 30 Tage nach Inbetriebnahme) zahlen. Bevor Sie den Auftrag annehmen, möchten Sie aber eine Referenz einholen.

Aufgabe:
– Bezug auf den o. a. Auftrag des irischen Kunden
– Da Sie noch nie mit dieser Gesellschaft Geschäfte gemacht haben, bitten Sie um detaillierte Auskunft über:
    a) Größe des Unternehmens
    b) Seit wann ist es auf dem Markt?
    c) Wer leitet die Firma?
    d) Jahresumsatz?
    e) Kreditwürdigkeit, Zahlungsmoral?
– Ist die erwünschte Zahlungsweise nach Meinung der Auskunftei riskant?
– Bitte um Bescheid, ob die Rechnung für die Auskunft per Visa-Kreditkarte beglichen werden kann.

2.

Name	eigener Name	Mr Bruce Foster
Position	Leiter/in der Auslandsabteilung	Credit Manager
Firma	Bürgschaftskredit GmbH	Australian Exports Pty Ltd
Anschrift	Bahnhofstr. 110,	45 Colonial Parade,
	74626 Bretzfeld, Germany	Milsons Point, NSW 2061,
		Australia
Fax	+49 (79 46) 21 41 80	+61 (2) 99 22 62 42
E-Mail	bsk.gmbh@t-online.de	austral.exports@aussiweb.au

Erteilung von Auskunft:

Geschäftsfall:
Die Auskunftei Bürgschaftskredit GmbH hat von der australischen Gesellschaft Australian Exports Pty eine Fax-Anfrage über die deutsche Gesellschaft Trautenberg & Schröder GmbH in München erhalten, die dem australischen Unternehmen einen Großauftrag über 125.000 Euro erteilt hat.

Aufgabe:
– Die infrage stehende Firma ist ein kleineres Unternehmen auf dem Gebiet des Im- und Exports von Maschinen
– Grundkapital des Unternehmens laut Handelsregisterauszug 50.000 Euro
– Vor größerer Kreditgewährung wird gewarnt
– Firma kommt ihren Zahlungsverpflichtungen nicht immer pünktlich nach
– Sie war in der Vergangenheit zweimal wegen nicht gezahlter Verbindlichkeiten vor Gericht

–   Auf jeden Fall sollten Sicherheiten verlangt werden
–   Ggf. nur Zahlung per bestätigtem unwiderruflichem Akkreditiv
–   Erteilung dieser Auskunft ist streng vertraulich und unverbindlich.

3.

Name	Rebecca (Simon) Christiansen	Ms Francis Packer
Position	Leiter/in der Kreditabteilung	Credit Manager
Firma	Atlas & Globus GmbH	Optical Instruments Ltd
Anschrift	Postfach 310719,	68 Grosvenor Gardens,
	42897 Remscheid, Germany	London SW1 4XX, England
Fax	+49 (21 91) 21 34 22	+44 (171) 3 42-76 50
E-Mail	atlas.globus@firmenetz.de	optic.inst@linkall.co.uk

Bitte um Auskunft:

Geschäftsfall:
Ihre Firma stellt optische Instrumente für die Schifffahrt her. Die irische Firma O'Connell Navigation Systems in Dublin hat Ihnen einen Auftrag im Gesamtwert von 27.500 Euro erteilt und die britische Firma Optical Instruments Ltd als Referenz benannt.

Aufgabe:
Formulieren Sie eine höfliche Bitte um Auskunft an die britische Gesellschaft unter Einbeziehung folgender Punkte:
–   Bezugnahme auf irische Firma, deren Namen auf beiliegendem Zettel steht, und den soeben erhaltenen Auftrag
–   Erwähnung, dass Ihnen die britische Firma als Referenz vom Kunden genannt wurde
–   Bitte um diskrete Auskunft über die Solvenz der genannten Firma
–   Liegt die Auftragssumme im Rahmen der Geschäftsmöglichkeiten?
–   Kann nach Meinung der Firma ein längeres Zahlungsziel risikolos gewährt werden?
–   Dank im Voraus für geleistete Hilfe
–   Vertrauliche Behandlung ist selbstverständlich
–   Zusicherung, dass Sie jederzeit zu Gegendiensten bereit sind.

4.

Name	eigener Name	Mr J. P. de Clerk
Position	Sachbearbeiter/in Abteilung Firmenkunden (Corporate Clients)	Credit Department
Firma	Hale Bank AG	Boyd Bank Pty
Anschrift	Münchner Str. 45, 60329 Frankfurt, Germany	Private Bag X08, Johannesburg, South Africa
Fax	+49 (89) 9 45-9 89	+27 (11) 9 89-4 32
E-Mail	hale.bank.ag@banknetz.de	body.bank.pty@linkbank.com

Erteilung von Auskunft:

Geschäftsfall:
Ihre Bank hat von der südafrikanischen Boyd Bank Pty eine Bitte um Auskunft über die deutsche Gesellschaft Nolde & Partner GmbH, Frankfurt, erhalten. Die Nolde & Partner GmbH hatte Ihre Bank als Referenz genannt.

Aufgabe:
Erteilen Sie die gewünschte Auskunft unter Berücksichtigung der folgenden Punkte:
– Nolde & Partner GmbH sind seit 1952 in Frankfurt / Main ansässig und vertreiben Schrauben und Muttern (*nuts, bolts and screws*)
– Die beiden Hauptgeschäftsführer sind die Brüder Stefan und Johann Nolde, 50 und 46 Jahre alt. Ein dritter Geschäftsführer ist Dipl.Kaufm. Dietrich Meyer, 40 Jahre alt
– Die Gesellschaft besitzt Immobilien im Wert von 3,5 Mio. Euro. Das Grundkapital der Gesellschaft beträgt 225.000 Euro
– Umsatz des Unternehmens im letzten Jahr: 42,5 Mio. Euro
– Wert des Lagerbestandes: 3,75 Mio. Euro
– Kreditrahmen (*credit facility*) bei der Bank: bis 1 Mio. Euro, der aber selten in Anspruch genommen wird
– Die Gesellschaft kommt allen finanziellen Verpflichtungen pünktlich nach
– Ihnen ist nichts Nachteiliges über die Firma bekannt
– Auskunft wird ohne Obligo erteilt.

5.

Name	eigener Name	–
Position	Leiter/in der Kreditabteilung	The Manager
Firma	Hotel Wiener Hof	Midland Bank
Anschrift	Freiligrathring 10,	Wimbledon Parkside,
	40878 Ratingen, Germany	London SW19 5NN, England
Fax	+49 (21 02) 34 25 56	+44 (1 81) 3 77 65 92
E-Mail	wiener.hof@t-online.de	midland.bank@banknet.co.uk

Bitte um Auskunft:

Geschäftsfall:
Ihr Hotel hat von einem britischen Unternehmen, der Thunderbird plc in Bristol, eine Bestellung für eine Tagung von 30 Zimmern und mehreren Tagungsräumen zuzüglich Verpflegung und Serviceleistungen für die Dauer von 5 Tagen erhalten. Gesamtpreis: ca. 32.500 Euro. Die Thunderbird plc will 10 % Anzahlung leisten, Rest zu Beginn der Tagung, Abrechnung der Zusatzleistungen (Telefon- und Faxgebühren, Minibar, zusätzliche Speisen und Getränke) nach Beendigung der Tagung. Als Referenz hat die Thunderbird plc die Midland Bank angegeben.

Aufgabe:
Wenden Sie sich an die Midland Bank in London und bitten Sie um eine Auskunft mit folgenden Angaben:
– Bezug auf die Bestellung der Thunderbird plc bei Ihnen und darauf, dass diese die britische Bank als Referenz genannt hat
– Schildern Sie den Umfang der Bestellung mit dem Auftragswert
– Ist die Firma gut für einen Kredit in dieser Höhe?
– Welchen Ruf genießt sie?
– Kann ohne Weiteres eine solche Bestellung ohne höhere Anzahlung akzeptiert werden?
– Kann die Bank (mit Genehmigung des Kunden) etwas über ihr Rating sagen?
– Sichern Sie strikte Vertraulichkeit zu
– Dank im Voraus für erteilte Auskunft
– Höflicher Schluss.

Unit 13

Job Applications

Applicant's Accompanying Letter

1. Source of employer's address (solicited / unsolicited application)*
2. Present situation
   - employment / training course
   - responsibilities / duties
   - details of promotion / progress within the company
   - unemployed
3. Reason(s) for leaving current job / seeking new activity*
4. Request to be considered for the post
   - availability for interview / aptitude test
5. Reference(s)/ testimonial(s)
6. Polite ending
7. Enclosure(s)

*As appropriate

Fig. 27

Curriculum Vitae

1. Name (first name + surname)*
   or
   First name(s)(Forenames / Christian name(s))*
   Surname (Family name / Last name)*
2. Address + Telephone number / Fax number / E-mail address / Internet (Home page)
3. Date of birth
4. Marital status
5. Nationality / Immigration status*
6. Driving licence(s)
7. Objective*
8. Education and Qualifications
   - primary school*
   - secondary school
   - higher education
   - vocational training course(s)
9. Employment
   - temporary work
   - permanent post(s)
   - company
   - position
   - responsibilities
   - achievements*
   - reason(s) for leaving*
10. National (Military) Service* / Community (Social) Service*
11. Community Work* / Other Skills and Experience*
12. Interests
13. Reference(s)

* As appropriate

Fig. 28

Employer's Reply

1. Reference to application
2. Invitation to
   - an aptitude test*
   - an initial interview
   - the final interview
3. Conditions*
   - qualifications
   - experience
   - references
   - nationality /
     immigration status
   - probationary period
   - salary
   - expenses
   - accommodation
4. Rejection
   - reason(s)
   - waiting list
   - referral to another
     employer
   - reference to return
     of application
     documents
5. Polite ending
6. Enclosure(s)
   (map / directions /
   airline ticket)

*As appropriate

Fig. 29

Writing a Reference / Testimonial

1. Date
2. Salutation (reference) /
   "To whom it may concern"
   (testimonial)
3. Subject line with name
   of candidate
4. Reference to request
   for reference
5. How well you know the
   candidate (time)
6. The candidate's work / position
   - quality
7. The candidate's nature
   (manner)
8. The candidate's character
9. Reason(s) for leaving*
10. Suitability for the position
    in question / Recommendation
    for further employment
    (testimonial)
11. Complimentary close and
    signature (reference) /
    Signature, name and position
    of person (testimonial)

*As appropriate

Fig. 30

Introduction

Applicant

The addresses of potential employers can be obtained:
1. from a private employment agency ("placement firm", "recruitment agency")
2. in the "Appointments" or "Situations Vacant" sections of a newspaper
3. through a recommendation.
4. from a state-run employment exchange (UK: "Jobcentre")

In addition to this there are also "head-hunters", i.e. employment agencies special-ising in finding executives for top jobs. "Head-hunters" approach top executives discreetly and make them an attractive offer on behalf of another company.

The company advertising the post in question is first contacted by the applicant, normally either by telephone or in writing and in some cases even by paying a personal visit to the company or its agent or representative. Sometimes an applica-tion form is sent to be filled in by the applicant and there can also be an aptitude test. If the aptitude test results are good, the candidate is invited to an initial inter-view. After this, the most promising candidates are short-listed and invited to a final interview.

The form the interview takes varies greatly. Some companies use an interview panel of several people, usually the personnel manager and sometimes even a psychologist. The interview can include a role-play or simulation. Some companies also pay candidates' expenses.

When making a written application for a job it is usual to send in a letter of application and a CV. The letter of application contains details of the applicant's current job, why he or she wishes to resign it, the period of notice that must be given and, unless the advertisement contains this information, what salary is expected. In addition, it should contain the names of people who are prepared to provide a reference. If the candidate has testimonials, these should be included, as should letters of recommendation.

Many advertisements also contain details of "fringe benefits" (also known as "perks" = perquisites). These can include such things as a company car, an interest-free car loan, a car allowance, private medical insurance, assistance with relocation costs, assistance with school fees and a gratuity.

Curriculum Vitae / Résumé

A CV (plural: CVs, AE: résumé / resume) is a document containing information on an applicant's career and personal background under separate headings. It is almost always typed and in tabular form. An English or American CV is not signed and dated as it is in German. In addition, American employers are not allowed to ask questions regarding the applicant's race, colour, creed, national origin, age (unless under 18), gender, marital status, disabilities and arrest record.

The purpose of a CV / résumé is to make it easy for a prospective employer to obtain an overall picture of the applicant before meeting him or her. It should be well laid-out and easy to read and also not have any significant omissions. In an English or American CV / résumé, however, details of primary (AE: elementary) school education need not be included unless they are of particular importance, e. g. in the case of bi-lingual applicants born abroad. The order in which activities are listed is usually chronological in a British CV, whereas an American résumé may be in reverse order. There are no hard and fast rules. The CV or résumé is one of the criteria used by employers to decide which candidates to invite to an interview and what questions to ask them.

Some CVs / résumés contain a paragraph entitled "**Objective**" or "**Occupational goal**" in which the applicant states what he or she hopes to achieve. This makes it easier for the employer to decide whether the new post will be suitable for the candidate or not. It is also important to include achievements and accomplishments in a CV / résumé. This is best done by giving relevant details under the heading "Successes" or "Achievements" in the **Employment** section.

It is customary to begin with the name. Here it is important to make it clear which name is which as there may be some confusion between the first name(s) / forename(s) / Christian name(s) (if the applicant is Christian) and the surname / family name / last name. If the names are easy for the employer to recognise (e. g. "Christine Braun" or "Thomas Schmidt"), the heading can be simply "Name:" If the names are hard for English-speaking employers to recognise, it is best to use two headings – "First name:" and "Surname:"

Some CVs are sent with photographs and others (especially in the USA) are not. It is less customary to have a photograph on a CV than on an application form, which may have space on it for this purpose. A female applicant can also add her title (Miss / Mrs / Ms) in brackets after her signature at the end of the covering letter.

The practice of underlining the first name by which one is generally known is not customary in English-speaking countries.

Employer

After contacting the prospective employer the applicant introduces himself / herself and finds out whether he / she is eligible for the job or not.

A written application consists of a CV / résumé, references, testimonials (see "**References / Testimonials**" on page 205), certificates and qualifications. The employer invites promising candidates to an aptitude test and / or an initial interview. Unsuitable candidates are informed that they unfortunately cannot be considered for the post in question. The best candidates are short-listed and invited to a final interview, after which one is given the job. Some companies only pay the expenses of the successful candidate, whereas others pay those of all candidates or of the short-listed ones.

Handwritten or typed?

In general, unless the employer specifically states that the covering letter should be handwritten, both the covering letter and the CV / résumé are typed. If an application form is enclosed, this may be filled in in the applicant's own writing.

How to look for a job

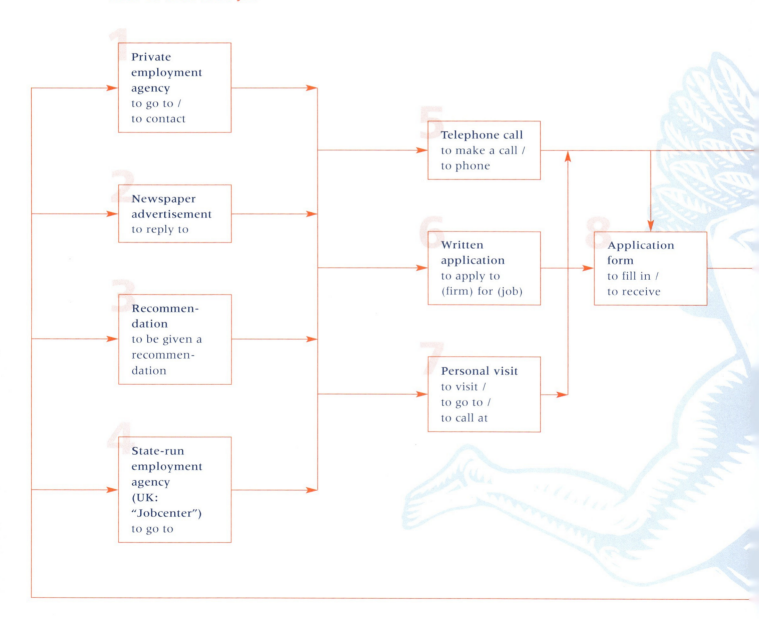

1 **Private employment agency**
to go to /
to contact

2 **Newspaper advertisement**
to reply to

3 **Recommendation**
to be given a recommendation

4 **State-run employment agency**
(UK: "Jobcenter")
to go to

5 **Telephone call**
to make a call /
to phone

6 **Written application**
to apply to
(firm) for (job)

7 **Personal visit**
to visit /
to go to /
to call at

8 **Application form**
to fill in /
to receive

Reference / Testimonials

A reference is a written report on the applicant's character and / or ability to do the job in question and is specifically written to be read by one particular employer for one particular job. A testimonial contains the same information but is of a general nature and may sometimes be addressed "To whom it may concern". It can be added to any application.

In general, it is customary and advisable only to include positive information when writing a reference because the person in question may find himself or herself disadvantaged by a negative reference and sue the referee for defamation of character.

In many cases a reference is more eloquent in its omissions than in its inclusions.

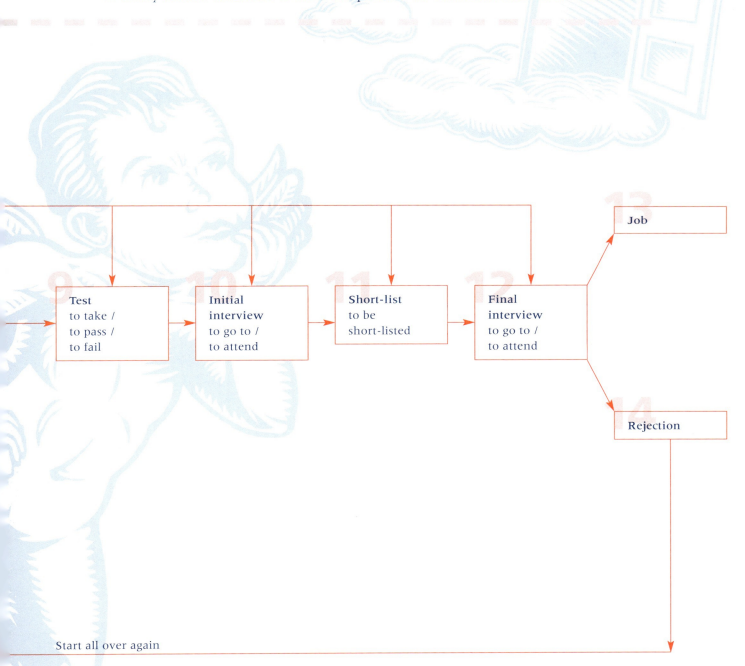

Job

Test
to take /
to pass /
to fail

Initial
interview
to go to /
to attend

Short-list
to be
short-listed

Final
interview
to go to /
to attend

Rejection

Start all over again

Specimen Letters

1. Accompanying letter.
See Unit 1 Layouts, **Fig. 4** on page 13 for the layout of a private letter.

Heinrich-Gustav-Str. 99
69121 Heidelberg
Germany

20 January ..

Ms Kate Williams
Human Resources Officer
PowerGen Plc
90–100 Coronation Street
LANCASTER
LA1 4GH
England

Dear Ms Williams

Your Advertisement on the Internet for the Post of European Sales Clerk

I am writing with reference to the above-mentioned advertisement and am most interested in applying for the post you offer.

I am currently employed as a business administration clerk at Neckarstahl AG in Heidelberg and have held this post for five years. Even though I am successful in my current position I would like to work for a firm at which I would be able to put my knowledge of English to good use.

I feel sure that your company has the opening I am looking for and would therefore be most grateful if you could consider my application.

I am available for interview at a week's notice.

I enclose my CV and copies of my qualifications. Should you require a reference Frau Wiebke Pütz, who teaches business administration theory and English at Heidelberg Vocational Training College, will be pleased to provide you with any information you may need.

I look forward to hearing from you at your earliest convenience.

Yours sincerely

Rita Räumschüssel
Rita Räumschüssel (Ms)

Encs:
CV
Certificates

Specimen CV

Curriculum Vitae

Name:	Rita Räumschüssel
Address:	Heinrich-Gustav-Str. 99
	69121 Heidelberg
	Germany
	Tel. +49 (62 21) 3 42 19
Date of birth:	26 March 19..
Marital status:	Divorced
Nationality:	German

Full car and motor cycle licence

Objective
To obtain a position with more scope for personal initiative in which I will be able to put my knowledge of English to good use.

Education & Qualifications
19..–19..   Maria-Wächtler Gymnasium, (grammar school), Heidelberg
Abitur (German university entrance qualifications)
Main subjects: Mathematics, Chemistry
Average grade: 1.4 (distinction)

Employment
19..–19..   Neckarstahl AG, Heidelberg
Training course to obtain a qualification from the Heidelberg Chamber of Commerce as a business administration clerk
Final assessment: Grade 1

Since ..	Permanent post in the Export Sales Department
Position:	Export Sales Clerk
Responsibilities:	Responsible for all sales transactions with foreign companies
Achievements:	During the time when I was responsible for exports a large number of major contracts were negotiated

Interests
Jazz dance, ballroom dancing and ice hockey

Reference
Frau Wiebke Pütz
Lutherstr. 99
69120 Heidelberg
Germany
Tel. +49 (62 21) 66 75 31

CyberPower

California Calling!

Cyber**Power** *Software Incorporated* needs you!

As a major software company in L.A., California we are looking for a commercial agent in Germany to market our latest products. You will be fluent in English and German, perfectly up-to-date with the latest developments in the field of business software and also have a network of customers in the construction industry.

Have we described you?

If so, contact our President, Jon Sayers, right now in Los Angeles, California with your résumé:

Cyber**Power** *Software Incorporated*
5330 Pacific Concourse Drive
280
Los Angeles, CA 90045
Tel: +1 (3 10) 2 97-79 88
Fax: +1 (3 10) 2 97-79 66
E-mail: cyber.power.la@compuserve.com
Web Site: http://www.cyberpower.com

2. Karl-Philipp Jaspers in Oberhausen responds to the above advertisement in the German American Chamber of Commerce publication "German American Business West".

First he writes his accompanying letter using the American layout (here in modified form for a private letter. See Unit 1 Layouts, **Fig. 4** on page 13).

Specimen letter 2

Karl Philipp Jaspers, Commercial Agent

Feldstr. 35
46149 Oberhausen
Germany

Tel: +49 (2 08) 30 98 16
Fax: +49 (2 08) 30 98 17
E-mail: jaspersoftware@t-online.de

January 2, ..

Mr. Jon Sayers, President
CyberPower Software Incorporated
5330 Pacific Concourse Drive
280
Los Angeles, CA 90045
U.S.A.

Dear Mr. Sayers:

I have seen your advertisement in the German American Chamber of Commerce publication "German American Business West" and am most interested in becoming your commercial agent in Germany.

As you can see from my enclosed résumé I am currently self-employed and have been running my own highly successful company for the past three years. Since demand for software applications for the construction industry is expanding faster than ever before, I very much hope that you will consider me for the post advertised.

I will call you Friday morning for further details.

Many thanks in advance for your attention to my application.

Sincerely,

Karl-Philipp Jaspers
Karl-Philipp Jaspers

Enclosure

His résumé is set out as follows:

Feldstr. 35
46149 Oberhausen
Germany

K a r l   P h i l i p p   J a s p e r s ,   Commercial Agent

Tel: +49 (2 08) 30 98 16
Fax: +49 (2 08) 30 98 17
E-mail: jaspersoftware@t-online.de

Occupational Goal

To expand my already flourishing software business with the addition of state-of-the-art applications for the construction industry in Germany, Austria and Switzerland

General Background

10 years' study and experience of computer software and hardware in both Germany and Britain

Professional Experience

3/98 – present	Sole proprietor of Jaspers Sofware GmbH in Oberhausen, with 4 employees, concentrating on importing software products from the U.S.A. and Britain to Germany (North-Rhine Westphalia)
3/98	Founding of Jaspers Software GmbH (Inc.) in Oberhausen
1/98	Return to Germany from Britain to set up my own company to market software products
9/95 – 12/97	Employment at Software Schöller Ltd in Britain, the Birmingham subsidiary of Schöller AG in Essen, Germany
8/94 – 8/95	Internship in the Information Technology section of Schöller AG in Essen

Education

10/88 – 6/94	Heinrich- Heine-University in Düsseldorf, Germany Master's Degree equivalent, majoring in Information Technology
6/87	Abitur (High School Diploma)
9/78 – 6/87	Gymnasium (Middle and High School) in Oberhausen

Military service

7/87 – 10/88	Conscript

Interests

Photography, soccer

References

Available on request

3. An employer invites a promising candidate to an interview

PowerGen Plc
90–100 Coronation Street
Lancaster
LA1 4GH
England

KW/TT
30 January ..

Ms Rita Räumschüssel
Heinrich-Gustav-Str. 99
69121 Heidelberg
Germany

Dear Ms Räumschüssel

Thank you for your letter dated 20 January .., in which you apply for the post of European Sales Clerk.

You are among the candidates who have been chosen to take part in an aptitude test as part of our selection procedure. The test will take place at 10 am on 15 February in the Hilton Hotel in Frankfurt. Successful candidates will then be invited to an initial interview that afternoon. Short-listed candidates will later be invited to attend the final interview, which will take place in London.

Directions to the Hilton Hotel are enclosed for your convenience. Please note that expenses will only be paid on presentation of appropriate receipts.

We look forward to meeting you personally in Frankfurt.

Yours sincerely

Kate Williams

Kate Williams (Ms)
Human Resources Officer

Enc

4. An employer rejects an application

POwerGen Plc
90–100 Coronation Street
Lancaster
LA1 4GH
England

KW/TT
30 January ..

Ms Rita Räumschüssel
Heinrich-Gustav-Str. 99
69121 Heidelberg
Germany

Dear Ms Räumschüssel

Thank you for your letter dated 20 January .., in which you apply for the post of European Sales Clerk.

We regret to inform you that only candidates with considerable experience in the field of European sales are eligible for this position and so, judging by your CV, it would consequently be unsuitable for you. Your application has, however, been filed and will be used at a later date if a suitable post becomes vacant.

We regret that we are unable to help you this time and wish you every success in the future.

Yours sincerely

Kate Williams

Kate Williams (Ms)
Human Resources Officer

5. Favourable reference on a former employee

Moritzstr. 98
10960 Berlin
Germany
Tel. +49 (30) 2 04 36 18

Export Bendorf KG

MS/TT
21 February ..

Mr Harry Wilberforce
Director of Human Resources
EuroTrade Ltd
98 Silver Street
CAMBRIDGE
CA4 9JK
England

Dear Mr Wilberforce

Silke Hermann

In reply to your request for a reference on Ms Hermann in connection with her application for a position as Export Sales Representative I am pleased to provide you with the following information.

Ms Silke Hermann worked for approx. five years in our company's Export Sales Department from .. – .. . Her work was always of an exceptionally high standard and she carried out her duties with imagination and intelligence. She speaks and writes both English and French fluently and is a cheerful personality with a natural skill with people. She is entirely trustworthy and reliable and also sensitive to other people's needs. Her loyalty to the company was unquestioning as was her commitment to the task at hand. She left the company in .. because she was expecting her first child.

I have no hesitation in recommending Ms Hermann for this post, for which I feel she would be ideally suited.

Yours sincerely

Marita Schlohmann
Marita Schlohmann
Personnel Director

6. Testimonial

Moritzstr. 98
10960 Berlin
Germany
Tel. +49 (30) 2 04 36 18

28 December ..

To whom it may concern

<u>Silke Hermann</u>

Ms Silke Hermann worked for five years in our company's
Export Sales Department from .. – .. . Her work was always
of an exceptionally high standard and she carried out her
duties with imagination and intelligence. She speaks and
writes both English and French fluently and is a cheerful
personality with a natural skill with people.

She is entirely trustworthy and reliable and also sensitive
to other people's needs. Her loyalty to the company was
unquestioning as was her commitment to the task at hand.

She left the company in .. because she was expecting her
first child.

I have no hesitation in recommending her for employment.

Marita Schlohmann
Marita Schlohmann
Personnel Director

Case Study

GlobalCard Europe Ltd

Has this caught your eye?

Would you like to improve your spoken and written business English?

We have a number of administrative posts at our European Service Centre in Brighton on the south coast of England.

We are a blue chip global financial services organisation with one of the most accepted and respected brand names in the world.

You will be fluent in German and have a good command of English. You will have university entrance qualifications and be in your early to mid-twenties. You will also preferably have some administrative experience.

You will be keen to acquire experience in the field of international business and be thinking in terms of spending a minimum of 18 months abroad, after which time you will have excellent promotion prospects.

We are offering a competitive package based on performance and length of service with an initial annual salary of £15K +, depending on experience. In addition, you will qualify for a bonus on completion of 12 and 18 months' service. Assistance will be provided with relocation expenses.

If you would like to be considered for one of these posts, please send your application to Mary MacNamara, our Human Resources Officer, by 31 January . . .

GlobalCard Europe Ltd
90–100 Regent's Park Drive   BRIGHTON   BN2 2LP   England

Henrietta Stratmann sees this advertisement in last Friday's edition of the *Frank-furter Allgemeine Zeitung* for a job in Britain with a major credit card company and decides to send in an application.

Write Henrietta's CV and covering letter using the following profile:

Profile

Henrietta was born on 26 June .., is German and lives in 44892 Bochum (Am Neggenborn 98, tel. (02 34) 33 38 21, fax (02 34) 33 39 00, e-mail: stratmann@t-online.de). She is single and has a full driving licence.

She now wants a new job which will enable her to use her English and commercial skills and, at the same time, offer her promotion prospects.

She attended the Lessing Gymnasium (explain) in Bochum and, after 8 years, obtained her Abitur (explain) specialising in English and biology, with an average grade of 1.5 (explain). She then went on to attend a full-time vocational course at the "Europäisches Berufskolleg der Stadt Essen" (explain) to become a "state-qualified commercial assistant with languages (English / French)". The course there lasted two years and she obtained an overall grade of 2.2 (explain). Whilst on this commercial course she learned to type at 50 w. p. m. (words per minute) and to use most major software packages and the Internet.

After completing the course she got a job as an export sales assistant at "Ehrenfeld und Kappel Rolltreppen (*escalators*) GmbH" in Wuppertal, where she has now been for the past two years. The section she works in deals with orders for lifts and escalators from the Middle East (Saudi Arabia, Kuwait, the United Arab Emirates). After a year there she was promoted to the position of sales clerk responsible for all Middle Eastern orders. Henrietta is successful at her work but would now like to work abroad in an English-speaking country for a few years. She has travelled widely in Europe and North America and also speaks Spanish fluently. Her hobbies are fencing, skiing, computers and painting.

As referee she gives the name of Frau Sabine Schulz, her old lecturer in modern languages at the "Europäisches Berufskolleg der Stadt Essen" (Sachsenstr. 27, 42158 Essen, tel. (02 01) 33 38 53, fax (02 01) 33 39 00, e-mail: s.schulz@aol.com).

Language

Use the "**Applicant's Accompanying Letter** Standard Expressions" table to find the words missing below.

1. **Verbs + nouns**
   Which verbs go with the following nouns?
   a. to ▨ a post (i. e. "occupy")
   b. to ▨ a company (i. e. "to start working for")
   c. to ▨ a company (i. e. "to make smaller")
   d. to ▨ an aptitude test

2. **Verbs + prepositions / particles**
   Which prepositions / particles go with the following verbs?
   a. to wind ▨ a company (i. e. "to close down")
   b. to take ▨ a challenge
   c. to be laid ▨ (i. e. "to lose your job")
   d. to specialise ▨ fashionwear
   e. "My salary amounts ▨ $50,000 p. a."

3. **Nouns + prepositions / prepositions + nouns / adjectives + prepositions**
   a. ▨ view of the fact that …
   b. to have shares ▨ a company
   c. "My current salary is ▨ for review in …"
   d. ▨ short notice
   e. ▨ your earliest convenience

4. Adjectives / adjectival phrases + nouns
   a. to seek ▨ employment (i.e. "different")
   b. to be made ▨ (i.e. "unemployed")
   c. "My salary at the moment" – "My ▨ salary"
   d. "My salary depends on how hard I work" – "My salary is ▨"
      (hyphenated expression)

Use the "**Curriculum Vitae**" and "**Employer's Reply** Standard Expressions" tables to find the words missing below.

5. Verbs + nouns
   Which verbs go with the following nouns?
   a. to make twice as much
   b. to make three times as much
   c. to make four times as much
   d. to ▨ a new product (i.e. "to put on the market for the first time")

6. Verbs + prepositions / particles
   Which prepositions / particles go with the following verbs?
   a. to take ▨ more responsibility
   b. to be considered ▨ this position
   c. to qualify ▨ a marriage allowance

7. Nouns + prepositions / prepositions + nouns / adjectives + prepositions
   a. scope ▨ personal initiative
   b. "Ms Jones is secretary ▨ the Managing director."
   c. to be ▨ charge of export sales

8. Adjectives / adjectival phrases + nouns
   a. to be conversant ▨ a software package
   b. to be bi-lingual ▨ German and Turkish
   c. ▨ request

9. Further points
   a. Give an expression in the "Employment: permanent post(s), achievements" section to mean "to make more efficient".
   b. If you can no longer rise to a higher position in a company you have reached the ▨ of the ▨.

Daniela Witkowski lives in Essen. She is 25 years old and, despite the fact that she is currently employed, she wishes to use her foreign-language skills to work abroad, preferably in the UK. She therefore registers with a number of Internet job search databases, one of which is called NetRecruit. Today she receives an e-mail with a job description so she phones NetRecruit.

Listen to the dialogue and answer the questions below.

Questions

1. What job is Daniela interested in?
2. What section is Daniela put through to?
3. Who does Daniela speak to?
4. What company has advertised the post?
5. What are they setting up in the UK?
6. What details is she given about the salary?
7. What will the company help Daniela to do if she gets the job?
8. Where will interviews take place?
9. How long has Daniela got to send in her application?
10. Who is she going to send her application to? Give the name of the company.

Now listen again and answer the following questions:

11. What must be included in a full application?
12. What type of work would Daniela be expected to do?
13. Explain why it might not be possible for Daniela to start work in the UK in a month's time.

Telephone Role Play

Rolle A

Sie sind Daniela (Otto) Spickernagel und arbeiten seit drei Jahren bei der Scholl Industriebedarf GmbH in München. Ihre Firma exportiert Werkzeuge (*tools*) in englischsprachige Länder (GB, USA, Kanada, Australien), hat aber keine eigene Vertretung im Ausland. Sie haben im *Job Seekers Weekly* von letzter Woche eine Stellenanzeige für eine/n „*European sales clerk*" bei der Firma Baring & Price Technology plc in Reading, GB, gelesen. Rufen Sie die Personalchefin, Frau Julia Parson, an, und berücksichtigen Sie dabei folgende Punkte:

– Beziehen Sie sich auf die o. a. Anzeige
– Beschreiben Sie Ihre Firma und Ihre Arbeit (viele englischsprachige Kunden, Schriftverkehr in Englisch, Besucher aus dem Ausland usw.)
– Sie möchten aber selber Auslandserfahrung sammeln
– Sie haben PC-Kenntnisse (Windows, Word, Excel)

- Sie haben Handelsenglisch in der Berufsschule (*at vocational training college*) und in der Firma (*in an in-house language course at work*) gelernt
- Sie haben auch das „*London Chamber of Commerce and Industry Certificate in English for Business*"
- Sie sind ledig und könnten in ca. 3 Monaten nach GB umziehen
- Für ein persönliches Vorstellungsgespräch stehen Sie jederzeit zur Verfügung, bitten aber um Erstattung der entstehenden Kosten
- Sie werden sofort Ihre Unterlagen an Baring & Price Technology plc schicken
- Wann würden Sie frühestens von der britischen Firma hören?

Role B

You are Julia Parson, the Personnel Manager at Baring & Price Technology plc in Reading. When Daniela (Otto) Spickernagel calls you from Munich, include the following points in your conversation:
- Experience in the export trade?
- Present job?
- Type of work?
- Reason for wanting to leave?
- Computer-literate? (programs?)
- Commercial English?
- Ready to move to the UK in the near future?
- Availability for interview?
- Your company would pay travel expenses if she / he is invited to an interview
- Ask for a written application (CV, qualifications, references, testimonials etc.)
- Say she / he will hear from you in three weeks' time after the closing date for applications.

Aufgaben

1.

Name	Helga Achenbacher	Mr Peter Hudson
Position	–	Director of Human Resources
Firma	–	Lion & Powell plc
Anschrift	Geiselheimer Str. 11	P.O. Box 261103
	64293 Darmstadt	Coventry CV4 7AL
Fax	+49 (61 51) 87 53 42	+44 (12 03) 64 97 08
E-Mail	achenbacher@t-online.de	lipo@wbs.warwick.ac.uk

Geschäftsfall:
Sie haben in der *Times* ein Stellenangebot der Firma Lion & Powell plc in Coventry gelesen. Die britische Firma sucht eine/n Sachbearbeiter/in für den europäischen Markt.

1. Aufgabe:
Schicken Sie Ihre Bewerbung an Lion & Powell plc und berücksichtigen Sie dabei folgende Punkte:
– Bezug auf die o. a. Anzeige
– Sie haben eine Ausbildung zur Groß- und Außenhandelskauffrau (*a recognised qualification in wholesaling and export sales*) bei der deutschen Firma Schaumann & Herpich GmbH in Frankfurt (Braubachstr. 30–40, 60311 Frankfurt) erfolgreich abgeschlossen
– Ihre Schullaufbahn und weitere Einzelheiten sind aus Ihrem Lebenslauf zu ersehen
– Sie haben jetzt bei Ihrem Ausbildungsbetrieb eineinhalb Jahre lang gearbeitet, möchten sich aber verändern und Auslandserfahrung sammeln
– Da Sie ledig sind, ist ein Umzug nach England kein Problem
– Sie haben bei Ihrem Unternehmen eine Kündigungsfrist von 6 Wochen zum Quartalsende
– Bei Erstattung der Reisekosten sind Sie jederzeit bereit, zu einem Vorstellungsgespräch nach England zu kommen
– Referenzen können bei Bedarf vorgelegt werden
– Bitte um Diskretion gegenüber Ihrem jetzigen Arbeitgeber.

2. Aufgabe:
Verfassen Sie den zu dieser Bewerbung gehörenden Lebenslauf. Die folgenden Angaben sind noch hinzuzufügen:
Geburtsdatum:	3. 10. ..
Telefon:	+49 (61 51) 87 53 41
Fax:	+49 (61 51) 87 53 42
Staatsangehörigkeit:	deutsch
Besuch des Gymnasiums:	.. – ..

Abitur:		Annette von Droste-Hülshoff Gymnasium in Ffm (Fächer: Englisch, Mathematik, Notendurchschnitt: 2,9)
Lehre (siehe Aufgabe 1):		Während der Lehre 3 Monate Praktikum bei der britischen Vertretung Ihrer Firma in Birmingham
Führerschein:		Klasse III
Hobbies:		Nähen, Lesen, Tanzen, Tennisspielen
Sprachkenntnisse:		Englisch, Französisch, Italienisch. In Englisch haben Sie darüber hinaus die Fremdsprachenkorrespondenten-prüfung vor der IHK Frankfurt abgelegt, Note: Gut.

2.

Name	Georg Lichtweg	Mr. Henry Chancellor
Position	selbständiger Vertreter	President
Firma	Lichtweg GmbH	Chancellor Inc.
Anschrift	Grabenstr. 40, 63450 Hanau	P.O. Box 4873, Big Bear Lake, California, CA 92315, U.S.A.
Fax	+49 (61 81) 45 11 37	+1 (9 09) 3 76 23 40
E-Mail	lichtweg@firmnetz.de	10443.8802@compuserve.com.

Geschäftsfall:
Sie arbeiten als selbständiger Vertreter im deutschen Raum. Sie vertreiben Produkte aus dem Kosmetikbereich, vorwiegend aus den USA und GB. Aus einer Anzeige in der Fachzeitschrift *Beauty* haben Sie erfahren, dass Chancellor Inc. einen Vertreter für Deutschland sucht.

1. Aufgabe:
Bewerben Sie sich auf die in *Beauty* erschienene Anzeige und richten Sie sich dabei nach folgenden Punkten:
- Bezug auf Anzeige
- Hinweis auf jahrelange Tätigkeit im Kosmetikbereich (siehe beiliegenden Lebenslauf!)
- Sie sind bei allen Großhändlern, Warenhäusern und Parfümerieketten in der BRD bestens eingeführt (auf Wunsch Referenzen)
- Sie fügen einen Prospekt Ihrer Firma bei
- Bieten Sie ein Treffen in Deutschland mit einem Besuch bei einigen Ihrer Großkunden an
- Bei Interesse ist auch ein Besuch in den USA möglich (Kostenerstattung).

2. Aufgabe:

Schreiben Sie den dazugehörigen Lebenslauf. Die folgenden Angaben sind dabei noch zu berücksichtigen:

Geburtsdatum: 18. 03. .. (vor ca. 30 Jahren)

Schulbesuch (Sek. II):   .. – .. (8 Jahre)

Wehrdienst: .. – .. (ca. 1 Jahr)

.. – ..   Studium der Volkswirtschaftslehre in Bremen, Abschluss als Dipl. Volkswirt (6 Jahre)

.. – ..   2 Jahre bei der deutschen Firma Stelzenberger GmbH in Herne (Schwerpunkt: Vertrieb von Seifen und Parfümerie-artikeln)

.. – ..   1 Jahr Auslandsaufenthalt in Bath / England bei der britischen Niederlassung der Stelzenberger GmbH (Bearbeitung des britischen Kundenstammes)

.. (letztes Jahr)   Rückkehr nach Deutschland und Übernahme einer Vertretung für die britische Firma Brook Ltd.

Seitdem: Ausweitung des Vertreternetzes und selbständige Tätigkeit im eigenen Unternehmen.

3.

Name	Paul (Paula) Gabler	Ms Geraldine Foster
Position	Personalleiter/in	
Firma	Upmarket GmbH	
Anschrift	Grillparzerstr. 11, 81675 München	34 Grosvenor Avenue, Jersey JE4 8XG, Channel Islands
Fax	+49 (89) 31 67 50	+44 (15 34) 73 09 61
E-Mail	upmarket.gmbh@online.de	g.foster@channelink.co.uk

Geschäftsfall:

Sie sind Personalchef/in bei der Firma Upmarket GmbH in München und hatten im *Guardian* ein Stellenangebot aufgegeben, in welchem Sie eine Fremdsprachen-korrespondentin für die Hauptsprache Englisch, Nebensprachen Deutsch und Französisch suchen. Geraldine Foster hat sich bei Ihnen beworben.

Aufgabe:

Schreiben Sie als Paul (Paula) Gabler einen Brief an Geraldine Foster und berücksichtigen Sie dabei folgende Punkte:
- Dank für Bewerbung
- Sie begrüßen sehr, dass Frau Foster als Muttersprache Englisch hat und 3 Jahre in Deutschland zur Schule gegangen ist

- Fügen Sie einen Personalfragebogen bei, den Frau Foster bitte ausfüllen und zurückschicken soll
- Laden Sie Frau Foster zu einem Vorstellungsgespräch am … um 9.00 Uhr in Ihrem Hause ein
- Fahrt- und Unterbringungskosten für 2 Nächte werden von Ihnen erstattet
- Sie werden sich auch um ein Hotel in der Nähe Ihrer Firma kümmern
- Weisen Sie darauf hin, dass Frau Foster sich auch einem Test unterziehen muss
- Das Vorstellungsgespräch wird wahrscheinlich erst am frühen Nachmittag beendet sein.

4.

Name	Stefan Angler	Mr Eric Johnston
Position	Personalleiter	Personnel Manager
Firma	Pharmafinanz AG	Pharmaceuticals plc
Anschrift	Postfach 3611,	46 Burnhill Road, Beckenham,
	65045 Wiesbaden	Kent BR3LA
Fax	+49 (6 11) 57 69 34	+44 (1 81) 7 63-92 46
E-Mail	phafin@netsurf.de	pharma.plc@firmlink.co.uk

Geschäftsfall:
Sie sind Stefan Angler und haben von Eric Johnston ein Schreiben erhalten, in dem er Sie um eine Referenz über Frank Küppersbusch bittet, der bei Ihnen mehrere Jahre als Exportsachbearbeiter tätig war und sich nun als Vertreter selbständig gemacht hat. Er will für die britische Firma pharmazeutische Produkte in Deutschland vertreiben.

Aufgabe:
Erteilen Sie der britischen Firma die gewünschte Auskunft unter Berücksichtigung folgender Punkte:
- Frank Küppersbusch hat bei Ihnen von .. – .. (4 Jahre) in der Abteilung Pharmazeutische Produkte Ausland gearbeitet
- Seine Aufgaben umfassten die gesamte Abwicklung von Exportaufträgen einschließlich der Einholung sämtlicher ggf. erforderlicher Genehmigungen und Gesundheitszeugnisse
- Er war sehr zuverlässig, pünktlich und auch bei schwierigen Fragen und Verhandlungen immer ein guter Ansprechpartner
- Sein Verhalten gegenüber Kunden, Kollegen und dem Arbeitgeber war stets loyal, zuvorkommend und einwandfrei
- Er war in der Lage, selbständig zu arbeiten
- Sie sind sicher, dass er als Vertreter gute Dienste leisten wird
- Ihre Auskunft ist selbstverständlich unverbindlich und wird vertraulich erteilt.

5.

Name	Sabine Jäger	Gerry Anderson
Position	Personalleiterin	Director of Human Resources
Firma	Hellweg Fashion KG	UpperCut Fashionwear Ltd
	Gumppenbergstr. 99	65 Old Mare Road,
	93053 Regensburg	Oxford OX5 8JJ, England
Fax	+49 (941) 547885	+44 (1865) 89453
E-Mail	hellweg.fashion.kg@linkall.de	uppercut@bizlink.co.uk

Geschäftsfall:
UpperCut Fashionwear Ltd sucht eine/n Muttersprachler/in Deutsch mit guten
Englischkenntnissen für eine Sachbearbeiterstelle im Export und gibt eine
entsprechende Annonce auf. Frau Gaby Bey bewirbt sich auf die Stelle und gibt
als eine ihrer Referenzen einen früheren Arbeitgeber, die Hellweg Fashion KG
in Regensburg, an. UpperCut Fashionwear wendet sich jetzt mit der Bitte um vertrauliche Auskunft über Frau Bey an die Hellweg Fashion KG.

Aufgabe:
Verfassen Sie als Personalleiter/in bei der Hellweg Fashion KG eine entsprechende
Referenz unter Berücksichtigung folgender Punkte:
–   Bedauern darüber, dass keine umfassende Auskunft gegeben werden kann
–   Beschäftigungsdauer von Frau Bey lediglich 10 Monate vor zwei Jahren
–   sehr gute Englischkenntisse
–   Aufgabengebiet: Export von Damenbekleidung nach Nordamerika
–   überdurchschnittlicher Erfolg auf diesem Gebiet
–   verließ die Firma auf eigenen Wunsch, weil sie ihr erstes Kind erwartete.

Unit 14

Forwarding and Insurance

Forwarding

Introduction

Goods are usually shipped by road, rail, inland waterway (river or canal), sea or air. If a company does not have its own means of transport, a shipping and forwarding agent (freight forwarding agent / freight forwarder) is used. Most such companies provide a comprehensive service, including:

*See Unit 6 "Delivery" for more details

- (international) air freight
- (international) sea freight
- containerisation
- trailer services
- storage and distribution
- packing and labelling

- assistance with shipping documents*
- legalisation and consularisation*
- provision of a certificate of origin* (from a chamber of commerce)
- customs clearance
- insurance

In the context of forwarding, care should be taken to distinguish between the following terms:

	Term	Meaning	Example
1	a Standard Shipping Note (Old term: "Mate's Receipt")	the 6-part document made up by the shipper with details of the goods to be forwarded	The carrier collects the goods, signs the SSN, gives a copy back to the shipper and uses the other copies to obtain further documentation needed.
2	a bonded warehouse	a warehouse where goods are stored until customs duties are paid	The goods will need to be stored in a bonded warehouse.
3	a cargo liner	a ship which operates on a particular route	There's a cargo liner on the Bremen–Cape Town route.
4	a charter party	a contract to hire out a ship or an aircraft to transport goods	The ship owner draws up the charter party and mails it to the charterer.
5	a depot	a place where containers and trailers are loaded and unloaded	The carrier will first take our goods to the depot.
6	a ferry	a boat or ship which carries passengers and goods across a stretch of water and back	the cross-Channel ferry
7	a Forwarder's Certificate of Receipt	a document confirming that the forwarder has received the goods "in apparent good order and condition"	According to the FCR the goods were undamaged.
8	a haulier a haulage contractor a haulage company	a company which transports goods by road	The haulier brings the goods to our premises.

	Term	Meaning	Example
9	a shipping conference	an association of shipowners whose liners sail the same routes	We normally use conference ships.
10	a tramp steamer	a cargo ship that does not operate on a fixed route	We'll have to charter a tramp steamer for this cargo.
11	a cargo	goods carried by a plane or a ship	a cargo of coal
12	demurrage	a charge paid to the owner of the ship if the charterer delays sailing	The demurrage charge is $100 per day.
13	lay-days	the days allowed for loading and unloading a ship	The time estimated includes 3 lay-days.
14	merchant shipping	cargo and passenger ships	This route is very popular with merchant shipping.
15	negotiable	can be sold	a negotiable bill of lading
16	received for shipment	the forwarder has received the goods but they are not on board a ship yet	We can only issue a received for shipment B/L at this stage.
17	ro-ro vessels	Roll-on / roll-off ferries enable vehicles to drive on board the ship at one end and off at the other without turning round, thus saving time.	Ro-ro ferries are faster.
18	a shipment	a quantity of goods	a shipment of wood
19	shipment	the act of loading goods on board a ship	The goods are ready for shipment.
20	shipment	the act of transporting goods by any commercial means	We require shipment by air.
21	the shipper	the person or company whose goods are transported	The shipper signs the bill of lading.
22	shipped on-board	the forwarder has received the goods and they are on board ship	Goods can be sold "on water" using a clean, shipped on-board B/L.
23	the carrier	the company that transports the goods	an airline
24	the consolidator	a company that combines consignments to fill cargo space economically	The consolidator puts similar goods together in one container or on one trailer.

The work of a freight forwarding agency

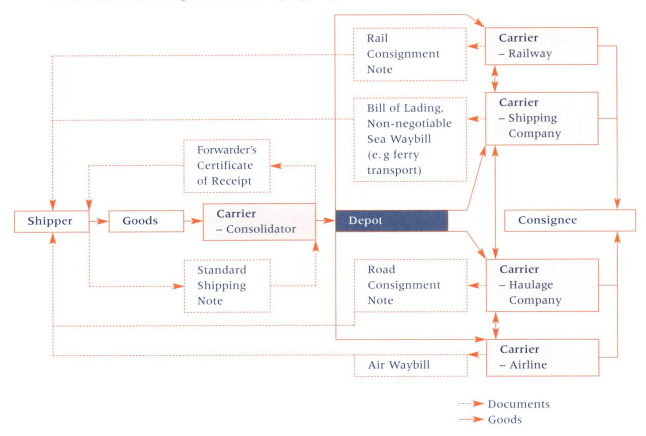

Shipper → Goods → Carrier – Consolidator → Depot → Consignee

Forwarder's Certificate of Receipt
Standard Shipping Note

Rail Consignment Note — Carrier – Railway
Bill of Lading, Non-negotiable Sea Waybill (e.g ferry transport) — Carrier – Shipping Company
Road Consignment Note — Carrier – Haulage Company
Air Waybill — Carrier – Airline

- - - → Documents
——→ Goods

Bills of lading

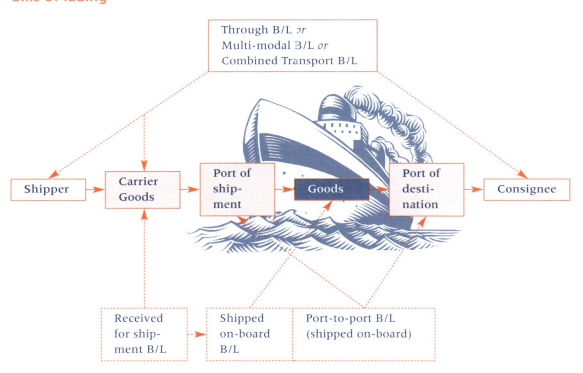

Through B/L *or*
Multi-modal B/L *or*
Combined Transport B/L

Shipper → Carrier Goods → Port of ship-ment → Goods → Port of desti-nation → Consignee

Received for ship-ment B/L → Shipped on-board B/L → Port-to-port B/L (shipped on-board)

Introduction

Goods in transit by road, rail, air, inland waterway or sea are insured against risks such as *damage, loss, fire* or *theft*. Insurance may be taken out from any of the major insurance companies specialising in cover for goods in transit and, also, with *Lloyd's of London*, which is an insurance *market* in Britain at which risks of almost any nature can be insured.

"*Marine insurance*" is the oldest category of insurance and was originally used to refer to sea voyages but is now also used to cover journeys by road, rail and air.

It is customary to base insurance cover for goods transported by ship upon the "*Institute Marine Cargo Clauses A, B, C, and War and Strikes Clauses*". Clause A is used for "all-risk" cover, whereas Clauses B and C offer less cover at a lower premium. Clauses A, B and C include such events as *collision damage, loss, theft, fire, explosion, sinking and natural catastrophes*.

In the context of marine insurance the word "*average*" is used to mean damage or loss resulting from an event at sea. "*General average*" means damage or loss brought about to prevent a catastrophe at sea, e.g. jettisoning the cargo to prevent a ship from sinking. Such a loss is borne by all parties to the voyage. "*Particular average*" means accidental damage to an insurer's cargo, e.g. breakage or damage by seawater. Such a loss is borne by the individual insurer.

In the following the terms most frequently used when referring to the different types of insurance cover are summarised.

Marine insurance cover

1. With particular average (WPA)
The insurer covers both total and partial loss.

2. With general average (WGA)
The insurer(s) must bear the costs incurred to save a voyage from complete destruction, e.g. if the cargo is jettisoned to save the vessel from total loss, or part of the cargo is lost while a fire on board is put out.

3. Free of particular average (FPA)
The insurer covers total loss but not partial losses to the cargo (e.g. damage by seawater, breakage on board) unless they result from stranding, sinking, burning or collision.

4. Free of particular average under 10% (FPA 10%)
Total loss is covered and partial losses resulting from particular average are also covered except the first 10%, which must be borne by the shipper (i.e. there is a deductible of 10%).

5. Free of all averages
Only total loss is covered.

6. Free of SR & CC
This means that strikes, riots and civil commotions are not covered.

7. FC&S
This stands for "free of capture and seizure", meaning that these events are not insured.

		Insured for total loss	Insured for partial loss incurred to prevent a catastrophe	Insured for partial loss (accidental damage to cargo)
1	With particular average	yes	yes	yes
2	With general average	yes	yes	–
3	Free of particular average	yes	yes	–
4	Free of particular average under 10 %	yes	yes	yes (but not the first 10 % of any accidental damage)
5	Free of all averages	yes	–	–

Marine insurance policies

A shipper may choose from the following policies when insuring his cargo:

A floating policy
The shipper pays a lump sum to the insurer in advance and each time a shipment is made the insurer issues an insurance certificate and deducts the premium from the lump sum. When the lump sum has been used up the policy is renewed.

An open policy
This is taken out by a shipper for a fixed period of time or until cancelled. It covers different types of goods. An insurance certificate is issued and a premium calculated for each consignment. The premium is paid in arrears.

A time policy
This covers a ship and / or its cargo for a particular period of time and not a particular voyage. A time policy may, in addition, only be valid in certain geographical areas.

A voyage policy
This is taken out for a particular voyage and has no specific time limit. The route stated may only be changed for an important reason, e.g. danger to life in the case of a ship in distress.

Customer's Enquiry about Freight Forwarding Services

1. Source of address*
2. Request for quotation*:
    – rates for single / regular shipment(s)
    – bulk rates
    – groupage rates
    – with / without insurance
    – charter rates
3. Details of goods to be transported:
    – quantity
    – weight
    – volume
    – dimensions
    – nature (e.g. hazardous)
4. Mode of transport required:
    – road
    – rail
    – sea
    – inland waterway
    – multi-modal
5. Location(s) / Date(s):
    – collection / delivery
    – storage
6. Documentation
7. Other formalities:
    – packing
    – customs clearance
    – collection service
8. Polite ending

*As appropriate

Fig. 31

Freight Forwarder's Offer

1. Reference to enquiry
2. Request for further information*:
    – weight
    – dimensions
    – special features of the goods
3. Mode of transport / insurance cover:
    – charges
4. Dates:
    – collection
    – raising documentation
    – storage
    – delivery
5. Reference to enclosure(s)*:
    – order form
    – shipping / packing instructions / packing
    – other information
6. Terms of payment
7. Validity of offer
8. Polite ending
9. Enclosure(s)

*As appropriate

Fig. 32

Specimen Letters

1. Freight forwarder's offer

Worldwide Shipping Services

Templeton House
Bridge Hall Road
Manchester
MR3 4JK
England
Tel. +49 (161) 2 26 89 45
Fax +49 (161) 2 26 89 40
E-mail: wss@cargolink.co.uk

SH/GF
2 December ..

Konrad GmbH
Spezial- und
Industrienähmaschinen
Pohlstr. 88
10785 Berlin
Germany

Dear Sir / Madam

Your Freight Enquiry dated 14 November ..

Thank you for the above-mentioned enquiry requesting us to quote you for a shipment of 100 industrial sewing machines to be delivered to O'Leary Bros in Dublin, Ireland.

Before we can send you our detailed quotation, we must ask you to specify the weight and dimensions of the consignment. We are able to tell you, however, that for shipping a load of approx. 2,000 kg by road and sea from Berlin to Dublin, Ireland franco to your customer's premises, we would charge ... euros per seafreight-tonne and ... euros per roadfreight-tonne.

We will require you fill in all sections of the enclosed order form when placing your order to enable us to book cargo space in good time. We would also draw your attention to the packing instructions enclosed.

Before we can start processing your shipment, we require an obligatory advance payment of 33 % of the final invoice amount. The balance is due when the goods reach their destination.

We look forward to receiving your order and enclose a brochure on our entire range of services for your convenience.

Yours faithfully
Worldwide Shipping Services

Shirley Harris

Shirley Harris
European Division

Encs

2. German company enquires about freight forwarding services

Fischer Wärmetechnik,
Benzstr. 88, 31135 Hildesheim, Germany
Tel.: +49 (51 21) 4 35 22, Fax: +49 (51 21) 4 35 18
E-mail: fischer.waermetechnik@firmenlink.de

FAO:	Ms Brenda Morgan
	Customer Services
	Fast Freight International
	Birmingham
	England
Fax No:	+44 (1 21) 76 19 22
From:	Martine Ullmann
	Export Sales Department
Date:	9 July ..
Subject:	Shipment of 10 domestic central heating units to Scotland
Total Pages:	1

Dear Ms Morgan

You have been recommended to us by Messrs. Stuart and Trimble in Glasgow, who have made use of your services in the past.

Please quote us your most favourable CIF rates for shipping 10 domestic central heating units (total weight approx. 7.5 tonnes) to Aberdeen, to be collected there by our customer, Dewar House Construction Ltd. We would require them to be transported in a separate container and stored in a locked warehouse at the port. The consignment is to be insured warehouse-to-warehouse against all risks, including particular average. We would also require you to crate each unit separately. As they are easily damaged we must point out that they must be handled with particular care. The goods are to be collected from our premises in good time to arrive in Scotland on 1 September at the latest. Our customer has also asked us if you are able to specify which vessel the load will be shipped on.

Please also let us know whether your service includes the provision of the requisite documentation, as payment has been agreed by documentary credit. Provided you are able to offer us the all-inclusive service we require, we will be pleased to commission you to forward this and other shipments.

A prompt reply to this enquiry would be most appreciated.

Yours sincerely

Martine Ullmann

3. German customer enquires about parcel rates

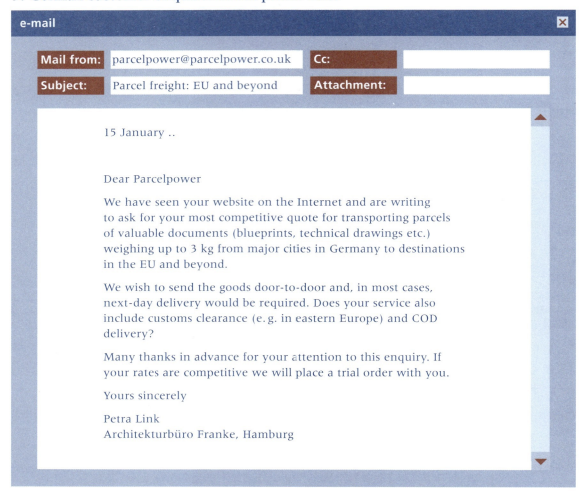

e-mail ☒

| **Mail from:** | parcelpower@parcelpower.co.uk | **Cc:** | |
| **Subject:** | Parcel freight: EU and beyond | **Attachment:** | |

15 January ..

Dear Parcelpower

We have seen your website on the Internet and are writing
to ask for your most competitive quote for transporting parcels
of valuable documents (blueprints, technical drawings etc.)
weighing up to 3 kg from major cities in Germany to destinations
in the EU and beyond.

We wish to send the goods door-to-door and, in most cases,
next-day delivery would be required. Does your service also
include customs clearance (e. g. in eastern Europe) and COD
delivery?

Many thanks in advance for your attention to this enquiry. If
your rates are competitive we will place a trial order with you.

Yours sincerely

Petra Link
Architekturbüro Franke, Hamburg

Case Study

Customer's enquiry

The Ohnesorg Dampfbierbrauerei in Hattingen in North-Rhine Westphalia was a small steam-beer brewery run by Herr Heinrich and Frau Agnes Ohnesorg as a family business for many years. Herr and Frau Ohnesorg are no longer alive and you, Michael(a) Ohnesorg, their only surviving heir, now wish to sell the brewery. Hank Brewster, an American businessman from Ithaca in New York State, USA, wants to set up a microbrewery there so he makes you an offer for the brewing equipment. You wish to accept his offer but one of his conditions is that you have to organise the transportation of all the beer-brewing equipment, which is highly delicate and over 100 years old.

The machinery has now been dismantled and you want to have it crated and transported as sea freight via Hamburg to the ocean port of Boston and then on to Ithaca by road. Payment is to be made partly by documentary credit.

You decide to obtain quotations from both German and American freight forwarders so you contact the German-American Chamber of Commerce in New York for addresses in the USA. You are given the address of CargoStar International in New York, whom you contact.

In your enquiry you include the fact that you want the forwarder to do everything for you, including the provision of all documentation. You add that the equipment needs to be in Ithaca within the next three months at the latest. You point out that the machinery may need to be stored in the USA if the weather conditions in New York State (November – March) are too dangerous to enable the equipment to be transported safely.

Freight forwarder's offer

You are Robin Parker and you work in the European Section of CargoStar International in New York. When you receive Michael(a) Ohnesorg's enquiry you quote him / her your standard freight rate of $60.00 per seafreight-tonne or $1m^3$ and $30.00 per roadfreight-tonne or $3m^3$, depending in either case, whichever is the greater. Crating would be charged separately. Your rates automatically include the raising of all standard documents, including Bs/L and L/C documentation. Storage would be charged separately but you point out that your company has warehouses and distribution centers all over the world, including Hamburg and Boston.

Your company operates a weekly shipping service from Hamburg to Boston. The transit time would be approximately 12 days and you would need 2 weeks' notice of the collection date required. You ask for the dimensions and weight of the machinery to enable you to send a detailed quotation. As regards insurance you recommend full insurance cover with particular average for the sea trip as the equipment is delicate.

You finish your letter by offering to provide any extra information needed by phone, fax, e-mail or letter and add that a catalog describing your company's entire range of services is being mailed separately.

Activities

Addresses:
- *Customer:*
  Ohnesorg Dampfbierbrauerei, Nierenhofer Str. 100, 45525 Hattingen,
  Fax: +49 (23 24) 3 09 41, e-mail: ohnesorg.dampfbier@t-online.de.
- *Forwarder:*
  CargoStar International, 20 East End Avenue, New York, NY 10028,
  fax +1 (7 72) 50 10, e-mail: cargo.star@bizlink.com

A. Customer's enquiry about freight forwarding services:
Using the "**Customer's Enquiry about Freight Forwarding Services** Letter Plan" in this Unit and the Standard Expressions write Michael(a) Ohnesorg's letter / fax / e-mail to CargoStar International in New York.

B. Freight forwarder's offer
Using the "**Freight Forwarder's Offer** Letter Plan" in this Unit and the Standard Expressions write Robin Parker's letter / fax / e-mail to Michael(a) Ohnesorg in Hattingen.

Language

Use the "**Customer's Enquiry about Freight Forwarding Services**" and "**Freight Forwarder's Offer** Standard Expressions" tables to find the words missing below.

1. Verbs + nouns
    Which verbs go with the following nouns?
    a. "Please ▒▒ us your best rates." (i. e. "Make us an offer")
    b. to ▒▒ a ship (i. e. "to hire")
    c. to ▒▒ documentation (i. e. "to make up")

2. Verbs + prepositions / particles
    Which prepositions / particles go with the following verbs?
    a. to consist ▒▒
    b. to pick ▒▒ the goods
    c. to dock ▒▒ Dover
    d. to attend ▒▒ import formalities
    e. to clear goods ▒▒ customs
    f. to entrust a carrier ▒▒ shipping the goods
    g. to quote a customer ▒▒ a consignment
    h. to amount ▒▒
    i. to speed ▒▒ the processing of your order
    j. to adhere ▒▒ regulations
    k. to insure ▒▒ all risks

3. Nouns + prepositions / prepositions + nouns / adjectives + prepositions
    a. ▒▒ transit
    b. in accordance ▒▒ Institute Cargo Clause A
    c. ▒▒ particular average (one word)
    d. to send goods ▒▒ the Channel Tunnel
    e. to send goods ▒▒ the Pyrenees
    f. harmful ▒▒ human beings
    g. susceptible ▒▒ fading
    h. 5 metres long ▒▒ 2 metres high (not "and")
    i. a quotation ▒▒ a shipment
    j. information as ▒▒ the weight of the load
    k. demurrage ▒▒ $10 per day
    l. ▒▒ an extra charge of $10
    m. "A copy is enclosed ▒▒ your reference."
    n. ▒▒ receipt of our invoice
    o. a remittance ▒▒ $1,000
    p. "This offer is ▒▒ engagement."

4. Adjectives / adjectival phrases + nouns
    a. the *necessary* documentation – the ▒▒ documentation
    b. a *customs* warehouse – a ▒▒ warehouse
    c. "There has been *great* demand." – "There has been ▒▒ demand."

5. **Further points**
   Which adjectives are used to mean the following?
   a. easily broken
   b. catches fire easily
   c. dangerous
   d. goes bad quickly (food / flowers)
   e. Something that destroys slowly by chemical action is ▬.
   f. Give 3 words used to mean different sorts of vessel.

13 Listening

Your name is Kathrin Lembeck and you work for EuroTransport GmbH Cologne. Today you get a phone call from an English customer about shipping some valuable items from Cologne to Yorkshire in the north of Britain.

Listen to the dialogue and answer the questions below.

Questions
   1. What sort of goods does Brian want to ship to Britain?
   2. How much is the load worth?
   3. What does the load consist of?
   4. Who will pack the goods?
   5. What sort of insurance does Brian want?
   6. What else will EuroTransport provide?
   7. What three methods of shipment does Kathrin suggest?
   8. How much time have EuroTransport got to transport the goods?
   9. What is Brian's phone number?
   10. What is Brian's fax number?

After studying the diagram on "The Work of a Freight Forwarding Agency" on page 228, listen again and answer the following questions.
   11. What transport document will be issued
       (a) if the goods are sent by ferry?
       (b) if the goods go through the Channel Tunnel?
       (c) if the goods go by air?
   12. What will the shipper receive in addition to copies of the transport document?
   13. Who is the shipper in this case?
   14. What is the name of the consignee?
   15. What must be clarified as regards insurance for the load?
   16. What will EuroTransport first do before they send Brian a quotation?
   17. When will Brian get a quotation from EuroTransport?

Telephone Role Play

Rolle A

Sie sind Nathalie (Jonas) Peters und arbeiten bei der Firma Schneider AG in Emmerich, Tel.: +49 (28 22) 27 44 11, Fax: +49 (28 22) 27 44 19. Rufen Sie die britische Spedition Nigel Foster Ltd, London, an. Es geht um Folgendes:

- Beziehen Sie sich auf die Speditionsaufträge, die Sie Foster letztes Jahr erteilt haben
- Sie haben wieder eine Sendung von 1.500 Kisten (*cases*) Wein, die nächste Woche in Emmerich per Lkw abzuholen wäre. Sie geht an Boosey Ltd in Chelsea, London
- Sie brauchen den Lkw in Emmerich am Dienstag nachmittag gegen 14.00 Uhr. Die Ware soll noch am gleichen Tag verladen werden
- Wann kann der Lkw losfahren und wann wird er in London ankommen?
- Was wird das Ganze kosten? Haben sich die Preise vom letzten Jahr geändert?
- Es handelt sich um 30 Paletten mit je (*each with*) 50 Kisten à (*containing*) 12 Flaschen
- Sie werden nach Erhalt des Fax Rücksprache mit Ihrem Chef nehmen, und wenn der Preis stimmt, den Auftrag schriftlich bestätigen. Welche Fax-Nr. hat Foster Ltd?
- Sie hoffen, die Sache klappt.

Role B

You are Lilly (Daniel) Whitehouse and work for Nigel Foster Freight Forwarders Ltd in London, fax: +44 (1 71) 4 99 63 50. When Natalie (Jonas) Peters phones you take the call.

- Say you are pleased to hear from Schneider AG again
- Tell them you'll be delighted to take another load for them
- You check on the computer and see that there is a lorry going to Germany next week. Ask when the German company would like it to pick up the wine in Emmerich
- The lorry can return to England on Tuesday evening, arriving in London mid-day Wednesday
- Explain that to work out the final price you need to know the number of pallets. Add that the prices are more or less the same as last year
- Ask for the German company's fax number and promise to fax them a quote in about an hour
- Say you would be pleased to transport the wine for them and guarantee that your quote will be competitive.

Aufgaben

1.

Name	Juliane (Herbert) Schaute	–
Position	Transportsachbearbeiter/in	–
Firma	Warensteiner & Co. KG	Gordon Shipping Service Ltd
Anschrift	Karl-Nagel-Str. 13,	P.O. Box 3408,
	86199 Augsburg	Plymouth PA5 8LV, England
Fax	+49 (8 21) 34 04 99	+44 (17 52) 84 05 12
E-Mail	warensteiner.kg@online.de	gordon.service@shipping.co.uk

Bitte um Frachtsätze an Spedition:

Geschäftsfall:

Sie müssen eine große, technisch sehr hochwertige Maschine, in Einzelteile zerlegt, an die Firma Preston plc in 34, Grange Road, Bristol BS8 2EA, England, schicken. Die Firma Preston hat Ihnen die Gordon Shipping Service Ltd genannt, die Erfahrung mit solchen Transporten hat und das Vertrauen von Preston genießt.

Aufgabe:

Schreiben Sie eine Anfrage nach Frachtsätzen an die Gordon Shipping Service Ltd und berücksichtigen Sie dabei folgende Punkte:
- Bezug auf Auftrag der Firma Preston
- Beschreibung der zu versendenden Ware
- Lieferung ist CIF Plymouth
- Es handelt sich um 15 Kisten, in welchen die zerlegten Teile transportiert werden, Abmessungen: 400 × 250 × 140 cm, Gesamtgewicht: ca. 30 Tonnen
- Wegen der Anfälligkeit der Teile müssten die Kisten unbedingt unter Deck (*below deck*) verstaut werden
- Bitte um Frachtsätze per Schiff von Hamburg bis Plymouth einschließlich Seeversicherung WPA
- Ware wird bis Hamburg per Lkw angeliefert
- Packliste wird vom Hafenspediteur 3 Tage vor Abreise übergeben.

2.

Name	Gabi (Christoph) Thomé	Ms Lydia (Mr Jeremy) Britton
Position	Transportsachbearbeiter/in	Transport Logistics
Firma	Deutsches Schifffahrtskontor	Steel Export Plc
Anschrift	Freihafenstr. 100,	P.O. Box 24605,
	20539 Hamburg	Bournemouth 6PH VR7,
		England
Fax	+49 (40) 64 57 10	+44 (2 02) 4 57 10
E-Mail	schifffahrtskontor@online.de	steel.export@steelex.co.uk

Frachtangebot an Exporteur:

Geschäftsfall und Aufgabe:
Sie haben eine Frachtanfrage der Firma Steel Export Plc erhalten, die Sie wie folgt bestätigen:
– Verschiffung von 2.000 Tonnen Stahlrohre (*steel tubes*), maximal 585 cm lang, gebündelt (*bundled*), nach Australien

Ihr Angebot war freibleibend bis zur endgültigen Auftragserteilung und Bestellung wie folgt:
– Verladung erfolgt in 20-Fuß-Containern von Hamburg nach Freemantle
– Kosten für Übernahme über Kai (*via quay*) in Hamburg 8,75 Euro pro Tonne
– Packen des Containers (*container stuffing*) 400 Euro pro 20-Fuß-Container
– Seefracht ab Hamburg bis Freemantle (FOB Hamburg bis CFR Freemantle): 1.800,00 US$ per 20-Fuß-Container
– THC (*terminal handling charges*) belaufen sich auf 145 Euro pro Container.

3.

Name	Margareta (Lutz) Hallenberger	Mr Albert Peters
Position	Exportsachbearbeiter/in	International Sea Freight
		Department
Firma	Bucher Handel AG	Clapton Ltd, Shipping Agents
Anschrift	Schmeddingstr. 130,	Column Drive,
	48149 Münster	Cardiff CF1 3EU, Wales
Fax	+49 (2 51) 13 60 09	+44 (12 22) 80 64 91
E-Mail	bucher.handel@online.de	clap.ship@shipnet.co.uk

Bestätigung einer Frachtbuchung:

Geschäftsfall und Aufgabe:
Sie haben heute mit Albert Peters gesprochen und bestätigen per Brief / Fax /

E-Mail die Buchung der Fracht wie folgt:

– Sie buchen auf der MV „Maersk Tokyo", die in 6 Wochen in Hamburg ausläuft, Frachtkapazität für folgende Ladung: 180 Bunde (*bundles*) 221,2 Tonnen Stahlrohre
– Die Verladung der Rohre erfolgt in 12 × 20 Fuß-Containern mit je 15 Bunden. Gesamtgewicht: 14,8 Tonnen
– Das Material wird bis zum ... (in 4 Wochen) (letzter Termin für Anlieferung: *closing date*) angeliefert bei: Hansa Umschlag GmbH, Schuppen (*shed*) 80 / 81, Hamburg-Freihafen
– Die Anlieferung erfolgt per Lkw durch Ihren Lieferanten, die Fa. Marcegaglia, Gazoldo Ippoliti, Italien
– Versender: Bucher Handel AG, Schmeddingstr. 130, Münster, Deutschland
– Empfänger: Prok Group Limited (Perth), 285 Collier Road, Bayswater, WA 6053, Australien
– Empfänger ist vom Ankunftsdatum zu unterrichten
– Die Fracht wird vorausbezahlt
– Das Akkreditiv trägt die Nr. 5873WB1912284/V, es liegt bei
– Bitten Sie um Übersendung eines Konnossements per Fax zwecks Überprüfung vor Verschiffung der Rohre.

4.

Name	Juliette (Henri) Godat	–
Position	Exportsachbearbeiter/in	–
Firma	Telekommunikation Odeon GmbH	Lloyd & Tudor Insurance Ltd
Anschrift	Dorpfeldstr. 30, 40699 Erkrath	33 Old Hall Street, Oxford OX1 PH3, England
Fax	+49 (21 04) 7 10 86	+44 (18 65) 57 93 10
E-Mail	telecom.odeon@online.de	lloyd.tudor@firmlink.co.uk

Brief an Versicherung mit der Bitte um ein Angebot:

Geschäftsfall:
Sie haben eine Warenladung von 5.000 Handys, die in 500 Kartons mit je 10 Stück verpackt sind, zu versenden. Spediteur ist die Fa. Transport Kugler & Co. KG, Brabandtstr. 18, 29221 Celle, Fax: +49 (51 41) 30 40 09, E-Mail: kugler.transport@firmenetz.de.

Aufgabe:
Schreiben Sie eine Anfrage an die Lloyd & Tudor Insurance Ltd und berücksichtigen Sie dabei folgende Einzelheiten:
– Sie bitten um ein Angebot für die Versicherung der 5.000 Handys (*cellphones, mobile phones*)

- Deckung gegen alle Risiken erwünscht, vom Lager Hamburg bis Lager Ihres Kunden, der Eric Johnson Ltd in 54 Grange Road, Bristol BS8 4EA, Fax: +44 (1 17) 8 51 30 90
- Transport als Sammelladung, die vom Spediteur in Hamburg übernommen und in Bristol ausgeliefert wird
- Warenwert: ca. 50.000 Euro
- Erbetene Versicherungsdeckung: Warenwert +10 %.

5.

Name	Sabine (Patrick) Quirinus	Ms Ruth (Mr Peter) Morton
Position	Transportsachbearbeiter/in	Commercial Policy Section
Firma	Schulz & Co. GmbH	Brompton Insurance Ltd
Anschrift	Hofallee 10,	P.O. Box 8365,
	32423 Minden	Manchester PG7 3LH, England
Fax	+49 (5 71) 33 11 89	+44 (1 61) 58 70 32
E-Mail	schulz.papier@online.de	brom.ins@firmlink.co.uk

Schadensmeldung an Versicherung (*insurance claim*):

Geschäftsfall:
Sie haben heute von der britischen Firma Citco Complex Plc eine Sendung Nähmaschinen (*sewing machines*) erhalten, die in 360 Kartons verpackt waren. Die Ware wurde CIP Ihrem Warenlager in Minden geliefert. Die Ware ist zum Teil beschädigt angekommen.

Aufgabe:
Schreiben Sie eine Schadensmeldung an die britische Versicherungsgesellschaft und erwähnen Sie dabei folgende Punkte:
- An ca. 10 Kartons sind Schäden entstanden
- Bericht eines Schadensgutachters (*claims assessor*) liegt bei
- Demnach war die Ladung auf dem Lkw, der die Kartons von Hamburg nach Minden brachte, durch einen Auffahrunfall verrutscht (*to slip in a nose-to-tail collision*), da sie offenbar nicht ausreichend gesichert war
- Dies führte zur Beschädigung einiger Nähmaschinen
- Liste der beschädigten Teile wurde bereits an Citco Complex Plc geschickt (Kopie anbei)
- Citco Complex Plc wird die Teile ersetzen und eine Zusatzrechnung an Sie schicken
- Sie werden diese an die Versicherungsgesellschaft weiterleiten
- Bitten Sie um Bestätigung der Schadensanerkennung (*confirmation that the claim has been granted*)
- Sie legen vorsichtshalber Kopien der Versanddokumente (Frachtbrief, Packliste, Versicherungszertifikat) bei.

6.

Name	Sabine (Georg) Henning	–
Position	Transportsachbearbeiter/in	–
Firma	Naturstein Müller KG	Interpacific Transport Ltd Shipping Agents
Anschrift	Nassauer Str. 110, 59065 Hamm	P.O. Box 241193, Brighton IH6 3PH, England
Fax	+49 (23 81) 24 90 15	+44 (2 72) 34 09 61
E-Mail	mueller.stein@online.de	interpacific@tradelink.co.uk

Bitte um Frachtsätze an Spedition:

Geschäftsfall:

Sie haben von der indischen Firma Mahami Ltd, 320 Narshinatha Street, Bangalore
400 009, Granitfliesen (*granite tiles*) der hochwertigen Sorte „Night Blue" gekauft. Es
werden 20 Verschläge (*crates*) à je 1 Tonne Gewicht, zusammen verpackt in einem
40 Fuß oben offenen Container (*open top container*) zum Versand gebracht. Die Ware
soll von Bangalore über den Hafen Mangalore verschifft werden.

Aufgabe:

Schreiben Sie an den Schiffsmakler Interpacific Transport Ltd einen Brief / ein Fax /
eine E-Mail mit folgendem Inhalt:
– Machen Sie die o. a. Angaben über Ihren Auftrag
– Beschreiben Sie, wie die Ware versandt werden soll
– Der indische Hersteller liefert FOB Mangalore
– Bitten Sie um ein Angebot von Frachtsätzen CFR Amsterdam mit alternativem
  Zusatzangebot für:
  a) Entladung des Containers in Antwerpen und Weiterführung per Lkw
     nach Hamm
  b) Abfertigung des Containers per Schiff, Bahn oder Lkw nach Hamm
– Im letzteren Fall muss der leere Container nach Antwerpen zurückgeführt
  werden.

Unit 15

Fairs, Exhibitions, Hotel Bookings and Making Arrangements

Introduction

Trade fairs and exhibitions give companies an opportunity to present their goods and services in the best light. Consequently. when choosing a suitable venue, a large number of factors must be considered, including how well-known and accessible the venue is and what facilities it offers. In addition to this, exhibitors and visitors will require a wide range of accommodation within easy reach of the event.

Some fair and exhibition organisers offer a planning service with CAD facilities enabling an exhibitor to look at a simulation of the site to see the exact location of his stand. In addition to this, CAD 3-dimensional technology can be used to simulate floor and wall coverings and create "walk-through" animations allowing the exhibitor to view different colours before making a final decision.

In many cases exhibitors are referred by the organisers to specialist firms which will tailor-make a stand to the exhibitor's specifications.

When writing your enquiry about trade fair, exhibition and conference facilities use the letter plans to structure your letter, fax or e-mail.

Enquiry about Trade Fair, Exhibition and Conference Facilities

1. Source of address*
2. Reason for enquiry:
   - conference facilities (seating capacity)
   - exhibition venue
   - stand at trade fair
3. Dates
4. Request for quotation for conference facilities* / exhibition space* / stand*
5. General requirements:
   - planning service
   - size / design of stand
   - size of exhibition area
   - location (on site)
6. Fixtures and fittings, i. e.
   - stage
   - (electrical) sockets
   - running water
   - lighting
   - floor covering
   - furniture
   - display panels
   - shelves
   - literature racks
7. Audio-visual facilities
8. (Tele)communication equipment:
   - telephone line(s)
   - fax machine(s)
   - ISDN lines
   - Internet link
   - e-mail
   - photocopying facilities
9. Advertising
10. Catering
11. Security
12. Transport
13. Accommodation
14. Polite ending

*As appropriate

Fig. 33

Hotel bookings / Making arrangements

When booking accommodation for business purposes it is important to state the number of rooms and guests, whether en-suite facilities are required and what meals are to be taken in the hotel. In some cases hotels offer corporate rates to companies booking accommodation for their employees. If a company books a large number of rooms or even a whole hotel for a particular event, the reservation can be treated as a block booking at a special rate.

Most hotels and guest-houses post, fax or e-mail a booking form and some require a deposit in advance. As company representatives frequently entertain clients, it is also important to state when booking whether the bill is to be sent to the company or paid by the guests themselves. In many cases payment by (corporate) credit card is accepted.

Hotel Bookings

1. Source of address*
2. Request for information*, e.g.
   - location
   - facilities
   - size of hotel
3. Type of accommodation required
   - rooms / number of beds
   - smokers / non-smokers
   - meals
4. Dates
5. Special requests
   - location of room
   - food (vegetarian / dietary restrictions)
   - disabled guests
6. Prices
   - corporate rates
   - block bookings
7. Payment
8. Polite ending

*As appropriate

Fig. 34

Making Arrangements

1. Reference to previous correspondence*
2. Reference to arrangement(s)*
3. Time and place
4. Confirmation of arrangement(s)*
   - mode of transport
   - estimated time of arrival
5. Change in arrangements*
   - apologise*
6. Cancellation of arrangement(s)*
   - apologise*
7. Request for confirmation*
8. Polite ending
9. Enclosures*

* As appropriate

Fig. 35

Specimen Letters

1. German exhibitor books a stand at a trade fair

Our ref. lang.25
Your ref. -
9 July ..

Mr Peter Jones
Harrogate International Centre
Kings Road
HARROGATE
HG1 SLA
North Yorkshire
England

Dear Mr Jones

Stand at the Natural Beauty Fair 1–5 December ..

My company will be exhibiting its products in Harrogate this December and wishes to be allocated a stand in the main exhibition area.

We will need one measuring 5 m × 4 m with a counter at the front and a back room. As regards fixtures and fittings we require :
– 3 electrical sockets
– a sink with hot and cold water taps
– bright lighting (halogen?) and fitted carpet throughout
– 2 display panels, measuring approx. 1.5 m × 2 m
– 2 literature racks

Will you also be able to put up posters to advertise our company's stand?
If so, we would like you to start advertising 2 months in advance, both locally and nationally.

If you are unable to supply any of the features requested we would be grateful if you would recommend suitable contractors to us.

We hope to hear from you shortly.

Yours sincerely

Theresa Langhardt
Theresa Langhardt (Mrs)
Proprietor

Langhardt Bio-Kosmetik
Sappelstr. 1 81369 München Germany
Fax: +49 (89) 57 3 22 E-mail: langhardt.bio@t-online.de
Tel.: +49 (89) 57 3 21

2. German company enquires about a hotel room for an executive

Bonita Moden GmbH,
Rottwinkelstr.3, 45897 Gelsenkirchen, Germany
Tel.:+49 (2 09) 54 78 81, Fax: +49 (2 09) 54 78 00
E-Mail: bonita.moden@firmenetz.de

FAO:	The Booking Clerk
	Park Hotel
	York
	UK
Fax No:	+44 (19 04) 8 97 45
From:	Birgit Beckstein
	Secretary to the Managing Director
Date:	3 June ..
Subject:	Room reservation 1–3 July ..
Total Pages:	1

Dear Sir / Madam

The Tourist Information Office in York has given us the address of your hotel, describing it as centrally located and well-equipped.

We are looking for a single, en-suite, non-smoking room for the Managing Director of our company, Mr Hubertus. He will require bed and breakfast for 2 nights from 1–3 July ..

Please make sure that the room has a balcony and is in a quiet part of the hotel. If it is on an upper floor, he would like to be near the lift.

We would like you to quote us corporate rates for the accommodation required as we anticipate using facilities in your area quite frequently in the near future.

We look forward to receiving your offer.

Yours faithfully

Birgit Beckstein
pp. Bonita Moden GmbH

3. British hotel makes offer of accommodation

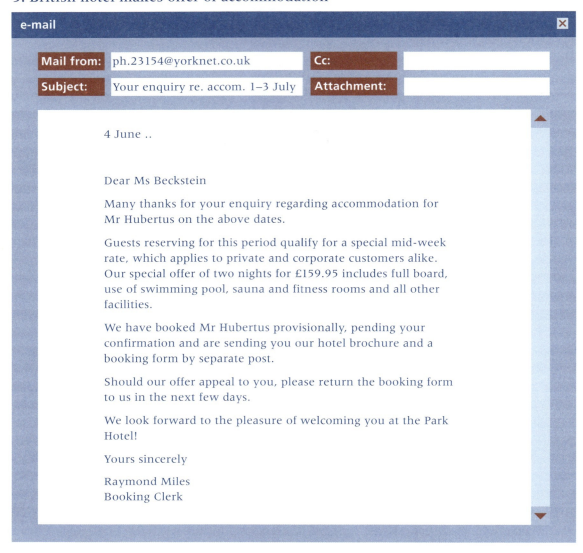

e-mail ☒

| **Mail from:** | ph.23154@yorknet.co.uk | **Cc:** | |
| **Subject:** | Your enquiry re. accom. 1–3 July | **Attachment:** | |

4 June ..

Dear Ms Beckstein

Many thanks for your enquiry regarding accommodation for Mr Hubertus on the above dates.

Guests reserving for this period qualify for a special mid-week rate, which applies to private and corporate customers alike. Our special offer of two nights for £159.95 includes full board, use of swimming pool, sauna and fitness rooms and all other facilities.

We have booked Mr Hubertus provisionally, pending your confirmation and are sending you our hotel brochure and a booking form by separate post.

Should our offer appeal to you, please return the booking form to us in the next few days.

We look forward to the pleasure of welcoming you at the Park Hotel!

Yours sincerely

Raymond Miles
Booking Clerk

Case Study Part 1

You are in the Marketing Department of Body-Kultur KG in 40227 Düsseldorf (Markenstr. 28, fax +49 (2 11) 77 95 43, e-mail: body.kultur@aol.com). Your company manufactures health drinks and health food and is now preparing to launch a new product called "Dietfree". Body-Kultur aim to sell their products all over Europe and beyond, so they decide to book a stand at the next "Health and Beauty Show" at the Earls Court Olympia site in London, England, in six months' time. You will be there for five days in all from 16–20 … (invent the month).

For this event you require a large stand 10 m wide × 8 m long × 3.50 m high with a roof over it. At the back of your stand you will need a small office, big enough for a table and four chairs. You want a fence around the stand and flood lights everywhere, except in the office, where you require there to be a centre light. In the middle of the stand you want a small stage with curtains and a spotlight for presentations. You will need two ISDN lines, four electrical sockets (220–240 V) in the office, six sockets on the stage and a sink with hot and cold water.

You think that plain synthetic carpeting in light brown would be best for the entire stand with wickerwork furniture (3 settees, 3 coffee tables and 8 armchairs) for the reception area. You will also require four white 1.50 m × 2 m (width × height) display panels and two literature racks for your company's leaflets. In between presentations you want to show video loops of your products so you will also need two large TV monitors and a video-player. For the live presentations you will require a public address system with two clip-on radio microphones.

Carola Klar, the famous German model, will be coming to open the stand at 10 am on the first day and do a presentation of "Dietfree" so you will need 10 attendants to control the crowd and press photographers, at least five security guards and video surveillance. You also want to have her picked up from her hotel by chauffeur-driven limousine.

Your guests on the first day are to be served cocktails at 11 am and a buffet lunch at 1 pm on the stand, so you will require a catering and waiter service.

You want to have posters put up all over London and radio and TV commercials to be made two weeks before the event.

Activity

Using the "**Enquiry about Trade Fair, Exhibition and Conference Facilities** Letter Plan" in this Unit and the Standard Expressions, write Body-Kultur KG's enquiry to Earls Court Olympia in London (Warwick Road, London SW5 9TA, England, fax +44 (1 71) 3 85-70 00, e-mail: poexwebmaster@eco.co.uk) as a letter / fax / e-mail.

Case Study Part 2

The organisers at Earls Court Olympia send you back a list of hotels in the vicinity so you draft the text of a letter / fax / e-mail to be sent out to cover the following points.

For the 15 and 16 … (month) you will need accommodation for Carola Klar and her bodyguard, Axel Schulte. You want a luxury suite (but no meals) for her and a single room with full board and access to a fitness room for her bodyguard. There must also be a communicating door between Axel Schulte's room and Ms Klar's suite for security reasons. Both Carola Klar and Axel Schulte are non-smokers.

For the rest of your company's party of four executives and two female trainees, you require 4 single rooms (en suite) and one double room (en suite) all with half board.

On the evening of the 16 … (month) you want to give a private dinner-party for 30 people with a floor show and dancing, so you ask the hotel if it can offer these facilities and, if so, to send you a choice of menus. One of the executives in your party doesn't eat meat.

When finishing your letter / fax / e-mail you enquire about corporate rates and how payment should be made. Finally, you point out that this may be the first of several visits by employees of your company to London.

Activity

Using the "**Hotel Bookings** Letter Plan", in this Unit and the Standard Expressions, write Body-Kultur KG's enquiry to the
Olympia Hotel, 87 Nevern Place, Earls Court, London SW5 9NP,
fax: +44 (1 71) 3 72-34 88, e-mail: olympia.hotel@hotelink.co.uk.

Language

Use the "**Enquiry about Trade Fair, Exhibition and Conference Facilities**" and "**Hotel Bookings** Standard Expressions" tables to find the words missing below.

1. **Verbs + nouns**
   Which verbs go with the following nouns?
   a. to ▩ a trade fair (i.e. "to go to")
   b. to ▩ a product (i.e. "to put on the market for the first time")
   c. to ▩ a sales convention (i.e. "to provide a venue for")
   d. to ▩ guests from one location to another (i.e. "to take them from place to place")
   e. to ▩ a crowd (i.e. "to attract")
   f. to ▩ a bill (i.e. "to pay")

2. Verbs + prepositions / particles
Which prepositions / particles go with the following verbs?
    a. to look ▦ (i. e. "to try to find")
    b. to put ▦ a stand
    c. to equip ▦
    d. "The steps lead ▦ to the stage."
    e. "Please dispose ▦ the carpet after the event."
    f. to put ▦ a poster
    g. to set ▦ a web site
    h. to put ▦ an appearance
    i. to pick ▦ people from the station
    j. "The room looks ▦ over the sea."
    k. to treat ▦ a block booking

3. Nouns + prepositions / prepositions + nouns / adjectives + prepositions
    a. ▦ the Internet
    b. 20 m long ▦ 15 m wide (not "and")
    c. "The event is due ▦ take place next week."
    d. to have ▦ mind
    e. 5,000 m² ▦ size
    f. ▦ easy reach of the restaurant
    g. access ▦ a cold water tap
    h. ▦ advance
    i. ▦ a major scale
    j. "The guard is ▦ duty." (i. e. "He's at work")
    k. ▦ the duration of the event
    l. ▦ the vicinity of
    m. ▦ the past
    n. allergic ▦
    o. ▦ a regular basis
    p. ▦ view of
    q. ▦ your earliest convenience
    r. ▦ return

4. Adjectives / adjectival phrases + nouns
    a. ▦ background lighting (i. e. "not easily noticed")
    b. an ▦ armchair (i. e. "covered in cloth")
    c. an ▦ shelf (i. e. "can be moved up and down")
    d. a ▦ shelf (i. e. "strong")
    e. a ▦ video screen (i. e. "huge")
    f. a ▦ person (i. e. "well-known, important")
    g. ▦ rates (i. e. "for business people")

5. **Further points**
   a. A carpet without a pattern is ▨.
   b. Give the names of some other natural materials furniture can be made of (apart from wood).
   c. Give another word for sofa.
   d. Give the names of three sorts of transport links.
   e. What expression is used to mean that a hotel room has its own private bathroom?
   f. What expression is used to mean "breakfast and one more meal"?
   g. What expression is used to mean "all meals"?

14 Listening

Before you listen to the dialogue, first read through the background information provided and the instructions following it.

Background information

Harald Peters works for Vogelsang Küchengeräte GmbH in Mannheim. His company wants to take a stand at the Housewares International Fair at the Harrogate International Centre in Yorkshire in the north of England so, using the list of stand contractors given to him by the fair organisers, he phones one of the firms listed.

Listen to the dialogue and answer the questions below.

Questions
 1. What is the name of the company Harald phones?
 2. Name two of the things the English company's service covers.
 3. What does Harald's company want for presentations?
 4. What else does the German company want?
 5. What does the stand contractor's "standard package" include?
 6. What will the English contractor install to give the stand running water?
 7. What type of furniture does Jill suggest for the stand?
 8. What kind of floor covering has been popular recently?
 9. What does Jill's "special offer" include apart from tables, chairs and floor covering?
10. What sort of lighting does she suggest?

Now listen again and answer the following questions:
11. What sort of work doesn't the English company do itself?
12. Would this mean that Harald's firm would need to sign contracts with a number of firms? Explain your answer.
13. How will Harald find out what decor the English stand contractor can offer?

14. Why will Harald's company need strong lights on the stand?
15. What does Jill promise to do soon?

Activity
Write Harald's summary of the telephone conversation in German. It is to be given to his boss, Frau Heymanns, the Sales Director.

Telephone Role Play

Rolle A
Sie sind Bettina (Claudius) Röttgemeier und arbeiten für die Firma Verpackungs-folien GmbH in Hagen. Ihre Firma möchte auf der British Home Exhibition einen Stand mieten. Rufen Sie das Buchungsbüro der Messeleitung in London an.
- Stellen Sie Ihre Firma vor und fragen Sie nach dem genauen Termin der nächsten British Home Exhibition
- Sie brauchen einen Stand, Größe ca. 4 × 5 m im Hauptausstellungsbereich
- Die angebotene Alternative ginge eventuell auch. Wie ist dieser Stand ausgerüstet?
- Könnte man Ihnen Adressen, Fax- und Tel.-Nummern von Messeausrüstern (*fair outfitters*) schicken, die sich um diese Dinge kümmern?
- Sie buchstabieren: Verpackungsfolien GmbH, Overbergstr. 27, 58099 Hagen
- Sie bitten um Zusendung eines Lageplans des Standes mit Unterlagen (*literature*) über die Messe
- Kann die Messeleitung auch Hotelbuchungen vermitteln?
- Sie bedanken sich im Voraus für die Zusendung der Unterlagen. Bis wann muss der Stand fest gebucht sein?
- Das geht in Ordnung. Wohin muss die Anzahlung überwiesen werden?
- O. K. Sie erwarten die Unterlagen.

Role B
You are Cynthia (Jonathan) Perry and work in the Booking Office of the London Trade Fair plc. When Bettina (Claudius) Röttgemeier phones, you take the call.
- The British Home Exhibition is from 13–19 … (in four months' time)
- Explain that the main exhibition area is fully booked. Recommend a similar stand near the entrance to the main exhibition area
- The stand has 6 sockets, cold water and fluorescent lighting throughout. The exhibitor has to provide the furniture and carpeting
- Say you'll send the German company a list of fair outfitters with the booking form. Ask for the company's name and address
- Say you'll also send them a plan of the site and some literature on the fair
- Explain that hotel bookings are made through an agency called Room Service Ltd. You'll include their leaflet in your letter
- You'll need a firm booking and a deposit of 20 % of the fee for the stand by 10 … (in three months' time) at the latest

–   Say that the account number is on the booking form
–   Say you look forward to receiving the German company's booking.

Aufgaben

1.

Name	Petra (Chris) Commodore	–
Position	Verkaufsleiter/in	–
Firma	Bunzmüller GmbH	National Fairs and Exhibition Centre plc
Anschrift	Obere Baustr. 48, 90478 Nürnberg	P.O. Box 1405, Birmingham RC6 1UZ, England
Fax	+49 (9 11) 47 30 06	+44 (1 21) 33 11 89
E-Mail	bunzmueller@online.de	nec.plc@bizlink.co.uk

Anfrage an Messeleitung zwecks Anmietung eines Standes:

Geschäftsfall:
Für die im Frühjahr dieses Jahres stattfindende „Household Fair" in Birmingham brauchen Sie einen Stand.

Aufgabe:
Schreiben Sie an die National Fairs and Exhibition Centre plc einen Brief / ein Fax / eine E-Mail unter Berücksichtigung folgender Punkte:
–   Für die Haushaltsmesse vom 5.–10. .. (Monat angeben) dieses Jahres brauchen Sie einen Stand mit folgender Ausrüstung:
    –   Standabmessungen: ca. 15 m × 10 m × 4 m
    –   Hinterzimmer für Konferenzen und Verkaufsgespräche, ausgestattet mit einem Konferenztisch aus Holz und 6 ledergepolsterten Stühlen
    –   abschließbarer Schrank
    –   Garderobenständer
    –   kleine Küche mit entsprechender Ausstattung (Kalt- und Warmwasser)
    –   normales Standmobiliar (gerne Rattanmöbel oder Ähnliches)
    –   zwei große Regale für Ihre Tischlampen
    –   Elektroanschlüsse 220–240 V in ausreichender Zahl für die Ausstellung Ihrer Lampen (mindestens 20 Steckdosen)
    –   Computer-, Fax- und Telefonanschluss auf dem Stand
–   Bitte um detailliertes Angebot und Übersendung des Messekatalogs mit allen Einzelheiten
–   Ist Standauf- und abbau im Preis inbegriffen?

2.

Name	Petra (Chris) Commodore	–
Position	Verkaufsleiter/in	–
Firma	Bunzmüller GmbH	Royal Park Hotel
Anschrift	Obere Baustr. 48,	P.O. Box 48,
	90478 Nürnberg	Birmingham PA3 5UL, England
Fax	+49 (9 11) 47 30 06	+44 (1 21) 64 31 05
E-Mail	bunzmueller@online.de	royal.park.hotel@hotlink.co.uk

Hotelreservierung für Messe:

Geschäftsfall:
Sie benötigen für die im 1. Geschäftsfall erwähnte Messe eine Hotelunterkunft.

Aufgabe:
Schreiben Sie eine Bestellung an das Royal Park Hotel unter Berücksichtigung folgender Einzelheiten:
–   Buchen Sie 6 Einzel- und 2 Doppelzimmer mit Bad / Dusche und WC für die Zeit vom 5. bis 10. .. (Monat angeben) (einschließlich)
–   Bitten Sie um Bestätigung der Buchung per Fax
–   Darüber hinaus benötigen Sie am 8. .. (des selben Monats) in der Zeit von 18.00 bis 22.00 Uhr einen Vorführraum mit Overhead-Projektor, Flipchart, Satelliten-Fernseher, einem Laser-Farbkopierer, Telefon- und Faxanschluss
–   Im Anschluss an diese Veranstaltung wollen Sie ein warmes Buffet für 30 Personen mit Getränken servieren
–   Für die Miete des Vorführraumes und das Buffet hätten Sie gern ein Festangebot
–   Sollte Ihnen dieses zusagen, erfolgt schriftliche Bestellung.

3.

Name	Ute (Arnold) Kirchwald	Mr. Charles Newport
Position	Sachbearbeiter/in Reservierungen	Executive Vice President
Firma	Hotel Lindenhof	Bloomington Computer Franchising Inc.
Anschrift	Gutzmannstr. 8–12, 14165 Berlin	8703 Bloomington Freeway, Minneapolis, MN 77420-8493, U.S.A.
Fax	+49 (30) 84 12 75	+1 (6 12) 7 73 40 19
E-Mail	lindenhof.berlin@online.de	bcf.inc@linkus.com

Hotelangebot für Vertreterkonferenz:

Geschäftsfall:
Sie haben eine Anfrage auf Reservierung von Unterkünften und Buchung von Konferenzräumen für die weltweite Vertretertagung (*Representatives World Convention*) der amerikanischen Firma Bloomington Computer Franchising Inc. bekommen.

Aufgabe:
Machen Sie der Firma folgendes Angebot:
- Einzelzimmer mit Bad / Dusche / WC / TV / Minibar für 60 Personen, Dauer 4 Tage, d. h. 26. bis einschl. 29. .. (Monat angeben), Sonderpreis je 60 Euro
- Während der 4 Tage zusätzliche Reservierung von:
  a) einem Konferenzraum für ca. 60 Personen
  b) einem Konferenzraum für ca. 20 Personen
- Beide Konferenzräume ausgestattet mit Videorecorder, Tafel, Overhead-Projektor
- Außerdem kleines separates Büro mit Computer (Internet, E-Mail), Fax, Telefonanschluss und Kopiergerät mit 2-sprachiger Bedienungskraft Deutsch / Englisch: 600 Euro pro Tag
- Die Konferenzräume werden kostenlos zur Verfügung gestellt, falls die Mahlzeiten im Hotel eingenommen werden
- Kleinbus für Stadtfahrten wird zur Verfügung gestellt
- Abholung der Gäste und Transfer zum Hotel wird garantiert
- Zahlungsbedingungen: ⅓ bei Buchung, ⅓ bei Ankunft der Gäste, Rest bei Abreise.

4.

Name	Anja (Norbert) Tröger	–
Position	Sachbearbeiter/in Akquisition	–
Firma	Deutsche Messe	Asian Travel Inc
Anschrift	Luxemburger Str. 80–82, 50674 Köln	1249/512 Charoen Koung Road, Bangkok 10500, Thailand
Fax	+49 (2 21) 48 13 56	+66 (22 24) 68 80
E-Mail	deutsche.messe@online.de	asia.travel.inc@asianet.com

Bestätigung der Standreservierung auf einer Messe:

Geschäftsfall:
Sie haben von der Asian Travel Inc einen Auftrag für eine Standreservierung der Internationalen Reise-Messe erhalten, die vom 13. bis 15. .. (Monat angeben) in Köln stattfinden wird.

Aufgabe:
Bestätigen Sie diese wie folgt:
– Standgröße: 3 × 6 m
– 3-stufiger Aufgang zum Stand
– Ein runder Tisch mit 6 Stühlen
– Mit Vorhang abgetrennte Kochnische (Kalt- und Warmwasser)
– Messe-Grundausstattung: Geschirr, Gläser usw., unbedingt Teekessel (*kettle*)!
– ausreichende Elektroanschlüsse
– Telefon, Fax, E-Mail-Anschluss
– Boden ausgelegt mit Teppichboden in dunkelblau
– Möglichkeit, Display-Tafeln anzubringen
– Gesamtpreis: 3 Tage inkl. Auf- und Abbau, 6.250 Euro im Voraus zahlbar per Banküberweisung
– Abrechnung der Telefon-, Stromkosten usw. am letzten Messetag
– Prospekt mit genauem Lageplan ist beigefügt
– Weiterhin fügen Sie einen Stadtplan von Köln, einen Hotelführer und weitere Listen mit Messefirmen bei, die Service-Leistungen für Aussteller erbringen.

5.

Name	Anja (Jörg) Lehmann	Miss Sandra Peters
Position	Sekretärin von Herrn Hartmann, Einkaufsleiter	Marketing Department
Firma	Schiffer KG	Electronics plc
Anschrift	Bachstr. 15, 99094 Erfurt	84 Sydney Street, London SW3 6NJ, UK
Fax	+49 (3 61) 4 87 49	+44 (1 71) 13 88
E-Mail	schiffer@comnet.de	electronics@scfgroup.com

Geschäftsfall:
Sie sind Anja (Jörg) Lehmann und arbeiten für die Firma Schiffer KG in Erfurt. Ihr Chef, Herr Hartmann, wollte die englische Firma Electronics plc in London besuchen. Durch eine Umdisponierung muss der Termin geändert werden. Er bittet Sie, dies der britischen Firma mitzuteilen.

Aufgabe:
Schreiben Sie einen Brief / ein Fax / eine E-Mail an Miss Sandra Peters in der Marketing-Abteilung der Electronics plc und berücksichtigen Sie dabei die folgenden Punkte:

– Beziehen Sie sich auf Ihren Brief von vor 8 Tagen und die Ankündigung des Besuchs von Herrn Dietmar Hartmann vom 14. bis 16. nächsten Monats sowie die Bestätigung per Fax der britischen Firma vor 7 Tagen
– Ihr Chef muss den Termin um 2 Tage verschieben (erfinden Sie einen triftigen Grund!)
– Bitte um Änderung aller Termine auf 16. bis 18. nächsten Monats
– Ist die Änderung ohne große Unannehmlichkeiten möglich?
– Kann Electronics plc bitte auch die Hotelbuchungsänderung veranlassen?
– Entschuldigen Sie sich für die verursachte Mehrarbeit
– Höflicher Schluss.

Appendix 1

- **Dictating Punctuation**
- **Telephone Phrases**
- **Glossary of Commercial Terms**

Dictating Punctuation

.	full stop / (AE: period)
,	comma
?	question mark
!	exclamation mark (AE: exclamation point)
-	hyphen (not normally dictated)
–	dash (dictated)
:	colon
;	semi-colon
"…"	open inverted commas / close inverted commas (quotation marks / quotes)
(…)	open brackets / close brackets (AE: parenthesis, plural: parentheses)
…	dot, dot dot
/	stroke / slash
\	backslash
'	apostrophe
w o r d	d o u b l e s p a c e d
word	*in italics*
word	**in bold type**
A	uppercase "a"
a	lowercase "a"
<u>dog</u>	underlined
→ "The music played."	indent (indent 5 spaces)

Text text text text text text text text text text text text text text text text text text text text text text text.

• *"Leave a line, new paragraph."*

Text text text text tex text text text text text text text text text text text text text text text text text text text text text text text text text text text …

8.3	eight <u>point</u> three
8,022.79	eight thousand and twenty-two point seven nine
&	ampersand
#	number (AE and computer language)
§	section ("section" symbol)
*	asterisk
@	at ("at" symbol)
h.jones@weblink.co.uk	h – dot – jones – at – weblink – dot – co – dot – uk
http://www.company.de	h – t – t – p – colon – forward slash– forward slash – www – dot – company – dot – d – e

Further useful expressions:
space   gap   margin   flush-left   flush-right

Telephone Phrases

Getting through to the right person

With a switchboard operator

	Caller	Switchboard Operator	Person you wish to speak to
1	(Dials the number)	Good morning / afternoon, EuroTrans. Can I help you?	
2	Good morning / afternoon, could I speak to Jane Grey in Exports, please?	Yes, sir / madam, I'll put you through.	Hello. Exports. Exports, can I help you?

Switchboard operator asks who's calling

	Caller	Switchboard Operator	Person you wish to speak to
3	(Dials the number)	Good morning, EuroTrans. Can I help you?	
4	Good morning, could I speak to Jane Grey in Exports, please?	Who shall I say is calling, please?	
5	It's Heinz / Heike Schulz from Designer Mode in Essen, Germany.	Putting you through now, sir / madam.	Hello. Hello Heinz / Heike. Exports. Exports, can I help you?

The person is not available

	Caller	Switchboard Operator	Person you wish to speak to
6	(Dials the number)	Good morning, EuroTrans. Can I help you?	
7	Good morning, could I speak to Jane Grey in Exports, please?	I'm sorry, she 's not available at the moment. Can I take a message?	
	Will you tell her Heike Schulz from Designer Mode in Essen, Germany, phoned, please and ask her to phone me back?	Yes, madam. I'll pass the message on to her.	
8	Thank-you. Goodbye.	Bye.	

Without a switchboard operator

	Caller	Person you wish to speak to (or a colleague)
9	(Dials the number)	Hello. EuroTrans. Exports.
10	Good morning, could I speak to Jane Grey in Exports, please? Good morning, this is Heike Schulz from Designer Mode in Essen, Germany. Could I speak to Jane Grey in Exports, please? Hello, Jane. Hello, Jane. It's Heike here. Hello, it's Heike Schulz from Designer Mode in Essen, Germany.	Speaking. Hello, Heike. It's Jane speaking. Hello, Heike. How are things? Hello, Miss / Mrs / Ms Schulz. What can I do for you? Just a moment, I'll put you through. Just a moment, I'll get her.

Small-talk before giving the reason for calling

	Caller	Other person
11	Hello Jane. How are things?	Fine. How about you?
12	Fine. Great! Marvellous! Not so bad. Mustn't grumble. Can't complain. Could be better.	Good.
	We've got a lot on at the moment. We're snowed under. We're up to our eyes in work.	Oh, I see. Oh, really!
13	How about you? How are things at your end?	Fine. Great! Marvellous! Not so bad. Mustn't grumble. Can't complain. Could be better.

The reason for calling

	Caller	Other person		
14		Now what can I do for you, Heike / Mr Jones / sir / madam?		
15	It's about … (details, e.g. our last order) I need some information on … There's (a bit of) a problem with … The reason I'm calling is to ask you … Can / could you tell me .. I'd like to know …	Right, could I have the order number, please? Could I have the date, please? Could you spell that for me, please?		
16	It's order number JGWV98 The date's (the)[1] 9th (of) September … It's spelt S - V - A - R - T - V - I - K	I'm just accessing it on the computer. I'll just get the file. All right, I've got that. Just give me a minute, will you?		
		Just give me a moment to	find the file, open the file, get the file, take a look at the file,	will you?
17	OK. All right. Yes, certainly.	Ah yes, here it is … Right, I've got it … It's just coming up now … Ah yes, I've got it on the screen now … Here we are. My secretary's just brought me it.		

Useful phrases

18 Could I have your phone / fax number, please?
Have you got e-mail?
Could I have your e-mail address, please?
Has your company got a web site? / Are you on the Internet?
What's the address, please?

19 Oh, I'm sorry. I must have dialled the wrong number!
I'm sorry. Could you say that again?
I'm sorry, I didn't catch that. Could you repeat it?
Could you spell that word for me, please?
What was the name again? I didn't catch it.

20 I'm sorry but it's a very bad line. Could you phone back in two minutes?
I'm sorry but it's a very bad line. Could you speak a little louder, please?
I'm sorry but I can't make out what you're saying. Would you like
    to call back later?
I'm sorry, but we seem to have been cut off last time. If it happens again I'll
    call you back.

1 The words in brackets are not normally written but are said when saying the date. An alternative form is 'September (the) 9th', in which case the word 'the' is also said but not written.

Are you phoning from a phone box? Perhaps you'd better give me the number so I can phone you back.

I'm sorry but there seems to be someone else on the line. Could you give me your number and I'll phone you back?

Asking for / promising action

	Caller		Other person	
21	When can we expect	the order? the goods? the consignment? the document(s)? the work to be done? an answer?	It's being dealt with at the moment. It's the next thing on our list. It'll take about … (e.g. 3 weeks). It'll take a few days. Not before the end of …(e.g. the week / the month). By … (date, e.g. June 15) at the latest. Within the next … (period of time, e.g. 10 days).	
22	When can you let me know? When can we expect an answer? I need to know very soon. How long will it take you to deal with this?		I'll get back to you I'll call you back I'll let you know	very soon. as soon as I can. within the next 24 / 48 hours. tomorrow. by the end of the week.

We're looking into it.
We're doing the best we can.
I've marked this matter "urgent".
Mr / Ms Hermann will look into it as soon as he / she comes in this morning.

Mr / Ms Hermann's	tied up not available in a meeting out of the office on leave off sick	at the moment.
I've passed the matter on to the person's who's	standing in for him / her. deputising for him / her. doing his / her work.	
Look, I'm sorry but	there's not much more I can do at the moment. It's out of my hands now. We'll have to wait to see what the insurance company says.	

Apologising

23 I'm very sorry about that.
I'm terribly sorry about that.
I fully understand the inconvenience this has caused.
I'm sorry but I'm afraid I can't help you.

I'm sorry but you'll have to talk to our … (name, e.g. Herr Schmidt) about that.
I'll put you through / I'll give you his number.

24 I'm very sorry about the delay / the mistake / the mix-up / the damage.

25 Please accept our apologies for this.

Finishing off the call

	Caller	Other person
26		Anything else I can do for you?
		Is there anything else I can do for you, Heike / Mr Jones / sir / madam?
27	That's all, thank you.	You're welcome.
	No, thank you very much.	You're welcome and thanks for the order.
		Thank you for calling.
		We'll get back to you as soon as we can.
		Have a nice day.
	Oh, by the way, there's just one more thing … (details).	All right, we'll look into that as well.
	Yes, there's just one more thing … (details).	
28	Bye.	Bye.
	Goodbye.	Goodbye.

Glossary of Commercial Terms

A

abbreviations for counties in England and Wales and states in the USA
See "counties" and "states".

Academic Performance Classification Table

German	German	English	English[1]	American[2]	American
Grade 1	very good	Grade A	distinction	Grade A	excellent
Grade 2	good	Grade B	merit	Grade B	good
Grade 3	satisfactory	Grade C	pass	Grade C	average
Grade 4	adequate			Grade D	poor
Grade 5	inadequate (fail)	Grade D	fail	Grade F	failing
Grade 6	extremely inadequate (fail)	Grade E	unclassified		

1   There are no 'official' classifications of performance using these descriptions in the UK. The words used here (e.g. 'fail') are intended as a guideline for foreign users of English.

2   The A–F system given here is typical of the US but varies from institution to institution.

University / Higher Education / College (US)					
English		**American**			
1 (a first)	A first class ([honours] degree) in … (subject)	A	Excellent	4.0	90–100 %
2.1 (a two-one)	An upper second ([honours] degree) in … (subject)	B	Good	3.0	80–89 %
2.2 (a two-two)	A lower second ([honours] degree) in … (subject)	C	Average	2.0	70–79 %
3 (a third)	A third class ([honours] degree) in … (subject)	D	Passing	1.0	(60–)65–69 %[3]
		F	Failing	0.0	0(–59)–64 %

The laude system at American universities:

3.80–4.0 summa cum laude

3.60–3.79 magna cum laude

3.40–3.59 cum laude

acceptance against documents see "documents against acceptance" (D/A)

accepting house a merchant bank in the UK which, for a fee, accepts a bill of exchange drawn on an exporter

act of God event caused by natural forces, e.g. earthquake, storm, hurricane etc. Often also referred to as "force majeure".

advertising the publication of information on goods or services to persuade people to buy them and, on occasion, to dissuade people from buying them. Whilst most advertising is persuasive, some is informative, as is the case with government health campaigns. For further information see "marketing".

agency see Unit 11 "Agency agreements"

AGM (annual general meeting) see "private enterprise"

air waybill see Unit 6 "Delivery"

amalgamation see "merger"

annual general meeting see "forms of private enterprise"

APR (annual percentage rate) see "bank services"

Articles of Association see "forms of private enterprise"

assets all things with a value owned by a person or company

---

3 The cut-off point for a passing grade varies from institution to institution.

asset and liability statement American expression for the British balance sheet

assurance (life assurance) see "insurance"

attorney see "power of attorney"

average loss or damage arising from an event at sea. See "Insurance" in Unit 14 "Forwarding and Insurance".

average adjuster an expert in marine insurance claims who calculates how much money the insured is to be paid by the insurer

aviation insurance see "Lloyd's of London"

avoirdupois see "measure"

B

balance sheet statement of the financial position of a company at the end of a certain period, usually a financial year. It is divided into assets and liabilities.

bank services
Private customers:
The "high street" or "clearing" banks offer a variety of services to private customers. The most important types of account offered are *current* accounts (US "checking accounts") and *deposit* accounts.

Whereas a *deposit* (savings) account is for people who wish to leave their money in it for a longer period of time and earn interest, a *current* account is to enable customers to handle their finances on a day-to-day basis, e.g. to receive their salaries and make cash withdrawals. In the UK current accounts are also offered by buildings societies (see "building society").

Current account holders can make payments by crossed cheque (which can only be paid into a bank account), *open cheque / bearer cheque* (which, in theory, could be cashed by anyone and is not usually issued by British banks to private account holders), *order cheque* (transferrable by endorsement) or *eurocheque* accompanied by a *eurocheque card*. In addition, they can pay by *standing order* (for fixed sums at regular intervals, e.g. the rent) or *direct debit* (for varying sums at irregular intervals, e.g. the telephone bill). They can also *transfer* money from one account to another (bank giro). International transfers can be made by SWIFT (the Society for World-wide Interbank Financial Telecommunication) – see Unit 7 "Payment".

Cashless payments are frequently made using plastic cards. Among the most important of these are *debit cards* (electronic cash cards), *credit cards* and *prepaid cards*.

When payment is made by *debit card* the amount is immediately debited electronically to the card holder's current account by "swiping" the debit card through a terminal (card-reader). In the case of a *credit card* the seller receives the sum in question from the credit card company some time after the transaction, minus a fee of 2–3 %. 4–6 weeks later the credit card holder can then either pay the whole amount owing, or pay it back in instalments. In this latter case, the outstanding amount incurs interest charged at a high APR (annual percentage rate). *Prepaid cards* contain a microchip which can be loaded with "electronic money". The card can then be used instead of cash in shops with the appropriate terminal.

Plastic cards can also be used to make withdrawals from cash dispensers (ATMs = automatic telling machines, cash machines) and obtain bank statements.

Banks also offer their customers overdraft facilities, traveller's cheques, foreign exchange, statements of account (bank statements) and advice on investment and savings and a developing range of homebanking or online banking services.

Corporate customers (*business* customers)
The most important services offered to corporate customers are *discounting* bills of exchange, opening / advising / confirming *letters of credit, underwriting* offers for sale when a company goes public (see "underwriting"), factoring services (buying a company's outstanding invoices for less than their nominal value) making payments to business partners (e.g. by SWIFT) and overdraft facilities.

In the UK there are also specialist banks called *merchant banks*. These only deal with business and corporate customers and specialise in *raising capital for industry, floating companies on the stock exchange* and *takeover bids*, accepting *bills of exchange*, arranging *long-term loans* and managing *investment portfolios*.

Baltic Exchange the Baltic Mercantile and Shipping Exchange in the City of London, the world's largest shipping market for the chartering, buying, selling and the insurance of ships and the chartering of aircraft. It is also a commodity market for grain, coal, timber and oilseeds.

bear an investor who has sold a security in the hope of buying it back at a lower price because he believes the market will fall

bear market a market in which prices are falling. See also "bull".

bid offer see "takeover bid".

bill of exchange (B/E, b/e, plural: Bs/E) (also referred to as a draft – see "draft")
A bill of exchange is defined as:
"An unconditional order in writing, addressed by one person to another, signed by the person giving it, requiring the person to whom it is addressed to pay on demand, or at a fixed or determinable future time, a sum certain in money
(a) to a specified person
(b) to the order of a specified person
(c) to bearer."

There are three parties to a bill of exchange, the *drawer*, the *drawee* and the *payee*. In many cases the drawer (the seller) is the payee (the beneficiary). However, the bill can also be made out to the order of the payee, i.e. to a person named by him. The drawee is the person who must pay (the buyer).

A *sight bill* is payable when it is presented to the drawee. Bills of exchange may also be payable at a certain time after sight, e.g. 90 d/s (90 days after sight) or at a certain time after date. In such cases they are known as *time bills*. Such bills are commonly used in export trade.

After receiving payment by B/E, the payee (beneficiary, seller) can:

1. *discount* it with his bank for the face value (nominal value) less interest (charges)
2. *negotiate* it (use it as a means of payment). To do this the payee (seller) must endorse it (sign it on the back) before passing it on to a business partner by way of payment.
3. *wait* for the drawee to honour (pay) the bill at maturity (on the due date).

The following diagram summarises the options open to the drawer.

Payment by Bill of Exchange

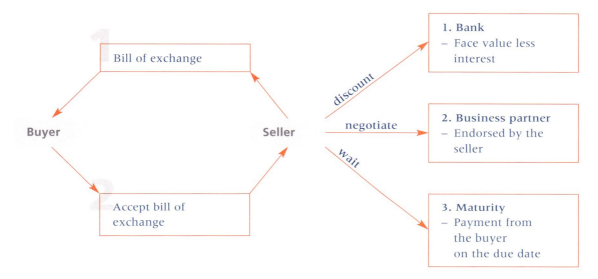

If the drawee fails to accept or pay a bill of exchange it is said to be *dishonoured*.

bill of lading (B/L, plural: Bs/L) see Unit 6 "Delivery" for a summary of the important features and the diagrams and explanations in Unit 14 "Forwarding and Insurance".

A bill of lading is the document issued by the carrier to the shipper upon delivery of goods for shipment by sea. It has three main functions. It is:

1. a document of title – if "to order" it is negotiable by endorsement
2. a contract of carriage
3. a receipt for the goods

Bs/L are normally made out by the shipping line singly or in signed sets of two, three or more original (negotiable) copies. There can also be further unsigned copies for reference purposes.

A "clean" or "unclaused" B/L contains the statement that the goods have been shipped "in apparent good order and condition", that none are missing and that the packaging shows no sign of damage. A "claused", "foul", "dirty" or "unclean" B/L contains a statement indicating that there is damage to the goods or that some are missing.

Bs/L can be :
1. received for shipment. This means that the goods are in the possession of the carrier but not on board ship yet,

or

2. shipped on-board. This means that the goods are actually on board ship. This type of B/L is more valuable than a "received for shipment" B/L.

Carriers can also take responsibility for the carriage inland as well as at sea, in which case a through, multi-modal or combined transport B/L is issued (see diagram in Unit 14 "Forwarding and Insurance"). A B/L only for transport by sea is known as a "port-to-port B/L".

blue chip term for the most highly regarded shares. Originally an American term, from the highest value poker chip.

bond a long-term, fixed-interest security issued by a government, municipality or company stating that the money borrowed from the investor will be repaid.

bonded warehouse a building in which goods are kept until customs duties have been paid

building society an organisation specialising in providing long-term loans (mortgages) to purchase property (i. e. buildings or land, AE: real estate). In the UK building societies are allowed to offer all the services offered by banks and vice versa.

bulk large size, volume or quantity. See "wholesaler".

bull an investor who has bought a security in the hope of selling it at a higher price because he believes the market will rise

bull market a market in which prices are rising. See also "bear".

C

cartage carriage over short distances, also used for the fee charged for this

cash against documents (CAD) see "documents against payment" (D/P) and Unit 7 "Payment"

Certificate of Incorporation see "private enterprise"

certificate of origin see Unit 6 "Delivery"

chamber of commerce voluntary association of businessmen, formed for the purpose of promoting the interests of its members and the trade of the country as a whole. They provide information and advice to members, settle commercial disputes, certify documents and issue certificates of origin. In addition to the national chambers of commerce, there are binational chambers of commerce (e. g. the German American Chamber of Commerce) which represent and further the interests of their respective countries. The International Chamber of Commerce in Paris has the additional function of bringing certain international rules and regulations up-to-date, such as the Incoterms (see Unit 3 "Offers") or the rules and regulations of the Documentary Letters of Credit (see entry in this Glossary), which are issued in several languages.

COD (cash on delivery) see Unit 7 "Payment"

collateral security in the form of property or an item of value that can be claimed by a lender if a loan is not repaid

commission fee charged to a client by a broker, solicitor or an institution for acting on the client's behalf

commodities commercial expression for raw materials, usually when they are sold, e.g. coffee, sugar, tin

consignment note see Unit 6 "Delivery"

convergence criteria economic criteria to be met for an EU country to take part in European Monetary Union, i.e. the introduction of the euro. The factors considered are:
1. inflation
2. long-term interest rates
3. budget deficits
4. government debt
5. exchange rate stability

counties abbreviations for counties in England and Wales

Bedfordshire	Beds	Northamptonshire	Northants
Berkshire	Berks	Northumberland	Northd
Buckinghamshire	Bucks	Nottinghamshire	Notts
Cambridgeshire	Cambs	Oxfordshire	Oxon
Gloucestershire	Glos	Shropshire	Shrops / Salop
Hampshire	Hants	South Glamorgan	S Glam
Hertfordshire	Herts	Staffordshire	Staffs
Lancashire	Lancs	West Glamorgan	W Glam
Leicestershire	Leics	Wiltshire	Wilts
Lincolnshire	Lincs	Worcestershire	Worcs
Mid Glamorgan	M Glam	Yorkshire	Yorks
Middlesex	Middx		

D

DAX (Deutscher Aktienindex) German index of the movement and yields of common stocks and shares. See also "Dow Jones Industrial Average" and "FTSE".

debenture a long-term, fixed-interest security issued by a company to raise capital and secured (in the UK) by the company's assets. Debentures are not shares, the holders are not members and they have no voting rights. Debenture holders are *creditors*. They must be paid a *fixed rate of interest* whether the company is making a profit or not and before any dividend is paid on shares. If the company fails to pay interest or repay the loan, debenture holders can *force a company into liquidation* in order to recover their funds.

delcredere commission see Unit 11 "Agency Agreements"

delivery note a document made out by the consignor of goods to advise the buyer that they have been delivered or despatched

despatch (dispatch) note see "delivery note"

documents (shipping documents) see Unit 6 "Delivery" and Unit 14 "Forwarding and Insurance"

documents against acceptance (D/A) a term of payment in foreign trade. The exporter sends the shipping documents to a bank or agent at the port of destination with instructions not to release them to the consignee until he has accepted a bill of exchange (draft). See "documentary collection".

documents against payment (D/P) a term of payment in foreign trade. The shipping documents are released (usually by a bank) to the buyer or his agent against payment of an agreed sum. See "documentary collection".

documentary collection
The Stages of a Documentary Collection

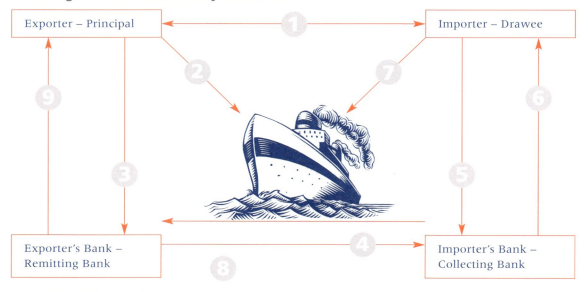

1. The exporter (principal) and importer (drawee) agree to pay by documentary collection.
2. The exporter ships the goods.
3. The exporter gives the documents (e.g. the B/L, commercial invoice, packing list, insurance certificate, certificate of origin etc.) and collection instructions to his bank (the remitting bank).
4. The exporter's bank sends the documents and instructions to the importer's bank (the collecting bank) by air mail.
5. The importer (drawee) either pays or accepts a bill of exchange in accordance with the collection instructions.
6. The documents are released to the importer.
7. The importer uses the documents to collect the goods.
8. The importer's bank transfers the amount collected or the accepted bill of exchange to the exporter's bank.
9. The exporter's bank pays the exporter in the agreed way.

documentary credit
The Stages of a Documentary Credit

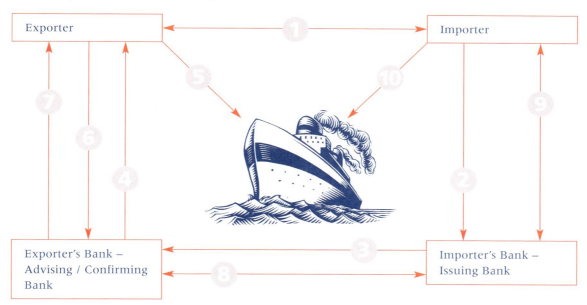

1. The exporter and importer agree to pay by documentary credit.
2. The importer instructs his bank (the issuing bank) to open an irrevocable and confirmed documentary credit in the exporter's favour.
3. The issuing bank opens the documentary credit and instructs its correspondent bank in the exporter's country (the advising / confirming bank), usually by electronic means, to confirm the credit to the exporter.
4. The exporter's bank confirms the credit to the exporter.
5. The exporter ships the goods.

6. The exporter presents the documents stipulated in the documentary credit to his bank, e.g. the B/L, commercial invoice, packing list, insurance certificate, certificate of origin etc.
7. The exporter's bank checks the documents and, if they are as specified, pays the exporter under the terms of the credit, e.g. by crediting the amount due to his account or by paying / accepting / negotiating his draft.
8. The account which the importer's bank has at the exporter's bank is debited with the amount paid to the exporter plus bank charges. The exporter's bank then forwards the documents to the importer's bank in two separate sets by separate air mail to avoid loss in transit.
9. The importer's bank debits the importer's account with the amount of the credit plus its bank charges and those of the exporter's bank and then hands over the documents to the importer.
10. The importer uses the documents to collect the goods.

A *revocable* credit may be cancelled or amended at any time. An *irrevocable* credit cannot be cancelled or amended without the approval of all parties concerned.

A *confirmed* credit means that the advising bank in the exporter's country has confirmed the credit and is obliged to pay the exporter if the terms of the credit are fulfilled. If, for example, the issuing bank is prevented from transferring the funds for political or economic reasons, the exporter will still receive payment.

Dow Jones Industrial Average American index of the movement and yields of common stocks and shares. See also "FTSE" and "DAX.

draft, banker's draft, b/e see bill of exchange and Unit 7 "Payment", "Methods of payment in foreign trade"

E

EMU European Monetary Union. The introduction of the euro in January 1999 as the common currency of EU member states meeting the convergence criteria. See "convergence criteria".

endorse to sign on the back. See "bill of exchange".

equities ordinary shares. See "private enterprise"

EU (European Union) association of western European countries originally formed under the Treaty of Rome in 1957. The main organs that govern the EU are: the Council of Ministers, the European Commission, The European Court of Justice and the European Parliament.

exchange rate value of one currency as compared to another at a specific time

E.C.G.D. (Export Credit Guarantee Department) see Unit 10 "Delay in Payment"

F

factoring see Unit 10 "Delay in Payment"

FED (Federal Reserve Bank) term commonly used to refer to the American central bank

FIATA (International Federation of Freight Forwarders' Associations) based in Zurich, Switzerland

floating policy see "Insurance" in Unit 14 "Forwarding and Insurance"

flotation when a company's shares are offered on the market for the first time this is referred to as a flotation. See also "offer for sale", "private enterprise" and "public issue".

force majeure see "act of God"

forfeited goods goods whose owners have lost the right of property since payment has not been made by them or they have failed to perform a duty

franchise authorisation given by one company to another to use its name and sell its goods. It also means a business operating in this way.

franchising arrangement whereby a franchiser gives another producer or trader (the franchisee) the exclusive right to manufacture or sell products in a specific area. The franchisee pays the franchiser a fee, the franchise, and thus obtains the right described above. In some instances the franchisee agrees to buy supplies and receive additional services from the franchiser, such as assistance with public relations and advertising.

FTSE (Financial Times Industrial Ordinary Share Index) *The Financial Times* publishes a number of indices (e.g. the FTSE 100) showing the performance of leading British shares. See also "Dax" and "Dow Jones Industrial Average".

futures securities or goods bought or sold at a fixed price for future delivery. In many cases the buyer or seller only intends to speculate with them by relying upon price changes in order to sell at a profit before delivery.

G

GATT (General Agreement on Tariffs and Trade) member states seek to abolish trade barriers and improve economic relations and conditions between themselves

general partner see "private enterprise"

giro account the UK post office equivalent to a current account at a bank

gilts fixed-interest, low-risk government securities

H

Hermes a German export credit insurance scheme. See Unit 10 "Delay in Payment".

high street bank see "bank services"

hire purchase a form of consumer credit whereby the buyer pays for goods over a period of time in instalments and does not become their legal owner until a fixed period of time has elapsed or a certain number of payments have been made.

holding company see "parent company"

I

immovables or **immovable assets** property that cannot be moved, e.g. land and buildings

INCOTERMS / Incoterms see Unit 3 "Offers"

industrial action see *Satzbausteine*, Unit 8 "Delay in Delivery" for examples

inland waterways the rivers, canals and lakes of a country, used to transport goods on inland waterway craft (e.g. barges and lighters)

Institute Cargo Clauses clauses defining marine insurance cover for goods. See "Insurance" in Unit 14 "Forwarding and Insurance".

insurance see "Insurance" in Unit 14 "Forwarding and Insurance" for details of insurance for goods in transit
   The purpose of insurance is to provide a sum of money as compensation for damage, injury, loss and death (the latter being known as life 'assurance'). The work of an insurance company is to set up a fund by inviting a large number of people to pay contributions called 'premiums'. The risk of loss is thus spread over as large a number of people as possible. The compensation paid to those who suffer loss is covered by the premiums collected.

The most important job for an insurance company is to assess risks accurately. This work is done by a person called an actuary. An actuary uses statistical evidence from the past to predict the probability of a hazard happening. Premium rates are calculated on this basis. Some risks are, of course, uninsurable. Examples of this are fashion trends in the retail trade or the possibility that a competitor may bring out a better product at a lower price.

The commonest forms of insurance are:
 1. medical insurance (health insurance)
 2. personal liability insurance
 3. household or glass insurance
 4. fire insurance
 5. insurance against theft or burglary
 6. pension schemes
 7. legal (costs and expenses) insurance
 8. third party insurance for motor vehicles
 9. fully comprehensive insurance for motor vehicles
10. life assurance
11. product liability insurance
12. export credit insurance (ECGD in the UK / "Hermes" in Germany)
13. Insurance for goods in transit

invoice see Unit 6 "Delivery" for the different types of invoice

IOU ("I owe you") a written ackowledgement of a debt signed by the debtor

ISO International Standards Organisation

issuing bank see "documentary credit"

issuing house see "offer for sale", "underwriter" and "underwriting"

J

joint-stock company a company whose members have limited liability. See "private enterprise" for further details regarding liability.

joint venture a business activity in which two or more people or organisations work together to make a product or provide a service

junk bonds bonds usually considered as being of little or no value. See "bond".

L

letter of credit a letter from a bank to another bank by which a customer named in the letter is given the right to obtain money. See "documentary credit".

liability responsibility to settle a debt or make good loss or damage. See "private enterprise".

liabilities debts owed by a business to its owners and creditors as shown on the company's balance sheet

lighter a small boat, similar to a barge, to carry cargoes over short distances, e. g. from an ocean-going vessel to land

limited companies see "private enterprise"

limited liability see "Lloyd's of London" and "private enterprise"

limited partner see "private enterprise"

liner a ship owned by a shipping company operating on a particular route. See Unit 14 "Forwarding" in "Forwarding and Insurance" for more details.

liquidator receiver, i. e. someone charged with the responsibility of liquidating (selling) a company's assets in the event of it being wound up, e. g. in the event of insolvency or bankruptcy

Lloyds Bank one of the major UK banks

Lloyd's of London the leading international insurance market. It began in 1689 when shipowners and merchants met in Edward Lloyd's coffee-house in the City of London to arrange insurance. In 1774 the insurers formed a body which in 1871 became the Corporation of Lloyd's by an Act of Parliament. Today, business is done by underwriters grouped in syndicates and insurance brokers who represent clients and collect their premiums.

Until the beginning of the 1990s Lloyd's underwriters had unlimited liability. The premiums they received were paid into a pool out of which claims had to be settled. If these funds were not sufficient, the underwriters' syndicates had to pay the claims using their members' personal wealth. In the course of time this proved impossible, since claims were becoming increasingly higher. To save Lloyd's, new rules were introduced, including the admission of corporate members (limited liability companies) in 1994. In addition to this a £3.2 bn reconstruction programme was implemented in 1995 and the market was entirely restructured.

Under the new arrangements, underwriting members and companies enjoy limited liability to a certain extent but are required to deposit substantial sums of money in the Premiums Trust Funds at Lloyd's, i. e. up to 50 % of the overall premium limit underwritten for private members and 50 % for corporate members. In addition to this, both private and corporate members are required to contribute annually to a Central Fund, which is used to cover claims if all other sources are insufficient (e. g. members' personal wealth).

The major areas of insurance dealt with at Lloyd's are marine, non-marine, aviation and motor insurance.

Lloyd's List and Shipping Gazette daily newspaper published by the Corporation of Lloyd's giving news of the movements of ships and aircraft and information about accidents

Lloyd's Register of Shipping a survey and classification of British and foreign ships. It also defines and maintains standards for the building, operating, and repair of ships.

M

marketing the process of finding out whether or not a market exists for particular goods or services and, if this is so, of determining the right price and sales methods to be used. The most important stages are:
- desk research (data, statistics etc.)
- field research (opinion polls, surveys, questionnaires etc.)
- marketing mix, i. e. how to combine the following marketing instruments: advertising, terms and services, distribution, public relations, price policy, product policy, sales promotion. See "advertising" for related details.

market maker a firm which is a member of the London Stock Exchange (see "stock exchange") which is committed to making firm buying and selling prices at all times for specific shares

marine insurance see "Insurance" in Unit 14 "Forwarding and Insurance" for details

measure (weights and measures) see *Satzbausteine* Unit 14 "Forwarding and Insurance"

Memorandum of Association see "private enterprise"

merchant banks see "bank services"

merger amalgamation. The joining together of two or more companies to become one.

minutes written summary of the important points discussed at a meeting

mortgage a long-term (usually) low-interest loan for the purpose of buying property (i. e. buildings and land). See "building society".

N

negotiate to use in exchange for money or goods. See "bill of exchange" and "bill of lading" for further details.

negotiable instrument a document that can be exchanged for goods or money. Typical examples are bank notes, cheques, bills of exchange, promissory notes, shares and bills of lading.

nominal value face value on (the value printed on) a banknote, share etc.

NVOCC non-vessel operating common carrier

O

OECD (Organisation for Economic Cooperation and Development) an international organisation which has the goal of improving economic growth and raising the standard of living of its member countries.

offer for sale a method of selling a company's shares on the stock exchange for the first time through a merchant bank (issuing house). The public can apply for shares directly at a fixed price. The offer is underwritten by the bank, meaning that it will take up any shares not bought by the public. A prospectus containing details of the sale must be printed in a national newspaper. See "underwriting".

OPEC (Organisation of Petroleum Exporting Countries) association set up in 1961 of the major petroleum-producing countries to increase their bargaining power.

open policy see "Insurance" in Unit 14 "Forwarding and Insurance"

overdraw to overdraw a bank account, to have an overdraft. See "bank services".

overheads the regular costs (fixed and variable) of running a business, e.g. rent, salaries, heat, light

oversubscribed if more applications are made to buy a security than there are securities available, the issue is said to be oversubscribed. See also "private enterprise" and "stag".

P

packing list shipping document. See Unit 7 "Delivery".

parent company holding company. A company that owns and controls a number of subsidiary companies.

portfolio usually referred to in business as the total of investments belonging to one investor or company. See also "bank services".

power of attorney formal document used in law authorising a person to act on behalf of another in all matters stipulated in this document

PR public relations

premium amount which is paid by the insured to the insurer to cover certain risks. See also "insurance".

principal see Unit 11 "agency Agreements"

private enterprise
The commonest forms of private enterprise in the UK are as follows:

– *Sole trader* (sole proprietor, sole proprietorship): A sole trader receives all profits made but takes all decisions alone and has *unlimited liability*, i.e. he is liable *to the extent of his personal wealth*.

– *Partnership:* Partners in a business have *unlimited liability*. They are both *individually* and *jointly* liable (i.e. liable for each other's actions) *to the extent of their personal wealth*. Their rights and responsibilities are set out in a *deed of partnership* (partnership agreement).

– *Limited partnership:* In a limited partnership the limited partner's liability for the debts of the firm is restricted to the amount of capital he has invested in the business. However, a limited partnership must have at least one *general (ordinary) partner*, who is *fully liable to the extent of his own personal wealth*. A *sleeping partner* invests money in a business and receives a share of the profits but takes no active part in the running of the firm.

– *Private limited company* (Ltd): Unlike a partnership, a private limited company is a separate legal entity. This means for example, that the company is sued and not its members in the event of a dispute. The shareholders ('Teilhaber') of a private limited company have limited liability, i.e. they are only *liable to the extent of their investment* in the company. The name of a private limited company must contain the letters "Ltd" to draw potential clients' attention to the fact that liability is limited.

  To obtain a *Certificate of Incorporation* from the *Registrar of Companies* a private limited company is required, among other things, to draw up a *Memorandum of Association* stating its business aims and *Articles of Association* regulating internal company affairs such as borrowing and rights and remuneration. After having completed these formalities it is allowed to start state trading.

  A private limited company must have at least two members but there is no upper limit. Shareholders can only sell their shareholdings ('Anteile') with the consent of the others and the company must *submit its accounts* to the Registrar of Companies each year. In the UK information on the company is available to the public from *Companies House* on payment of a fee (see Unit 12 "Credit Enquiries" and Unit 12 in *Satzbausteine* for more details).

— *Public limited company* (plc): A plc is a separate legal entity and its shareholders ('Aktionäre') have *limited liability*. Like a private limited company, a plc has a *Memorandum and Articles of Association*, which, after other formalities have been completed, must be presented to the *Registrar of Companies*, who then gives the company a *Certificate of Trading*. The name of a public limited company must contain the letters "plc" to draw potential clients' attention to the fact that liability is limited.

A company opts to become a plc (*go public*, be *floated* on the stock exchange) in order to raise additional capital. It may wish, for example, to expand, to bring out a new product or to finance research and development (R & D). Companies sell *shares in themselves* to members of the general public through the *stock exchange* (see "stock exchange" for more details). Shareholders are free to buy or sell shares whenever they wish.

Plcs offer investors two ways of making a profit. Firstly, shareholders receive a share of the company's profits called a *dividend*. Secondly, they can *speculate* by trying to sell their shares for more than they paid for them. There are various different types of share, the main ones being *preference shares* with a fixed rate of dividend, *ordinary shares (equities)* without a fixed rate of dividend and *deferred shares*, which are last in line to receive a dividend.

In addition to shares, a company may also sell *debentures*. A debenture is not a share. It is a *security with a fixed rate of interest*. Debenture holders are *creditors* and are first in line to receive the interest they are entitled to before shareholders receive dividends.

Control over a plc is exercised by the directors and shareholders, who meet at the AGM (annual general meeting). At the AGM votes are taken on matters concerning the company. As they bear most risk, the ordinary shareholders (equity holders) and deferred shareholders have most voting rights, whereas the preference shareholders have few or no rights.

At the AGM the board of directors is discharged ('Entlastung des Vorstands'), the company's performance is discussed, a new board is elected and dividends are announced.

profit and loss account accounting summary which usually forms part of the balance sheet to calculate the net profit or loss of a business before taxation

promissory note document containing an unconditional promise to pay a certain sum of money to the order of someone. Its major difference from a bill of exchange is that in a promissory note the drawer is identical to the drawee.

proxy authority given in writing by a shareholder to another person, usually to his / her bank, to act on his/her behalf in the Annual General Meeting of a plc

public issue a method of floating a company on the stock exchange. The company offers its shares to the public who can apply for them directly at a fixed price. A prospectus containing details of the sale must be printed in a national newspaper.

Q

quorum the minimum number of people who must be present at a meeting of an organisation for it to take legally valid decisions

R

Registrar of Companies see "private enterprise"

registered capital authorised capital of a company

R & D research and development

retailer a trader who buys goods from a wholesaler and sells them to consumers in shops or markets. The most frequently used retail outlets are corner shops, supermarkets, multiples (i. e. supermarkets with different names over their doors but owned by one large company) chain stores, department stores, hypermarkets (large stores outside of town or on the outskirts of town centres), shopping malls, mail order companies and the Internet (armchair shopping).

rights issue an invitation to existing shareholders to purchase additional shares in the company

S

SEAQ (Stock Exchange Automated Quotations) see "stock exchange"

securities stocks, shares, bonds and debentures traded on the stock exchange. See "private enterprise" and "stock exchange".

shares see "private enterprise"

shipping documents see Unit 6 "Delivery" and Unit 14 "Forwarding and Insurance"

sight bill see "bill of exchange"

SITPRO The Simpler Trade Procedures Board, an organisation based in London, England

states abbreviations for states in the USA

Alabama	AL	Delaware	DE
Alaska	AK	District of Columbia	DC
Arizona	AZ	Florida	FL
Arkansas	AR	Georgia	GA
California	CA	Guam	GU
Canal Zone	CZ	Hawaii	HI
Colorado	CO	Idaho	ID
Connecticut	CT	Illinois	IL

Indiana	IN	North Dakota	ND
Iowa	IA	Ohio	OH
Kansas	KS	Oklahoma	OK
Kentucky	KY	Oregon	OR
Louisiana	LA	Pennsylvania	PA
Maine	ME	Puerto Rico	PR
Maryland	MD	Rhode Island	RI
Massachusetts	MA	South Carolina	SC
Michigan	MI	South Dakota	SD
Minnesota	MN	Tennessee	TN
Mississippi	MS	Texas	TX
Missouri	MO	Utah	UT
Montana	MT	Vermont	VT
Nebraska	NE	Virginia	VA
Nevada	NV	Virgin Islands	VI
New Hampshire	NH	Washington	WA
New Jersey	NJ	West Virginia	WV
New Mexico	NM	Wisconsin	WI
New York	NY	Wyoming	WY
North Carolina	NC		

special markings on letters see list below and Unit 1 "Layout"

AIR MAIL	POSTE RESTANTE
BY COURIER	PRINTED MATTER
BY HAND	PRINTED MATTER REDUCED RATE
REGISTERED	PLEASE FORWARD
REGISTERED POST	TO BE FORWARDED
REGISTERED MAIL	IF UNDELIVERED PLEASE RETURN
RECORDED DELIVERY	PRIVATE
EXPRESS	PRIVATE AND CONFIDENTIAL
EXPRESS DELIVERY	URGENT
FAXED AND POSTED	PERSONAL
SPECIAL DELIVERY	

spot market buying and selling goods, currencies or securities for immediate delivery

spot price the price paid for immediate delivery

stag speculator on the Stock Exchange who applies for newly issued shares in the expectation that he will be able to sell them at a profit if they are oversubscribed.

stock exchange market in which securities can be bought and sold freely. The most common forms of securities are bonds (fixed-interest government or company securities), gilts (low-risk but low-return government securities), debentures (fixed-interest securities issued by private enterprise), equity/equities (normal shares). See "private enterprise" for further details on shares.

The London Stock Exchange was reformed in 1986 to abolish minimum commission, to admit both private and corporate membership and to allow all members to buy and sell shares both wholesale and retail. All members are now called "broker / dealers". Members committed to buying and selling specific shares at all times are known as market makers.

The inscription outside the London Stock Exchange is "Dictum meum pactum" "My word is my bond" because deals are struck verbally and only later confirmed in writing.

Broker / dealers are required by law to give their clients the best deal possible and a computer system called SEAQ (Stock Exchange Automated Quotations) checks all transactions and has them investigated if there is an irregularity.

subsidiary company partly or wholly owned by a parent or holding company. It has an independent management and is run as a separate legal entity, in contrast to a branch, which reports directly to the head office of its parent or holding company.

SWIFT Society for Worldwide Interbank Financial Telecommunication. See Unit 7 "Payment".

T

takeover bid an offer made by one company to the shareholders of another with a view to gaining control of the company

trade union association of employees working in the same industry or job. It represents members' interests in matters such as the improvement of working conditions, better pay etc. Trade unions use collective bargaining, as opposed to individual discussions at company level, to secure better results for all their members. The association of representatives of British trade unions is the TUC (Trades Union Congress).

transport The advantages and disadvantages of the major forms of transport are listed below.

	Advantages	Disadavantages
air	fast, good for perishable goods	expensive
ship	good for heavy / bulky goods, cheap	slow
lorry	door-to-door service	pollution, delays caused by traffic jams
rail	good for heavy / bulky goods, cheap	not door-to-door service

U

union see "trade union"

underwriter 1. a person who assesses and accepts risks for the purpose of insurance. See also "Lloyd's of London". 2. an organisation, such as an issuing house or a merchant bank, which guarantees to buy unsold shares when a company is floated on the stock exchange. See "offer for sale", "private enterprise" and "underwriting".

underwriting an arrangement whereby a company is guaranteed that an issue of shares will raise a given amount of cash. The underwriters (an issuing house, usually a merchant bank) undertake to subscribe for any of the issue not taken up by the public. They charge commission for this service. See "offer for sale".

V

VAT (value added tax) an indirect tax levied by the government as a percentage of the selling price of a product or service. It is payable at each stage of production and distribution but can be claimed back by traders and producers. It is finally paid by the consumer.

visible exports goods, as opposed to services, that are sold to other countries

visible imports goods, as opposed to services, that are bought from other countries

vocational training training in a trade or profession, e.g. a traineeship (general) or an apprenticeship (craft trades, industry). It can take place at work, at a vocational training college or at both.

W

warranty a guarantee that an article is free of defects and that faulty parts will be replaced free of charge

waybill a shipping document used in transport by road and rail, also called a consignment note. When goods are transported by air it is known as an air waybill. See Unit 6 "Delivery" for further details.

weights and measures see *Satzbausteine* Unit 14 "Forwarding and Insurance"

wholesaler person or company who buys goods in large quantities from the manufacturer and sells them to retailers. A wholesaler also provides additional services, such as transport, storage and the breaking of bulk into smaller quantities.

wholesaling buying from the manufacturer in bulk (in large quantities) and selling to the retailer in bulk (in large quantities)

Appendix 2

- **Vocabulary Unit by Unit**
- **Vocabulary A–Z**

Vocabulary – Unit by Unit

Unit 1 *Layouts*

abbreviated	*abgekürzt*
accountant	*Buchhalter/in, Rechnungsführer/in*
addressed, to be ~ (a woman)	*hier: angesprochen werden*
advisable	*ratsam*
attention line	*Zeile „zu Händen von"*
body of the letter	*Brieftext*
bold type, in ~	*fett gedruckt*
brief	*kurz*
brochure	*Broschüre, Prospekt*
business administration clerk	*Industriekaufmann/ kauffrau*
business administration theory	*Betriebswirtschaftslehre*
business associates	*Geschäftspartner (Plural)*
capitalised	*großgeschrieben*
carbon copy	*Durchschlag, Kopie*
chief executive officer	*Vorstandsvorsitzende/r; Generaldirektor/in; Hauptgeschäfts- leiter/in*
circulate	*in Umlauf bringen*
complimentary close	*Schlussformel*
confirmation	*Bestätigung*
consist of	*bestehen aus*
consultant	*Berater/in, Beratungs- firma*
contents	*Inhalt*
continuation pages	*Folgeseiten*
convenience, at your earliest ~	*so bald wie möglich*
convention	*Tagung*
current	*zur Zeit, aktuell*
CV (curriculum vitae)	*Lebenslauf*
delivery, take ~ of	*in Empfang nehmen, Lieferung annehmen*
dial (to)	*wählen (Telefon)*
duly	*ordnungsgemäß*
e-mail subscriber	*E-Mail-Teilnehmer/in*
enclosure	*Anlage*
environmental technology consultant	*Berater/in, Beratungs- firma für Umwelt- technologie*
equipment	*hier: Geräte*
fax transmission	*Faxübertragung*
feature (of a letter)	*Bestandteil (eines Briefes)*
file (a)	*Datei; Ordner*

freight forwarding agency	*Spedition*
further details	*weitere Einzelheiten*
glance, at a ~	*auf einen Blick*
hitch (a)	*Problem*
human resources officer	*Personalleiter/in*
indent (to)	*einrücken*
inhabitants	*Einwohner (Plural)*
inside address	*Empfängeranschrift*
interrupt	*unterbrechen*
legally binding (document)	*gesetzlich bindend (Dokument)*
link (to)	*verbinden*
managing director	*Geschäftsführer/in*
margin	*Rand*
message	*Mitteilung*
on behalf of	*für, im Auftrag von*
postcode	*Postleitzahl (britisch)*
pre-printed stationery	*vorgedrucktes Brief- papier*
previous	*vorherig, früher*
provide with	*ausstatten mit*
query (a)	*Frage*
quote (to)	*zitieren, angeben*
recipient	*Empfänger/in*
reference initials	*Bezugsinitialen*
salutation	*Anrede*
sample (a)	*Muster*
signatory	*Unterzeichner*
site plan	*Lageplan*
special marking (e.g. "urgent")	*besondere Markierung (z. B. „Eilt!")*
spreadsheet	*Tabelle(nkalkulation)*
stand out, to make ~	*hervorheben (lassen)*
subject line	*Betreff*
subsidiary	*Tochtergesellschaft*
summarise	*zusammenfassen*
support (to)	*unterstützen*
terms	*Bedingungen*
terms, on first name ~	*sich mit Vornamen anreden*
trust (to)	*hoffen, glauben, vertrauen*
underlined	*unterstrichen*
unmarried	*ledig, unverheiratet*
ZIP code	*Postleitzahl (amerikanisch)*

Unit 2 *Enquiries*

accountable to	(jmdm.) verantwortlich, rechenschaftspflichtig (sein)
appliance, household ~	Haushaltsgerät
approval	Zustimmung
as appropriate	wie geeignet, wie passend
based in Düsseldorf	mit Sitz in Düsseldorf
chamber of commerce	Handelskammer
charge (a)	Gebühr
civil engineering company	(Hoch-, Tief- und Straßen)Baufirma
commercial directory	Branchenverzeichnis
common	häufig
complete break-down	Zusammensetzung (hier: alles angeben was im Lack enthalten ist)
construction kit	Bausatz
construction project	Bauprojekt
contractor	Unternehmer
demand	hier: Nachfrage
desire (to)	wünschen
discount (a)	Nachlass
distributor	Vertriebsfirma, Großhändler
embassy	Botschaft
enquiry	Anfrage
establish	hier: herstellen
estimate (an)	Kostenvoranschlag
exhibition	Ausstellung
furniture	Möbel
garment	Kleidungsstück
grateful	dankbar
huge	riesig
hyphenated	mit Bindestrich versehen
indicate	angeben
initial order	Erstauftrag
involve	beteiligen; beinhalten
large-scale	groß (angelegt)
latest edition (of a publication)	letzte, neueste Ausgabe (einer Publikation)
link (a)	Verbindung
local government authorities	Kommunalbehörden
major	führend
necessitate	benötigen
non-refundable	ohne Rückerstattung
note (to)	feststellen
obtain	erhalten, bekommen, erwerben
operate	hier: arbeiten, tätig sein
overall responsibility	Gesamtverantwortung
particular	bestimmt
pattern	Muster
perform	ausführen
premises	Geschäftsräume
provide with	zur Verfügung stellen
quotation	(Preis)Angebot
range (a)	Auswahl, Produktpalette, Lieferprogramm
reasonable	vernünftig, angemessen
recommendation	Empfehlung
registered	eingetragen
requirements	Bedarf
retail chain	Einzelhandelskette
retailer	Einzelhändler
run low	zur Neige gehen
sale-or-return basis, on a ~	auf Verkaufs- oder Rückgabebasis
sample (a)	Muster
source (a)	Quelle
state (to)	angeben
stock, from ~	ab Lager
stock up	sich eindecken
stocks	Lagerbestand
submit	vorlegen
supply (to)	liefern, beliefern
tender, (to) put out to ~	zur Ausschreibung freigeben
terms of delivery	Lieferbedingungen
terms of payment	Zahlungsbedingungen
theme park	Themenpark, Freizeitpark
throughout (Germany)	in ganz (Deutschland)
to date	bis jetzt
trade fair	Handelsmesse, Fachmesse
trade journal	Fachzeitschrift
treat (to)	behandeln
trial order	Probeauftrag
unique	einzigartig
varnish (a)	Lack
work closely (to)	eng zusammenarbeiten
workmanship	Verarbeitung

Unit 3 *Offers*

accessories	Accessoires
agency	Agentur, Vertretung
appointment	Termin

appropriate destination	geeigneter Bestimmungsort
authorities	Behörden
available	erhältlich, verfügbar
avoid	vermeiden
bear the risk	das Risiko tragen
border	Grenze
carrier	Frachtführer
case	Kiste
choice selection	auserlesenes Sortiment
civil engineering company	(Hoch-, Tief- und Straßen)Baufirma
comprehensive	umfassend
confectionery	Süßigkeiten
consignment	Sendung
custody, in the ~ of the carrier	Gewahrsam (im Gewahrsam des Frachtführers)
customs duty	Zoll(gebühren)
depot	Lager, Warendepot
eligible	geeignet
encourage	ermutigen
entire	ganz, vollständig
exceed	übersteigen
excluding	ausschließlich
exclusive right of sale	Alleinverkaufsrecht
extensive sales network	weitreichendes Verkaufsnetz
fashionwear	modische Kleidung
favourable	günstig, preiswert
hesitate (to)	zögern
including	einschließlich
INCOTERMS (Incoterms)	INCOTERMS (Internationale Lieferbedingungen)
1. ex works	ab Werk
2. free alongside ship	frei Längsseite Schiff
3. free on board	frei an Bord
4. cost and freight	Kosten und Fracht
5. cost, insurance, freight	Kosten, Versicherung, Fracht
6. delivered ex ship	Lieferung ab Schiff
7. delivered ex quay	Lieferung ab Kai
8. free carrier	frei Frachtführer
9. carriage paid to ...	frachtfrei
10. carriage and insurance paid to ...	frachtfrei versichert
11. delivered at frontier	geliefert Grenze
12. delivered duty unpaid	geliefert unverzollt
13. delivered duty paid	geliefert verzollt

inland waterway port	Binnenschifffahrtshafen
introductory offer discount	Angebots-Einführungs-rabatt
jewellery	Schmuck
leaflet	Broschüre, Faltblatt
marine insurance	Seeversicherung
obligations	Pflichten
passing of risk	Gefahrenübergang
port of destination	Bestimmungshafen
port of shipment	Verschiffungshafen
printed matter	Drucksache
prospective	potentiell
quay	Kai
recommend	empfehlen
regarding	bezüglich
reputation	Ruf
request, on ~	auf Wunsch
responsibility	Verantwortung
retail outlet	Verkaufsstelle
revised	neu bearbeitet
rights	Rechte
rock-bottom	äußerst, niedrigst (bei Preisen)
rush delivery	eilige Lieferung
sea voyage	Seereise
ship's rail	Reling (des Schiffes)
shipping arrangements	Versandvorkehrungen
solicited	verlangt
subject to favourable references	unter der Bedingung günstiger Referenzen
substantial	beträchtlich
unload	entladen
unsolicited	unverlangt
up to	bis
validity	Gültigkeit
value-added tax (VAT)	Mehrwertsteuer (MwSt.)
wholesaler	Großhändler
without engagement	unverbindlich
work specifications	Spezifizierung der Arbeitsleistung

Unit 4 *Orders*

advise	benachrichtigen, informieren
air freight	Luftfracht
appreciate	hier: zu schätzen wissen
backpack	Rucksack
bill of exchange	Wechsel
camping gear	Campingausrüstung
carriage forward	unfrei

check (AE) (BE: cheque)	Scheck
competitive edge	(Preis)Vorteil
confectionery	Süßwaren
drawn on a German bank	gezogen auf eine deutsche Bank
equipment	Ausrüstung
floor tiles	Bodenfliesen
foam-lined cardboard boxes	mit Schaumstoff ge-polsterte Kisten
international money order	internationale Zahlungsanweisung
legally binding	gesetzlich bindend
light bulbs	Glühbirnen
qualifications	Bedingungen, Auflagen
qualify for (to)	Anspruch haben auf
remit (to)	überweisen
roughly	ungefähr
tabular form, in ~	in tabellarischer Form
transfer, by ~	durch Überweisung
unit price	Stückpreis, Preis pro Einheit
urgent	dringend
vice president	Direktor/in; Hauptab-teilungsleiter/in; Bereichsleiter/in
wall tiles	Wandfliesen

Unit 5 Acknowledgements

accordance, in ~ with	in Übereinstimmung mit
acknowledgement	Bestätigung
consent (to)	zustimmen
counter-offer	Gegenangebot
dock (to)	anlegen
domestic trade	Inlandshandel
due to open, to be ~	öffnen sollen
get sth up and running	etwas auf die Beine stellen
guard against knocks (to)	stoßsichern
lampshade	Lampenschirm
laser lighting equipment	Laserbeleuchtung
modification	Änderung
noted for later delivery, to be ~	für spätere Lieferung vorgemerkt (werden)
padding, with thick ~	mit dicker Wattierung
purchase (to)	kaufen
refusal	Ablehnung
substitute a new product for an old one	ein altes Produkt durch ein neues ersetzen

substitutes	Ersatz
summarise (to)	zusammenfassen
technicalities	technische Einzelheiten
time lag	(zeitliche) Verzögerung
towel-rail	Handtuchhalter
washbasin	Waschbecken

Unit 6 Delivery

advice of despatch	Versandavis
air-tight	luftdicht
approval, on ~	zur Ansicht, zur Probe
assess	feststellen
canvas	Leinen; Segeltuch
cardboard	Pappe
cargo	Fracht, Ladung
certify	bescheinigen
claused (B/L)	unrein
clean (B/L)	rein
common, to have in ~	etwas gemeinsam haben
consignee	Empfänger (einer Warensendung)
consignor	Absender (einer Waren-sendung)
contract of carriage	Frachtvertrag
corrugated	aus Wellpappe
crate	(Latten)Kiste, Holz-verschlag
damaged	beschädigt
decontamination unit	Dekontaminierungs-, Entgiftungsanlage
dirty (B/L)	unrein
endorsement	Indossament
ensure (to)	sicherstellen
estimated time of arrival	geschätzte Ankunftszeit
feature (a)	Merkmal
foam	Schaum
foam-lined	mit Schaumstoff ge-polstert
forwarder	Spediteur
foul	unrein
freight paid or unpaid	Fracht bezahlt oder nicht bezahlt
import restrictions	Einfuhrbeschränkun-gen
issue (to)	ausstellen
label (to)	etikettieren
life-jacket	Schwimmweste
marks	(Versand)Markierungen
multi-copy document	Dokument mit mehreren Kopien
negotiable	negoziierbar; begebbar

non-negotiable	*nicht negoziierbar; nicht begebbar*
non-returnable	*Einweg…*
objection	*Einwand*
on-board B/L	*Bordkonnossement*
outstanding balance	*ausstehender Saldo*
ownership (of the goods)	*Eigentum (an der Ware)*
part container load	*Teilcontainerladung*
prove	*beweisen, nachweisen*
quotation	*(Preis)Angebot*
receipt	*Empfangsbescheinigung, Quittung*
received-for-shipment B/L	*Übernahme-konnossement*
refund (a)	*(Rück)Erstattung*
request for payment	*Zahlungsaufforderung*
set sail	*auslaufen*
settlement	*Begleichung*
shipper	*Versender*
stainless	*rostfrei*
stipulate	*festsetzen*
sturdy	*stabil, kräftig*
sum due	*fällige Summe*
sworn and certified statement	*eidliche und beglaubigte Erklärung*
tin	*Dose*
transfer (to)	*übertragen; überweisen (Geld)*
triplicate, in ~	*in dreifacher Ausfertigung*
unit price	*Stückpreis*
weapons	*Waffen*
wet suit	*nässeabweisender Anzug, Neopren-Anzug*

Unit 7   *Payment*

active-carbon water filter	*Aktivkohle-Wasserfilter*
amendment	*Änderung*
carbonated water	*kohlensäurehaltiges Wasser*
clear a cheque	*einen Scheck einlösen*
correspondent bank	*Korrespondenzbank*
credit note	*Gutschrift, Gutschriftsanzeige*
currency	*Währung*
debit note	*Lastschrift, Lastschriftanzeige*
deduct	*abziehen*
earthenware bowl	*Steingutschüssel*
fragile	*zerbrechlich*
honour a draft	*einen Wechsel einlösen*

invoice amount	*Rechnungsbetrag*
maturity, at ~	*bei Fälligkeit*
omit to do sth	*vergessen, unterlassen etwas zu tun*
overcharge	*zu viel berechnen*
rate, at the normal ~	*zum normalen Satz, Preis*
short-ship a customer	*einem Kunden zu wenig liefern*
take into account	*in Betracht ziehen, berücksichtigen*
tally with	*übereinstimmen mit*
wholesale (to)	*im Großhandel vertreiben*

Unit 8   *Delay in Delivery*

apologetic, to be ~	*sich entschuldigen*
apology	*Entschuldigung*
fault, to be at ~	*im Unrecht (sein)*
awning	*Markise*
breach of contract	*Vertragsbruch*
charge expenses to someone	*jmdm. Ausgaben auferlegen, in Rechnung stellen*
commitment	*Verpflichtung*
compensation	*Entschädigung*
concession	*Zugeständnis*
contemporary	*zeitgenössisch*
D.I.Y. store	*Baumarkt, Do-it-yourself-Geschäft*
deadline	*letzter Termin*
despite	*trotz*
expire	*auslaufen*
foundation	*Stiftung*
inconvenient	*unpassend, ungünstig*
incur expenses	*Aufwendungen machen*
industrial action	*Arbeitskampfmaßnahme(n), gewerkschaftliche Kampfmaßnahmen*
insolvency	*Insolvenz, Zahlungsunfähigkeit*
instalment	*Teillieferung*
interest rates	*Zinssätze*
investigate	*untersuchen*
mere	*nur, lediglich*
mishap	*Missgeschick*
overdue	*überfällig*
promote	*fördern*
raspberry juice	*Himbeersaft*
raw materials	*Rohstoffe*
receipt	*Empfangsbescheinigung, Quittung*

regardless of whether …	*ungeachtet dessen, ob …*	furniture restorer	*Möbelrestaurator*
release from a contract (to)	*aus einem Vertrag entlassen*	gesture of goodwill	*Zeichen des guten Willens*
sue	*(gerichtlich) verfolgen, verklagen*	height	*Höhe*
		humidity	*Feuchtigkeit*
threaten	*(be)drohen*	illegible	*unlesbar, unleserlich*
utmost, to do one's ~	*sein Bestes tun*	impatient	*ungeduldig*
validity	*Gültigkeit*	impolite	*unhöflich*
		inaccurate	*ungenau*
		incapable	*unfähig*
		incompetent	*unfähig, inkompetent*

Unit 9 Complaints

		inefficient	*leistungsschwach, ineffizient*
appreciate, we would very much ~ it if …	*schätzen (wir würden es sehr schätzen, wenn …)*	inferior	*schlecht(er)*
		insolent	*unverschämt*
arbitration	*Schiedsgerichts(ver-fahren)*	investigate	*untersuchen*
		judging by … (your description)	*nach … (Ihrer Beschrei-bung) zu urteilen*
badly designed	*schlecht gestaltet, schlecht geplant*	leaky	*leck, undicht*
balance (the)	*Restbetrag*	length	*Länge*
benefit, give someone the ~ of the doubt	*im Zweifelsfall zu Gunsten von jmdm. entscheiden*	likely	*wahrscheinlich*
		matter (the)	*Angelegenheit*
		measurements	*Maße, Abmessungen*
bent	*krumm, verbogen*	meet someone's approval	*Zustimmung, Beifall finden*
business relations	*Geschäftsbeziehungen*		
china	*Geschirr*	messy	*unordentlich, schlampig*
chipped (china)	*angeschlagen (Geschirr)*	narrow	*schmal*
cloth	*Stoff*	needless to say	*unnötig zu sagen*
clothing	*Kleidung*	negligent	*nachlässig*
clumsy	*plump, ungeschickt*	noticeable	*erkennbar*
competitor	*Konkurrent, Mitbe-werber*	off-hand	*hier: brüsk, unhöflich*
		offensive	*anstößig, ausfällig*
complaint	*Beschwerde*	out of shape	*aus der Form*
cracked (china)	*gesprungen sein (Geschirr)*	pattern	*Muster*
		perform	*hier: funktionieren*
crooked	*hier: nicht gerade*	performance	*Ausführung*
crushed	*zerdrückt*	perished (rubber)	*spröde, brüchig (Gummi)*
damaged	*beschädigt*		
deduct	*abziehen*	promote	*fördern*
deformed	*deformiert*	proof	*Beweis*
dented	*eingebeult*	re-adjust	*hier: wieder in Ordnung bringen*
deposit (a)	*Anzahlung*		
disappointed	*enttäuscht*	regret (to)	*bedauern*
discoloured	*verfärbt*	release from contract	*aus dem Vertrag entlassen*
dishonest	*unehrlich*		
dismayed	*bestürzt*	remove	*entfernen*
dissatisfied	*unzufrieden*	rough	*rauh*
endanger	*gefährden*	roughly handled	*grob, unsachgemäß behandelt*
estimate (an)	*Kostenvoranschlag*		
factually	*sachlich*	rude	*grob, unverschämt*
faded	*ausgebleicht, verblasst*	rusty	*rostig*
faulty	*fehlerhaft*	scratched	*zerkratzt*
flooding	*Überschwemmung*	settlement	*Lösung*
frayed	*ausgefranst*	sloppy	*schlampig, nachlässig*

smudged	verschmiert	hospital equipment	Krankenhausaus-rüstung
solution	Lösung	instalment	Rate (Zahlung)
specifications	Angaben	legal proceedings	gerichtliche Schritte
squashed	zerquetscht, eingedrückt	neither … nor	weder … noch
stained	mit Flecken versehen	office staff	Büropersonal
tarnished	angelaufen (Metall)	outstanding balance	ausstehender Saldo
torn	zerrissen	overdue	überfällig
transit, in ~	auf dem Transport	oversight	Versehen
twisted	verdreht, verkrümmt	patch, to go through a bad ~	eine Pechsträhne haben
unavailable	nicht verfügbar		
uncommunicative	wenig mitteilsam, verschlossen	previous correspon-dence	vorheriger Schriftver-kehr
unpunctual	unpünktlich	regret (to)	bedauern
unreliable	unzuverlässig	reminder	Mahnung, Er-innerungsschreiben
unsaleable	unverkäuflich		
unsatisfactory	unzufriedenstellend		
unsuitable	ungeeignet	schedule, on ~	planmäßig
untidy	unordentlich, schlampig	senior executive	leitende/r Angestellte/r
untrained	ungeschult	subsidiary	Tochtergesellschaft
untruthful	unaufrichtig	swiftly	schnell
unusable	unbenutzbar	temporary office staff	Büropersonal auf Zeit
up-market	für höhere Ansprüche	trade mission	Handelsmission
upholstery	Polsterung	trusted	jmd., dem man vertraut
warped	verzerrt, verzogen		
weight	Gewicht	unfamiliar with	nicht vertraut mit
width	Breite	unreliable	unzuverlässig
wrong finish	hier: falsche Lackierung		

Unit 10 *Delay in Payment*

affect (to)	beeinflussen		
apologetic (to be)	sich entschuldigen		
application	hier: Erinnerung		
attempt (an)	Versuch		
backlog	Rückstand		
charge interest	Zinsen berechnen		
collection agency	Inkassoagentur		
commission	Provision		
computerised accounting system	computerisiertes Buch-haltungssystem		
concession	Zugeständnis		
confidential	vertraulich		
deadline, to set a ~	eine letzte Frist setzen		
delay (a)	Verzögerung, Ver-spätung		
diplomatic mission	diplomatische Stelle		
executive vice president	Direktor/in, Haupt-abteilungsleiter/in, Bereichsleiter/in		
face value	Nennwert		
fee	Gebühr		
final demand	letzte Aufforderung		
forthcoming, to be ~	hier: eingehen		

Unit 11 *Agency Agreement*

account, for his own ~	auf eigene Rechnung
account sales	Abrechnung (des Ver-kaufskommissionärs)
acquainted with	bekannt mit
applicant	Bewerber/in
assume the risk	das Risiko übernehmen
availability for interview	Verfügbarkeit für ein Vorstellungsgespräch
behalf, on someone's ~	für jemanden (im Auf-trag von jmdm.)
boost (to)	fördern, ankurbeln
commission	Provision
corporate customer	Firmenkunde
current sales volume	laufendes Verkaufs-volumen
deal, a great ~	eine große Menge, viel
degree in leather processing and shoe technology	(akad.) Ausbildungs-grad für Lederverar-beitung und Technik für Schuhwaren
distribution network	Vertriebsnetz
extension of the agreement	Verlängerung des (Ver-treter)Vertrags

fieldworker	Außendienstmitar-beiter/in
human resources department	Personalabteilung
indent for (to)	anfordern, bestellen
leisure	Vergnügen, Freizeit
newcomer	Neuling
personal qualities	persönliche Eigen-schaften
plumber	Installateur, Klempner
portable buildings	bewegliche Gebäude
praise	Lob
pre-suppose	voraussetzen
progress (to)	hier: weiterbearbeiten
rapidly	rasch, schnell
salary	Gehalt
settle a dispute	eine Streitigkeit bei-legen, schlichten
similar lines	ähnliche Produkte
solicited	verlangt
sound knowledge	fundierte Kenntnis(se)
submit an application	eine Bewerbung vor-legen
target (to)	abzielen, im Visier haben
termination of the agreement	Beendigung des (Ver-treter)Vertrags
territory	Gebiet
turnover (a)	Umsatz
unsolicited	unverlangt

Unit 12 *Credit Enquiries*

accessible	zugänglich
advisable	ratsam
arrears, to be in ~	im Rückstand (sein)
balance sheet	Bilanz
bankruptcy filing	Konkursantrag
catering / food processing equipment	Ausrüstung für die Lebensmittelver-arbeitung
cautious	vorsichtig
compile a report	einen Bericht zu-sammenstellen
comply with	übereinstimmen mit
confidentially	vertraulich
county court judgement	Urteil eines erstinstanz-lichen britischen Gerichts
credit line	Kreditlinie
credit reference agency	Auskunftei
customary	üblich
data protection laws	Datenschutzgesetze

derogatory legal filings	schlechte Gerichtsbilanz hinsichtlich der Zahlungsmoral
derogatory payment performance	amerikanisch: schlechte Zahlungsgewohn-heiten
disclaimer	Verzichterklärung, Haftungsausschluss-erklärung
excessive	überhöht
go public	an die Börse gehen
goal	hier: Ziel
highly sensitive	sehr empfindlich
in the strictest confidence	streng vertraulich
incur heavy losses	schwere Verluste erleiden
liability, with no ~ at all	mit keinerlei Haftung
lien on (against) property	Pfandrecht auf Besitz, dingliche Sicherheit
non-committal	nicht verbindlich
on the assumption that	in der Annahme, dass
open account terms, on ~	mit offenem Zahlungs-ziel
payment behaviour	Zahlungsmoral
payment habits	Zahlungsmoral
pool information (to)	Informationen sammeln
prior to	hier: (be)vor ...
profit and loss account	Gewinn- und Verlust-rechnung
reciprocation (of a favour)	Erwiderung (einer Gefälligkeit)
secure financial footing, on a ~	auf einer sicheren finanziellen Grund-lage
senior member (of a company)	leitendes Mitglied (einer Gesellschaft)
slip (a)	hier: Zettel
solicitor	(Rechts)Anwalt / Anwältin
trade reference	Handelsreferenz
unsecured basis, on an ~	ohne Sicherheiten
unsecured quarterly credit line	ungesicherte Quartals-kreditlinie
without any obligation whatsoever	ohne irgendwelche Verpflichtung
without obligation	ohne Verpflichtung, unverbindlich

Unit 13   Job Applications

£15K — 15.000 £

accommodation — *Unterbringung*

accomplishments — *Fertigkeiten; Kennt- nisse; Leistungen*

achievements — *Leistungen, Errungen- schaften*

acquire experience (to) — *Erfahrung erwerben, sammeln*

administrative post — *Verwaltungsposten*

allowance (car) — *Kilometergeld*

annual salary — *Jahresgehalt*

appointments, situations vacant — *(in einer Zeitung) Stellenanzeigen*

aptitude test — *Eignungstest*

arrest record — *Akten, Unterlagen über eventuelle Verhaftun- gen*

attend a course — *einen Lehrgang besuchen*

attend the final interview — *das endgültige Vor- stellungsgespräch haben*

be in charge of — *verantwortlich sein für*

become vacant (a post) — *frei werden (eine Stelle)*

bi-lingual — *zweisprachig*

blue chip — *erstklassig*

brand name — *Markenname*

business administra- tion clerk — *Industriekaufmann/ kauffrau*

business administra- tion theory — *Betriebswirtschaftslehre*

challenge — *Herausforderung*

cheerful personality — *freundliches Wesen*

commercial agent — *Handelsvertreter/in*

commitment to the task at hand — *Engagement für die vorliegende Aufgabe*

community (social) service — *Zivildienst*

community work — *etwa: Sozialarbeit auf freiwilliger Basis (in einem Altersheim, Behindertenarbeit usw.)*

confusion — *Verwechslung (z. B. zwischen Vor- und Zuname)*

construction industry — *Baugewerbe*

covering letter — *Begleitbrief*

creed — *Glaube, Konfession*

criterion (plural: criteria) — *Kriterium*

curriculum vitae — *Lebenslauf*

customary — *gewöhnlich, üblich*

database — *Datenbank*

defamation of character — *Verleumdung, Beleidi- gung*

disabilities — *Behinderungen*

divorced — *geschieden*

duties — *(hier) Aufgaben*

education and qualifications — *(Überschrift im Lebens- lauf:) Bildung (Aus- bildung) und Qualifi- kationen*

eligible for (a post, position) — *geeignet für (einen Posten, eine Position)*

executive (an) — *leitende/r Ange- stellte/r*

expenses — *Ausgaben, Spesen*

fencing — *Fechten*

filed, your applica- tion has been ~ — *Wir haben Ihre Bewer- bung zu den Akten genommen*

final assessment — *Endbeurteilung*

fluent in English — *in Englisch fließend*

for your convenience — *zum gefälligen Ge- brauch, um … zu erleichtern, der Ein- fachheit halber …*

fringe benefits — *(zusätzliche) Neben- leistungen*

gender — *Geschlecht*

gratuity — *Entschädigung*

hard and fast rules — *bindende, unumstöß- liche Regeln*

head-hunter — *jemand, der Top- Positionen für Führungskräfte ver- mittelt, Headhunter*

higher education — *höhere (Schul)Bildung*

human resources officer — *Personalleiter/in*

in reverse order — *in umgekehrter Reihen- folge*

information technology — *Informatik*

internship (AE) — *Praktikum*

interview — *Vorstellungsgespräch*

judging by — *nach … zu urteilen*

letter of recommen- dation — *Empfehlungsschreiben*

marital status — *Familienstand*

marriage allowance — *„Zuschlag" für Ver- heiratete*

national (military) service — *Wehrdienst*

natural skill with people	*natürliche Fähigkeit, mit Leuten umzugehen*
negotiate	*aushandeln*
objective	*(Überschrift im Lebenslauf) Zielsetzung*
occupational goal	*Berufswunsch, Berufsziel*
omission	*Auslassung*
on behalf of	*für, im Auftrag von*
on presentation of appropriate receipts	*bei Vorlage geeigneter Belege*
overall grade	*Gesamtnote*
panel	*Ausschuss, Gremium*
permanent post	*dauerhafte Stelle*
permanent post, to be given a ~ by the company at which you trained	*von der Firma, bei der man ausgebildet wurde, in Festanstellung übernommen werden*
perquisites ("perks")	*(zusätzliche) Vergünstigungen*
placement firm	*Firma, die Arbeitsstellen für bestimmte Gruppen vermittelt (z. B. Führungskräfte)*
private employment agency	*private Arbeitsvermittlungsagentur*
probationary period	*Probezeit*
professional experience	*Berufserfahrung*
progress	*Fortschritt(e)*
promising candidates	*vielversprechende Kandidaten und Kandidatinnen*
promotion	*Beförderung*
purpose	*Zweck*
put to good use	*gut verwerten*
race	*Rassenzugehörigkeit*
recruitment agency	*Arbeitsvermittlung*
refer someone to another employer (referral)	*jmdn. an einen anderen Arbeitgeber verweisen (Weiterleitung)*
reference	*Referenz*
reference to	*Bezugnahme auf*
rejection	*Absage, Ablehnung*
relocation costs	*Umzugskosten*
resign a job	*eine Stelle aufgeben*
responsibilities	*(hier) Aufgaben*
résumé (AE)	*amerikanisch: Lebenslauf*
salary	*Gehalt*
school fees	*Schulgebühren*
scope for personal initiative	*Raum für persönliche Initiative*
selection procedure	*Auswahlverfahren*
sensitive to other people's needs	*den Wünschen anderer Leute aufgeschlossen*
short-listed, to be ~	*in die engere Wahl kommen*
significant	*bedeutsam, wichtig*
skills	*Fähigkeiten*
software applications	*Software-Anwendungen*
sole proprietor	*Einzelkaufmann, Alleininhaber/in*
solicited	*verlangt*
source (a)	*Quelle*
space	*hier: Feld, Kasten*
specifically	*besonders*
state-run employment exchange	*(staatliches) Arbeitsamt*
subsidiary	*Tochtergesellschaft*
surname	*Familienname*
testimonial	*Arbeitszeugnis*
trustworthy	*vertrauenswürdig*
unemployed	*arbeitslos, ohne Beschäftigung*
unless	*es sei denn, dass …*
unsolicited	*unverlangt*
vocational training course	*Ausbildung, Lehre*
waiting list	*Warteliste*

Unit 14 *Forwarding and Insurance*

adhere to (regulations)	*(Vorschriften) entsprechen*
all-inclusive service	*Service alles inklusive*
average	*hier: Havarie*
bear, bore, borne (a risk)	*(ein Risiko) tragen*
blueprint	*Blaupause; Entwurf*
bonded warehouse	*Zollverschlusslager*
brewing equipment	*Brauereiausrüstung*
bulk rates	*Tarife für große Mengen*
cargo	*Fracht; Ladung*
cargo liner	*Frachtschiff*
cargo space	*Frachtraum*
charter party	*Charterpartie*
combined transport bill of lading	*Konnossement für kombinierten Transport*
commission someone to do something	*jmdn. beauftragen, etwas zu tun*

consignment note, road ~	*Straßenfrachtbrief*	mail (to)	*per Post schicken*
consolidator	*Sammelgutspediteur*	merchant shipping	*Handelsschifffahrt*
consularisation	*konsularische Be-glaubigung*	microbrewery	*Mikrobrauerei*
		multi-modal bill of lading	*multimodales Konnossement*
crate (to)	*mit einem Verschlag versehen*	non-negotiable sea waybill (e. g. for ferry transport)	*nicht negoziierbares Seefrachtpapier (z. B. für den Fährentrans-port)*
customs clearance	*Verzollung*		
damage	*Schaden*		
deductible of 10 % (a)	*mit 10 % Selbstbeteili-gung, 10 % abzieh-bar*	obligatory advance payment	*obligatorische Voraus-zahlung*
demurrage	*Überliegezeit*	open policy	*Generalpolice*
depot	*Ladestelle (für Contai-ner und Anhänger)*	particular average	*besondere Havarie*
		port of destination	*Bestimmungshafen*
dismantle	*abbauen, demontieren*	port of shipment	*Verschiffungshafen*
distinguish between (to)	*unterscheiden zwischen*	provided (that)	*vorausgesetzt, dass*
		quote (a)	*(Preis)Angebot*
distress, in ~	*in Seenot*	raising documenta-tion	*Zusammenstellung der Dokumente*
distribution	*Vertrieb; Verteilung*		
distribution centre	*Vertriebszentrum*	rates for single / regular shipments	*Tarife für einfache / regelmäßige Verschif-fungen*
domestic central heating unit	*Hauszentralheizungs-anlage*		
entrust someone with doing something	*jmdm. eine Aufgabe anvertrauen*	requisite documen-tation	*erforderliche Dokumen-tation*
ferry (a)	*Fähre*	riots and civil commotions	*Aufruhr und Bürger-krieg*
floating policy	*Abschreibepolice*		
forward (to)	*befördern*	ro-ro vessel	*Roro-Schiff*
forwarder's certificate of receipt	*Spediteurübernahme-bescheinigung*	roadfreight-tonne	*Straßenfracht-Tonne*
		seafreight-tonne	*Seefracht-Tonne*
free of capture and seizure	*frei von Aufbringung und Beschlagnahme (Ausschluss von Kriegsrisiko im See-versicherungsrecht)*	sewing machine	*Nähmaschine*
		shipment	*Verladung; Verschiffung*
		shipment (a)	*Lieferung, Ladung*
		shipping conference	*Schiffskonferenz*
		shipping note	*Warenbegleitschein*
general average	*allgemeine Havarie*	specify	*(genau) aufführen*
groupage rates	*Sammelladungstarife*	steam-beer brewery	*Dampfbierbrauerei*
haulier, haulage contractor, a haulage company	*Lkw-Unternehmer, Lkw-Spediteur*	storage	*Lagerung*
		stranding	*Stranden*
		stretch of water	*Wasserfläche*
hazardous	*gefährlich*	surviving heir	*überlebende/r Erbe/ Erbin*
highly delicate	*höchst delikat, empfindlich*		
		technical drawing	*technische Zeichnung*
human being	*Mensch*	theft	*Diebstahl*
insurance premium	*Versicherungsprämie*	through bill of lading	*Durchkonnossement*
jettison	*über Bord werfen*	time policy	*Zeitpolice*
labelling	*Etikettierung*	total and partial loss	*Gesamt- und Teilverlust*
lay-days	*Liegetage*	trailer	*Anhänger (z. B. Lkw)*
legalisation	*Legalisierung, Beurkundung / Beglaubigung*	tramp steamer	*Tramp(dampf)schiff*
		valid	*gültig*
		valuable	*wertvoll*
loss	*Verlust*	warehouse	*Lager*
lump sum	*Pauschalbetrag*		

Unit 15   Fairs, Exhibitions, Hotel Bookings and Making Arrangements

access to	Zugang zu
accessible	zugänglich
accommodation	Unterbringung
alike, private and corporate customers ~	hier: sowohl Privat- als auch Geschäftskunden
all over Europe and beyond	in ganz Europa und darüber hinaus
allocate	zuteilen
anticipate (to expect)	hier: erwarten
apart from	abgesehen von
apologise	sich entschuldigen
apply to	gelten für
area	Fläche
attendant	hier: Ordner (Person)
bill (a)	Rechnung
business purposes, for ~	für Geschäftszwecke
CAD (computer aided design) facilities	computerunterstützte Design-Anlagen
catering	Belieferung (mit Speisen und Getränken)
clip-on radio microphone	Ansteckmikrofon
communicating door	Verbindungstür
conference	Konferenz, Sitzung
confirmation	Bestätigung
contractor	Unternehmer, Firma
corporate rate	Firmentarif
counter	Theke
deposit (a)	Anzahlung
dietary restrictions	Diätvorschriften
disabled	behindert
display panel	Displaytafel
dispose of	entsorgen
draft (to)	entwerfen
duration	Dauer
en-suite facilities	Zimmer mit Bad (Hotel)
estimated time of arrival	geschätzte Ankunftszeit
executive	leitende/r Angestellte/r
exhibition	Ausstellung
exhibitor	Aussteller
facilities	Einrichtungen
fair outfitters	Messeausstatter
female	weiblich
fence (a)	Zaun
fitted carpet	Teppichboden
fixtures and fittings	Einrichtung, bewegliche und unbewegliche Einrichtungsgegenstände
floor show	eine Show im Haus (z. B. bei einem Abendessen)
fluorescent lighting	Leuchtstofflampen, -leuchten
half board	Halbpension
Internet link	Internetverbindung
location	Standort
pattern	Muster
pending your confirmation	bis zu(m) (Erhalt) Ihrer Bestätigung
pp	per procurationem, in Vollmacht; in Vertretung
proprietor	Besitzer/in
provisionally	vorläufig, provisorisch
public address system	Lautsprechersystem
quotation	Angebot
rack, literature ~	Prospektstand, -ständer
refer someone to (a firm) (to)	jmdn. an (eine Firma) verweisen
shelf, shelves	Regal, Regale
sink (a)	Waschbecken
size	Größe
socket	Steckdose
space	Fläche
specifications, to someone's ~	nach Angaben von jmdm.
stage (a)	Bühne
tailor-make	speziell anfertigen
trade fair	Fachmesse, Handelsmesse
trainee	Auszubildende/r
treat (to)	behandeln
upper floor	oberes Stockwerk
venue	Tagungs-, Ausstellungsort
vicinity, in the ~	in der Nähe, in der Nachbarschaft
video loop	Video-Schleife
video surveillance	Video-Überwachung
wickerwork	Korbgeflecht
within easy reach	leicht erreichbar

Vocabulary A–Z

A

abbreviated *(Unit 1)*
access to *(Unit 15)*
accessible *(Unit 12)*
   (Unit 15)
accessories *(Unit 3)*
accommodation
   (Unit 13), *(Unit 15)*
accomplishments
   (Unit 13)
accordance, in ~ with
   (Unit 5)
account sales *(Unit 11)*
account, for his own ~
   (Unit 11)
accountable to *(Unit 2)*
accountant *(Unit 1)*
achievements *(Unit 13)*
acknowledgement
   (Unit 5)
acquainted with
   (Unit 11)
acquire experience
   (to) *(Unit 13)*
active-carbon water
   filter *(Unit 7)*
addressed, to be ~
   (a woman) *(Unit 1)*
adhere to (regula-
   tions) *(Unit 14)*
administrative post
   (Unit 13)
advice of despatch
   (Unit 6)
advisable *(Unit 1)*,
   (Unit 12)
advise (to) *(Unit 4)*
affect (to) *(Unit 10)*
agency *(Unit 3)*
air freight *(Unit 4)*
air-tight *(Unit 6)*
alike, private and
   corporate customers
   ~ *(Unit 15)*
all over Europe and
   beyond *(Unit 15)*
all-inclusive service
   (Unit 14)
allocate (to) *(Unit 15)*
allowance (car)
   (Unit 13)
amendment *(Unit 7)*

annual salary *(Unit 13)*
anticipate (to expect)
   (Unit 15)
apart from *(Unit 15)*
apologetic, to be ~
   (Unit 8), *(Unit 10)*
apologise *(Unit 15)*
apology *(Unit 8)*
appliance, household
   ~ *(Unit 2)*
applicant *(Unit 11)*
application *(Unit 10)*
apply to *(Unit 15)*
appointment *(Unit 3)*
appointments, situa-
   tions vacant
   (Unit 13)
appreciate *(Unit 4)*
appreciate, we would
   very much ~ it if …
   (Unit 9)
appropriate destina-
   tion *(Unit 3)*
approval *(Unit 2)*
approval, on ~ *(Unit 6)*
aptitude test *(Unit 13)*
arbitration *(Unit 9)*
area *(Unit 15)*
arrears, to be in ~
   (Unit 12)
arrest record *(Unit 13)*
as appropriate *(Unit 2)*
assess *(Unit 6)*
assume the risk
   (Unit 11)
attempt (an) *(Unit 10)*
attend a course (to)
   (Unit 13)
attend the final
   interview *(Unit 13)*
attendant *(Unit 15)*
attention line *(Unit 1)*
authorities *(Unit 3)*
availability for
   interview *(Unit 11)*
available *(Unit 3)*
average *(Unit 14)*
avoid (Unit 3)
awning (Unit 8)

B

backlog *(Unit 10)*

backpack *(Unit 4)*
badly designed *(Unit 9)*
balance (the) *(Unit 9)*
balance sheet *(Unit 12)*
bankruptcy filing
   (Unit 12)
based in Düsseldorf
   (Unit 2)
be in charge of (to)
   (Unit 13)
bear the risk (to)
   (Unit 3)
bear, bore, borne
   (a risk) *(Unit 14)*
become vacant
   (a post) *(Unit 13)*
behalf, on someone's
   ~ *(Unit 11)*
benefit, give someone
   the ~ of the doubt
   (Unit 9)
bent *(Unit 9)*
bi-lingual *(Unit 13)*
bill (the) *(Unit 15)*
bill of exchange
   (Unit 4)
blue chip *(Unit 13)*
blueprint *(Unit 14)*
body of the letter
   (Unit 1)
bold type, in ~ *(Unit 1)*
bonded warehouse
   (Unit 14)
boost (to) *(Unit 11)*
border *(Unit 3)*
brand name *(Unit 13)*
breach of contract
   (Unit 8)
brewing equipment
   (Unit 14)
brief *(Unit 1)*
brochure *(Unit 1)*
bulk rates *(Unit 14)*
business administra-
   tion clerk *(Unit 1)*,
   (Unit 13)
business administra-
   tion theory *(Unit 1)*,
   (Unit 13)
business associates
   (Unit 1)

business purposes,
   for ~ *(Unit 15)*
business relations
   (Unit 9)

C

CAD (computer aided
   design) facilities
   (Unit 15)
camping gear *(Unit 4)*
canvas *(Unit 6)*
capitalised *(Unit 1)*
carbon copy *(Unit 1)*
carbonated water
   (Unit 7)
cardboard *(Unit 6)*
cargo *(Unit 6)*,
   (Unit 14)
cargo liner *(Unit 14)*
cargo space *(Unit 14)*
carriage and insurance
   paid to … *(Unit 3)*
carriage forward
   (Unit 4)
carriage paid to …
   (Unit 3)
carrier *(Unit 3)*
case *(Unit 3)*
catering *(Unit 15)*
catering / food
   processing equip-
   ment *(Unit 12)*
cautious *(Unit 12)*
certify (to) *(Unit 6)*
challenge *(Unit 13)*
chamber of commerce
   (Unit 2)
charge (a) *(Unit 2)*
charge expenses to
   someone *(Unit 8)*
charge interest (to)
   (Unit 10)
charter party *(Unit 14)*
check (AE) (BE:
   cheque) *(Unit 4)*
cheerful personality
   (Unit 13)
chief executive officer
   (Unit 1)
china *(Unit 9)*
chipped (china)
   (Unit 9)

choice selection
(Unit 3)

circulate (Unit 1)

civil engineering
company (Unit 2),
(Unit 3)

claused (B/L) (Unit 6)

clean (B/L) (Unit 6)

clear a cheque (to)
(Unit 7)

clip-on radio
microphone
(Unit 15)

cloth (Unit 9)

clothing (Unit 9)

clumsy (Unit 9)

collection agency
(Unit 10)

combined transport
bill of lading
(Unit 14)

commercial agent
(Unit 13)

commercial directory
(Unit 2)

commission (Unit 10),
(Unit 11)

commission someone
to do something (to)
(Unit 14)

commitment (Unit 8)

commitment to the
task at hand
(Unit 13)

common (Unit 2)

common, to have in ~
(Unit 6)

communicating door
(Unit 15)

community (social)
service (Unit 13)

community work
(Unit 13)

compensation (Unit 8)

competitive edge
(Unit 4)

competitor (Unit 9)

compile a report
(Unit 12)

complaint (Unit 9)

complete break-down
(Unit 2)

complimentary close
(Unit 1)

comply with
(Unit 12)

comprehensive
(Unit 3)

computerised
accounting system
(Unit 10)

concession (Unit 8),
(Unit 10)

confectionery (Unit 3),
(Unit 4)

conference (Unit 15)

confidential (Unit 10)

confidentially (Unit 12)

confirmation (Unit 1),
(Unit 15)

confusion (Unit 13)

consent (to) (Unit 5)

consignee (Unit 6)

consignment (Unit 3)

consignment note,
road ~ (Unit 14)

consignor (Unit 6)

consist of (Unit 1)

consolidator (Unit 14)

construction industry
(Unit 13)

construction kit
(Unit 2)

construction project
(Unit 2)

consularisation
(Unit 14)

consultant (Unit 1)

contemporary (Unit 8)

contents (Unit 1)

continuation pages
(Unit 1)

contract of carriage
(Unit 6)

contractor (Unit 2),
(Unit 15)

convenience, at your
earliest ~ (Unit 1)

convention (Unit 1)

corporate customer
(Unit 11)

corporate rate
(Unit 15)

correspondent bank
(Unit 7)

corrugated (Unit 6)

cost and freight
(Unit 3)

cost, insurance, freight
(Unit 3)

counter (Unit 15)

counter-offer (Unit 5)

county court
judgement (Unit 12)

covering letter
(Unit 13)

cracked (china),
(Unit 9)

crate (to) (Unit 14)

crate (a) (Unit 6)

credit line (Unit 12)

credit note (Unit 7)

credit reference
agency (Unit 12)

creed (Unit 13)

criterion (plural:
criteria) (Unit 13)

crooked (Unit 9)

crushed (Unit 9)

currency (Unit 7)

current (Unit 1)

current sales volume
(Unit 11)

curriculum vitae
(Unit 13)

custody, in the ~ of
the carrier (Unit 3)

customary (Unit 12),
(Unit 13)

customs clearance
(Unit 14)

customs duty (Unit 3)

CV (curriculum vitae)
(Unit 1)

D

D.I.Y. store (Unit 8)

damage (Unit 14)

damaged (Unit 6),
(Unit 9)

data protection laws
(Unit 12)

database (Unit 13)

deadline (Unit 8)

deadline, to set a ~
(Unit 10)

deal, a great ~
(Unit 11)

debit note (Unit 7)

decontamination unit
(Unit 6)

deduct (to) (Unit 7),
(Unit 9)

deductible of 10%
(Unit 14)

defamation of
character (Unit 13)

deformed (Unit 9)

degree in leather
processing and shoe
technology (Unit 11)

delay (a) (Unit 10)

delivered at frontier
(Unit 3)

delivered duty paid
(Unit 3)

delivered duty unpaid
(Unit 3)

delivered ex quay
(Unit 3)

delivered ex ship
(Unit 3)

delivery, take ~ of
(Unit 1)

demand (Unit 2)

demurrage (Unit 14)

dented (Unit 9)

deposit (a) (Unit 9),
(Unit 15)

depot (Unit 3),
(Unit 14)

derogatory legal filings
(Unit 12)

derogatory payment
performance
(Unit 12)

desire (to) (Unit 2)

despite (Unit 8)

dial (to) (Unit 1)

dietary restrictions
(Unit 15)

diplomatic mission
(Unit 10)

dirty (B/L) (Unit 6)

disabilities (Unit 13)

disabled (Unit 15)

disappointed (Unit 9)

disclaimer (Unit 12)

discoloured (Unit 9)

discount (a) (Unit 2)

dishonest (Unit 9)

dismantle (to)
(Unit 14)

dismayed (Unit 9)

display panel (Unit 15)

dispose of *(Unit 15)*
dissatisfied *(Unit 9)*
distinguish between
    (Unit 14)
distress, in ~ *(Unit 14)*
distribution *(Unit 14)*
distribution centre
    (Unit 14)
distribution network
    (Unit 11)
distributor *(Unit 2)*
divorced *(Unit 13)*
dock (to) *(Unit 5)*
domestic central
    heating unit
    (Unit 14)
domestic trade *(Unit 5)*
draft (to) *(Unit 15)*
drawn on a German
    bank *(Unit 4)*
due to open, to be ~
    (Unit 5)
duly *(Unit 1)*
duration *(Unit 15)*
duties *(Unit 13)*

E

earthenware bowl
    (Unit 7)
education and
    qualifications
    (Unit 13)
eligible *(Unit 3)*
eligible for (a post,
    position) *(Unit 13)*
e-mail subscriber
    (Unit 1)
embassy *(Unit 2)*
enclosure *(Unit 1)*
encourage *(Unit 3)*
endanger *(Unit 9)*
endorsement *(Unit 6)*
enquiry *(Unit 2)*
en-suite facilities
    (Unit 15)
ensure *(Unit 6)*
entire *(Unit 3)*
entrust someone with
    doing something
    (Unit 14)
environmental
    technology
    consultant *(Unit 1)*

equipment *(Unit 1)*,
    (Unit 4)
establish *(Unit 2)*
estimate (an) *(Unit 2)*,
    (Unit 9)
estimated time of
    arrival *(Unit 6)*,
    (Unit 15)
ex works *(Unit 3)*
exceed *(Unit 3)*
excessive *(Unit 12)*
excluding *(Unit 3)*
exclusive right of sale
    (Unit 3)
executive (an)
    (Unit 13), *(Unit 15)*
executive vice
    president *(Unit 10)*
exhibition *(Unit 2)*,
    (Unit 15)
exhibitor *(Unit 15)*
expenses *(Unit 13)*
expire *(Unit 8)*
extension of the
    agreement *(Unit 11)*
extensive sales
    network *(Unit 3)*

F

face value *(Unit 10)*
facilities *(Unit 15)*
factually *(Unit 9)*
faded *(Unit 9)*
fair outfitters *(Unit 15)*
fashionwear *(Unit 3)*
fault, to be at ~
    (Unit 8)
faulty *(Unit 9)*
favourable *(Unit 3)*
fax transmission
    (Unit 1)
feature (a) *(Unit 6)*
feature (of a letter)
    (Unit 1)
fee *(Unit 10)*
female *(Unit 15)*
fence (a) *(Unit 15)*
fencing *(Unit 13)*
ferry (a) *(Unit 14)*
fieldworker *(Unit 11)*
file (a) *(Unit 1)*
filed, your application
    has been ~ *(Unit 13)*

final assessment
    (Unit 13)
final demand *(Unit 10)*
fitted carpet *(Unit 15)*
fixtures and fittings
    (Unit 15)
floating policy
    (Unit 14)
flooding *(Unit 9)*
floor show *(Unit 15)*
floor tiles *(Unit 4)*
fluent in English
    (Unit 13)
fluorescent lighting
    (Unit 15)
foam *(Unit 6)*
foam-lined *(Unit 6)*
foam-lined cardboard
    boxes *(Unit 4)*
for your convenience
    (Unit 13)
forthcoming, to be ~
    (Unit 10)
forward (to) *(Unit 14)*
forwarder *(Unit 6)*
forwarder's certificate
    of receipt *(Unit 14)*
foul *(Unit 6)*
foundation *(Unit 8)*
fragile *(Unit 7)*
frayed *(Unit 9)*
free alongside ship
    (Unit 3)
free carrier *(Unit 3)*
free of capture and
    seizure *(Unit 14)*
free on board *(Unit 3)*
freight forwarding
    agency *(Unit 1)*
freight paid or unpaid
    (Unit 6)
fringe benefits
    (Unit 13)
furniture *(Unit 2)*
furniture restorer
    (Unit 9)
further details *(Unit 1)*

G

garment *(Unit 2)*
gender *(Unit 13)*
general average
    (Unit 14)
gesture of goodwill

    (Unit 9)
get sth up and
    running *(Unit 5)*
glance, at a ~ *(Unit 1)*
go public *(Unit 12)*
goal *(Unit 12)*
grateful *(Unit 2)*
gratuity *(Unit 13)*
groupage rates
    (Unit 14)
guard against knocks
    (to) *(Unit 5)*

H

half board *(Unit 15)*
hard and fast rules
    (Unit 13)
haulier, haulage
    contractor, a
    haulage company
    (Unit 14)
hazardous *(Unit 14)*
head-hunter *(Unit 13)*
height *(Unit 9)*
hesitate (to) *(Unit 3)*
higher education
    (Unit 13)
highly delicate
    (Unit 14)
highly sensitive
    (Unit 12)
hitch (a) *(Unit 1)*
honour a draft *(Unit 7)*
hospital equipment
    (Unit 10)
huge *(Unit 2)*
human being *(Unit 14)*
human resources
    department *(Unit 11)*
human resources
    officer *(Unit 1)*,
    (Unit 13)
humidity *(Unit 9)*
hyphenated *(Unit 2)*

I

illegible *(Unit 9)*
impatient *(Unit 9)*
impolite *(Unit 9)*
import restrictions
    (Unit 6)
in reverse order
    (Unit 13)

in the strictest confidence *(Unit 12)*
inaccurate *(Unit 9)*
incapable *(Unit 9)*
including *(Unit 3)*
incompetent *(Unit 9)*
inconvenient *(Unit 8)*
INCOTERMS (Incoterms) *(Unit 3)*
incur expenses *(Unit 8)*
incur heavy losses *(Unit 12)*
indent (to) *(Unit 1)*
indent for (to) *(Unit 11)*
indicate *(Unit 2)*
industrial action *(Unit 8)*
inefficient *(Unit 9)*
inferior *(Unit 9)*
information technology *(Unit 13)*
inhabitants *(Unit 1)*
initial order *(Unit 2)*
inland waterway port *(Unit 3)*
inside address *(Unit 1)*
insolent *(Unit 9)*
insolvency *(Unit 8)*
instalment *(Unit 8), (Unit 10)*
insurance premium *(Unit 14)*
interest rates *(Unit 8)*
international money order *(Unit 4)*
Internet link *(Unit 15)*
internship (AE) *(Unit 13)*
interrupt *(Unit 1)*
interview *(Unit 13)*
introductory offer discount *(Unit 3)*
investigate *(Unit 8), (Unit 9)*
invoice amount *(Unit 7)*
involve *(Unit 2)*
issue (to) *(Unit 6)*

J
jettison *(Unit 14)*
jewellery *(Unit 3)*

judging by … (your description) *(Unit 9), (Unit 13)*

L
label (to) *(Unit 6)*
labelling *(Unit 14)*
lampshade *(Unit 5)*
large-scale *(Unit 2)*
laser lighting equipment *(Unit 5)*
latest edition (of a publication) *(Unit 2)*
lay-days *(Unit 14)*
leaflet *(Unit 3)*
leaky *(Unit 9)*
legal proceedings *(Unit 10)*
legalisation *(Unit 14)*
legally binding (document) *(Unit 1)*
legally binding *(Unit 4)*
leisure *(Unit 11)*
length *(Unit 9)*
letter of recommendation *(Unit 13)*
liability, with no ~ at all *(Unit 12)*
lien on (against) property *(Unit 12)*
life-jacket *(Unit 6)*
light bulbs *(Unit 4)*
likely *(Unit 9)*
link (a) *(Unit 2)*
link (to) *(Unit 1)*
local government authorities *(Unit 2)*
location *(Unit 15)*
loss *(Unit 14)*
lump sum *(Unit 14)*

M
mail (to) *(Unit 14)*
major *(Unit 2)*
managing director *(Unit 1)*
margin *(Unit 1)*
marine insurance *(Unit 3)*
marital status *(Unit 13)*
marks *(Unit 6)*
marriage allowance *(Unit 13)*
matter (the) *(Unit 9)*

maturity, at ~ *(Unit 7)*
measurements *(Unit 9)*
meet someone's approval *(Unit 9)*
merchant shipping *(Unit 14)*
mere *(Unit 8)*
message *(Unit 1)*
messy *(Unit 9)*
microbrewery *(Unit 14)*
mishap *(Unit 8)*
modification *(Unit 5)*
multi-copy document *(Unit 6)*
multi-modal bill of lading *(Unit 14)*

N
narrow *(Unit 9)*
national (military) service *(Unit 13)*
natural skill with people *(Unit 13)*
necessitate (to) *(Unit 2)*
needless to say *(Unit 9)*
negligent *(Unit 9)*
negotiable *(Unit 6)*
negotiate *(Unit 13)*
neither … nor *(Unit 10)*
newcomer *(Unit 11)*
non-committal *(Unit 12)*
non-negotiable *(Unit 6)*
non-negotiable sea waybill (e. g. for ferry transport) *(Unit 14)*
non-refundable *(Unit 2)*
non-returnable *(Unit 6)*
note (to) *(Unit 2)*
noted for later delivery, to be ~ *(Unit 5)*
noticeable *(Unit 9)*

O
objection *(Unit 6)*
objective *(Unit 13)*

obligations *(Unit 3)*
obligatory advance payment *(Unit 14)*
obtain (to) *(Unit 2)*
occupational goal *(Unit 13)*
offensive *(Unit 9)*
off-hand *(Unit 9)*
office staff *(Unit 10)*
omission *(Unit 13)*
omit to do sth (to) *(Unit 7)*
on behalf of *(Unit 1), (Unit 13)*
on presentation of appropriate receipts *(Unit 13)*
on the assumption that *(Unit 12)*
on-board B/L *(Unit 6)*
open account terms, on ~ *(Unit 12)*
open policy *(Unit 14)*
operate *(Unit 2)*
out of shape *(Unit 9)*
outstanding balance *(Unit 6), (Unit 10)*
overall grade *(Unit 13)*
overall responsibility *(Unit 2)*
overcharge (to) *(Unit 7)*
overdue *(Unit 8), (Unit 10)*
oversight *(Unit 10)*
ownership (of the goods) *(Unit 6)*

P
padding, with thick ~ *(Unit 5)*
panel *(Unit 13)*
part container load *(Unit 6)*
particular *(Unit 2)*
particular average *(Unit 14)*
passing of risk *(Unit 3)*
patch, to go through a bad ~ *(Unit 10)*
pattern *(Unit 2), (Unit 9), (Unit 15)*
payment behaviour *(Unit 12)*

short-ship a customer
  (Unit 7)
signatory (Unit 1)
significant (Unit 13)
similar lines (Unit 11)
sink (a) (Unit 15)
site plan (Unit 1)
size (Unit 15)
skills (Unit 13)
slip (a) (Unit 12)
sloppy (Unit 9)
smudged (Unit 9)
socket (Unit 15)
software applications
  (Unit 13)
sole proprietor
  (Unit 13)
solicited (Unit 3),
  (Unit 11), (Unit 13)
solicitor (Unit 12)
solution (Unit 9)
sound knowledge
  (Unit 11)
source (a) (Unit 2),
  (Unit 13)
space (Unit 13),
  (Unit 15)
special marking (e. g.
  "urgent") (Unit 1)
specifically (Unit 13)
specifications (Unit 9)
specifications, to
  someone's ~
  (Unit 15)
specify (Unit 14)
spreadsheet (Unit 1)
squashed (Unit 9)
stage (a) (Unit 15)
stained (Unit 9)
stainless (Unit 6)
stand out, to make ~
  (Unit 1)
state (to) (Unit 2)
state-run employment
  exchange (Unit 13)
steam-beer brewery
  (Unit 14)
stipulate (Unit 6)
stock up (Unit 2)
stock, from ~ (Unit 2)
stocks (Unit 2)
storage (Unit 14)
stranding (Unit 14)

stretch of water
  (Unit 14)
sturdy (Unit 6)
subject line (Unit 1)
subject to favourable
  references (Unit 3)
submit (Unit 2)
submit an application
  (Unit 11)
subsidiary (Unit 1),
  (Unit 10), (Unit 13)
substantial (Unit 3)
substitute a new
  product for an old
  one (Unit 5)
substitutes (Unit 5)
sue (Unit 8)
sum due (Unit 6)
summarise (to)
  (Unit 1), (Unit 5)
supply (to) (Unit 2)
support (to) (Unit 1)
surname (Unit 13)
surviving heir
  (Unit 14)
swiftly (Unit 10)
sworn and certified
  statement (Unit 6)

T

tabular form, in ~
  (Unit 4)
tailor-make (to),
  (Unit 15)
take into account
  (Unit 7)
tally with (Unit 7)
target (to), (Unit 11)
tarnished (Unit 9)
technical drawing
  (Unit 14)
technicalities (Unit 5)
temporary office staff
  (Unit 10)
tender, (to) put out
  to ~ (Unit 2)
termination of the
  agreement (Unit 11)
terms (Unit 1)
terms of delivery
  (Unit 2)
terms of payment
  (Unit 2)

terms, on first name ~
  (Unit 1)
territory (Unit 11)
testimonial (Unit 13)
theft (Unit 14)
theme park (Unit 2)
threaten (Unit 8)
through bill of lading
  (Unit 14)
throughout
  (Germany), (Unit 2)
time lag (Unit 5)
time policy (Unit 14)
tin (Unit 6)
to date (Unit 2)
torn (Unit 9)
total and partial loss
  (Unit 14)
towel-rail (Unit 5)
trade fair (Unit 2),
  (Unit 15)
trade journal (Unit 2)
trade mission (Unit 10)
trade reference
  (Unit 12)
trailer (Unit 14)
trainee (Unit 15)
tramp steamer
  (Unit 14)
transfer (to) (Unit 6)
transfer, by ~ (Unit 4)
transit, in ~ (Unit 9)
treat (to) (Unit 2),
  (Unit 15)
trial order (Unit 2)
triplicate, in ~ (Unit 6)
trust (to) (Unit 1)
trusted (Unit 10)
trustworthy (Unit 13)
turnover (a) (Unit 11)
twisted (Unit 9)

U

unavailable (Unit 9)
uncommunicative
  (Unit 9)
underlined (Unit 1)
unemployed (Unit 13)
unfamiliar with
  (Unit 10)
unique (Unit 2)
unit price (Unit 4),
  (Unit 6)
unless (Unit 13)

unload (Unit 3)
unmarried (Unit 1)
unpunctual (Unit 9)
unreliable (Unit 9),
  (Unit 10)
unsaleable (Unit 9)
unsatisfactory (Unit 9)
unsecured basis, on
  an ~ (Unit 12)
unsecured quarterly
  credit line (Unit 12)
unsolicited (Unit 3),
  (Unit 11), (Unit 13)
unsuitable (Unit 9)
untidy (Unit 9)
untrained (Unit 9)
untruthful (Unit 9)
unusable (Unit 9)
up to (Unit 3)
upholstery (Unit 9)
up-market (Unit 9)
upper floor (Unit 15)
urgent (Unit 4)
utmost, to do one's ~
  (Unit 8)

V

valid (Unit 14)
validity (Unit 3),
  (Unit 8)
valuable (Unit 14)
value-added tax (VAT)
  (Unit 3)
varnish (a) (Unit 2)
venue (Unit 15)
vice president (Unit 4)
vicinity, in the ~
  (Unit 15)
video loop (Unit 15)video surveillance
  (Unit 15)
vocational training
  course (Unit 13)

W

waiting list (Unit 13)
wall tiles (Unit 4)
warehouse (Unit 14)
warped (Unit 9)
washbasin (Unit 5)
weapons (Unit 6)
weight (Unit 9)
wet suit (Unit 6)
wholesale (to) (Unit 7)

Appendix 3

– Documents

Certificate of Insurance

ORIGINAL

Lloyd's Agent at...................
is authorised to adjust and settle on behalf
of the Underwriters, and to purchase on
behalf of the Corporation of Lloyd's, in
accordance with Lloyd's Standing
Regulations for the Settlement of Claims
Abroad, any claim which may arise on this
Certificate.

LLOYD'S

Exporters
Reference

**THIS CERTIFICATE
REQUIRES ENDORSEMENT**

Certificate of Insurance No. C 7088/

This is to Certify that there has been deposited with the Committee of Lloyd's an Open Cover effected by *G. P. Turner & Co., Ltd.,* *per Atkin Raggett Ltd.,* of Lloyd's, acting on behalf of *Kolmar Cosmetics (England) Ltd. and/or Associated and/or Subsidiary Companies,* with Underwriters at Lloyd's, dated the *First day of November, 1976,* and that the said Underwriters have undertaken to issue to *G. P. Turner & Co., Ltd., per Atkin Raggett Ltd.,* Policy/Policies of Marine Insurance at Lloyd's to cover, up to £50,000 *(or equivalent in other currencies)* in all by any one steamer *or sending by air and/or road and/or rail and/or post and/or conveyance and/or held covered, Cosmetics and/or similar Interest and/or Raw Materials and/or Stationery and/or Machinery, other Interest held covered* to be shipped on or before the *Thirty-first* day of *October, 1981,* from any port or ports, place or places in *the United Kingdom* to any port or ports, place or places in *the World* excluding *Nigeria and/or Ethiopia),* including transhipment if and when required; and that *Kolmar Cosmetics (England) Ltd. and/or Associated and/or Subsidiary Companies* are entitled to declare against the said Open Cover the shipments attaching thereto.

Dated at Lloyd's, London, 26th January, 1979.

for the Committee of Lloyd's

Conveyance		From		
Via/To		To		INSURED VALUE/Currency:
Marks and Numbers			Interest	

Specimen

We hereby declare for Insurance under the said Cover interest as specified above so valued subject to the terms of the Standard Form of Lloyd's Marine Policy providing for the settlement of claims abroad and to the special conditions stated below and on the back hereof.

Institute Cargo Clauses (All Risks) (1.1.63) or Institute Air Cargo Clauses (All Risks) (15.6.65) (Clause 10 deleted) as applicable.
Institute War Clauses (1.7.76) or Institute War Clauses (including on-carriage by Air) (1.7.76) or Institute War Clauses (Air) (excluding sendings by Post) (1.1.71) or Institute War Clauses for the insurance of sendings by Post (1.1.71) as applicable.
Institute Strikes, Riots and Civil Commotions Clauses (1.1.63).
Institute Classification Clause (1.7.78) or held covered.
Risk to attach from time of leaving the Assured's premises and to continue until delivered to final destination including whilst at packers premises for packing and awaiting shipment.
Shipments on deck:—Including the risk of jettison and washing overboard.
General Average, Salvage and Special Charges payable as provided in the Contract of Affreightment and/or in accordance with laws and usages at port of destination and/or in accordance with foreign statement. In the event of the contributory value exceeding the insured value for the purpose of contribution to General Average or Salvage Charges, it is agreed that any amount due shall be paid in full by Underwriters. General Average Deposits Payable on production of General Average Deposit Receipts.

Underwriters agree losses, if any, shall be payable to the order of.. on surrender of this Certificate.

In the event of loss or damage which may result in a claim under this Insurance, immediate notice should be given to the Lloyd's Agent at the port or place where the loss or damage is discovered in order that he may examine the goods and issue a survey report.

(Survey fee is customarily paid by claimant and included in valid claim against Underwriters.)

This Certificate not valid unless the Declaration be signed by

KOLMAR COSMETICS (ENGLAND) LTD.
and/or Associated and/or Subsidiary Companies.   Dated at

Commercial Invoice

INVOICE	RECHNUNG FACTURE FACTURA فاتورة

Seller (name, address, VAT reg no.)		
SITPRO The Simpler Trade Procedures Board 151 Buckingham Palace Road, London SW1W 9SS VAT Reg. No. 241 8235 77	Invoice number JP-IV2167	
	Invoice date (tax point) 10.08.94	Seller's reference JP-IV2167
	Buyer's reference P.O.4123	Other reference

(c) SITPRO 1992

UNIC

Consignee VAT no.	Buyer (if not consignee) VAT no.
Aikashinko Shibakhoen Inc. 6-1, Honcho Kanamatsu Cho, Naka-Ku Kyoto Japan	Aikashinko Group Holdings Inc. 1-11-3 Shiba-Daimon Kitatoneyama, Toyonaka City Osaka Japan

Country of origin of goods	Country of destination
UK (EEC)	Japan

Terms of delivery and payment
DDP - Delivered Duty Paid Kyoto. Payment via: Bank of Foreign Trade 18-22 Valentine Place, London WC2 Account no. 120 7532 68

Vessel/flight no. and date	Port/airport of loading
Gala Del Mar	Liverpool

Port/airport of discharge	Place of delivery
Osaka	Kyoto

Shipping marks; container number	No. and kind of packages; description of goods	Commodity code	Total gross (Kg)	Total cube (m3)
Aikashinko P.O.4123 Kyoto via Osaka Japan	26 Cases Lamp accessories and advertising material		Kilos 82.75 Total net wt (Kg) 75.75	

Specimen

Item/packages	Gross/net/cube Description	Quantity	Unit price	Amount
1) 10 Cases	Cat. E/558W. 3 terminal angle batten lampholder - long skirt	250	1.60 each	400.00
2) 15 Cases	Cat. E/42W. 3 terminal angle batten lampholder - short skirt	400	1.26 each	504.00
				--------- 904.00
	1 case of advertising/ promotional literature.			

We warrant that the goods described above comply with regulation 4092 of 13 May 1981, and that packaging and labelling are to the specifications laid down in regulation 248 of 11 February 1987.	Invoice total GBP 904.00

	Name of signatory B Zbyszewski, Accountant
	Place and date of issue Orpington 10.08.94
	Signature *B. Zbyszewski*

It is hereby certified that this invoice shows the actual price of the goods described, that no other invoice has been or will be issued, and that all particulars are true and correct.

SITPRO Licensee No. 000.

V5

Certificate of Origin

1 Consignor	No. DA	ORIGINAL
2 Consignee	**EUROPEAN COMMUNITY**	
	CERTIFICATE OF ORIGIN	
	3 Country of Origin	
4 Transport details (Optional)	5 Remarks	
6 Item number; marks; numbers; number and kind of packages; description of goods		7 Quanti...

Specimen

8 THE UNDERSIGNED AUTHORITY CERTIFIES THAT THE GOODS DESCRIBED ABOVE ORIGINATE IN THE COUNTRY SHOWN IN BOX 3

Place and date of issue, name, signature and stamp of competent authority

.... 19 ....

DTI/VJ5/5/1

Road Consignment Note

LETTRE DE VOITURE INTERNATIONALE	CMR	INTERNATIONAL CONSIGNMENT NOTE	

(c) SITPRO, FTA, RHA 1992

Sender (name, address, country) Expediteur (nom, adresse, pays) **1**	Sender's/agent's reference Reference de l'expediteur/de l'agent **2/3**	
Consignee (name, address, country) Destinataire (nom, adresse, pays) **4**	Carrier (name, address, country) Transporteur (nom, adresse, pays) **5**	
Place & date of taking over the goods (place, country date) ILieu et date de la prise en charge des marchandises (lieu, pays, date) **6**	Successive carriers Transporteurs successifs **7**	
Place designated for delivery of goods (place, country) Lieu prevu pour la livraison des marchandises (leiu, pays) **8**	This carriage is subject, notwithstanding any clause to the contary, to the Convention on the Contract for the international Carriage of Goods by Road (CMR) Ce transport est soumis nonobstant toute clause contaire a la Convention Relative au Contrat de Transport International de Marchandises par Route (CMR)	

COPY 1 SENDER
COPY 2 CONSIGNEE
COPY 3 CARRIER

*NB FOR DANGEROUS GOODS SPECIFY:

1. Substance identification number (if applicable)
2. Substance description.
3. Class.
4. Item number and letter (if any).
5. The initials 'ADR' or 'RID'.
6. Other statements as required by ADR or RID.

Shipping marks; no & kind of packages; description of goods * Marques et nos; no et nature des colis; designation des marchandises* **9**	Gross weight **10** poids brut kg	Volume (m3) Cubage (m3) **11**

Specimen

Carriage charges Prix de transport **12**	Senders instruction for customs etc.. Instruction de l'expediteur (optional) **13**	
Reservations Reserves **14**	Document attached Documents annexes (optional) **15**	
	Special agreements Conventions particulieres (optional) **16**	
Goods received Marchandises recues **17**	Signature of carrier Signature du transporteur **18**	Company completing this note Societe emettrice **19**
		Place and date; signature Lieu et date. signature **20**

SITPRO Licensee No. 000.

Standard Shipping Note

(c) SITPRO 1991

STANDARD SHIPPING NOTE - FOR NON-DANGEROUS GOODS ONLY

Exporter 1	**Customs reference/status** 2 — PRE-ENTRY
SITPRO The Simpler Trade Procedures Board — 151 Buckingham Palace Road, London SW1W 9SS — VAT Reg. No. 241 8235 77	**Booking number** 3 — ACL - 418964P / **Exporter's reference** 4 — JP-IV2167
6 — Aikashinko Shibakhoen Inc. 6-1, Honcho Kanamatsu Cho, Naka-Ku Kyoto Japan	**Forwarder's reference** 5 — JP6943
Freight forwarder 7 — Dolphin Freight Limited 56 James Selvey Road Ashford, Kent	**International carrier** 8
Other UK transport details (eg. ICD, terminal, vehicle bkg. ref. receiving dates) 9	For use of receiving authority only
Vessel/flight no. and date Gala Del Mar / **Port/airport of loading** 10 — Liverpool	**10A** The Company preparing this note declares that, to the best of their belief, the goods have been accurately described, their quantities, weights and measurements are correct and at the time of despatch they were in good order and condition; that the goods are not classified as dangerous in any UK, IMO, ADR, RID, or IATA/ICAO regulation applicable to the intended modes of transport
Port/airport of discharge Osaka / **Destination** 11 — Kyoto	TO THE RECEIVING AUTHORITY - Please receive for shipment the goods described below subject to your published regulations and conditions (including those as to liability).

Shipping marks	Number and kind of packages; description of goods' non-hazardous special stowage requirements 12	Gross 13A	Cube (m3) of goods 14
Aikashinko P.O.4123 Kyoto via Osaka Japan	25 Cases Electrical apparatus (lampholders)	Kilos 77.75	
Aikashinko P.O.4123 Kyoto via Osaka Japan	1 Case Advertising material	5.00	

Specimen

We warrant that the goods described above comply with regulation 4092 of 13 May 1981, and that packaging and labelling are to the specifications laid down in regulation 248 of 11 February 1987.

For use of Shipping company only.	Total gross weight of goods — 82.75	Total cube of goods

PREFIX and container/trailer numbers 16	Seal number(s) 16A	Container/trailer size(s) and type(s) 16B	Tare wt(kg) as marked on CSC plate 16C	Total of boxes 13A and 16C 16D

DOCK/TERMINAL RECEIPT RECEIVING AUTHORITY REMARKS — Received the above number of packages/containers/trailers in good order and condition unless stated hereon.

Haulier's name	Name of company preparing this note 17
Vehicle reg. no.	Xephon Limited 91 87348 HA Evans, Export Clerk
	Date Orpington 10.08.94
DRIVER'S SIGNATURE / SIGNATURE AND DATE	(Indicate name and telephone number of contact) — HA Evans

630 Non-completion of any boxes is a subject for resolution by the contracting parties.   SITPRO Licensee No. 000.

Sea Waybill

© C of S 1979/1987

* Applicable only when document used as a Through Sea Waybill

Particulars declared by shipper

Shipper	VAT no.	**NON-NEGOTIABLE** **SEA WAYBILL**	SWB No.

Shipper's reference

Forwarder's reference

Consignee	VAT no.

Name of carrier

Notify Party and Address

The contract evidenced by this Waybill is subject to the exceptions, limitations, conditions and liberties (including those relating to pre-carriage and on-carriage) set out in the Carrier's Standard Conditions of Carriage applicable to the voyage covered by this Waybill and operative on its date of issue: if the carriage is one where had a Bill of Lading been issued the provisions of the Hague Rules contained in the International Convention for unification of certain rules relating to Bills of Lading, dated Brussels, 25th August, 1924, as amended by the Protocol signed at Brussels on the 23rd February, 1968 (the Hague Visby Rules) are compulsorily applicable under Article X, the said Standard Conditions contain or shall be deemed to contain a Clause giving effect to the Hague Visby Rules. Otherwise the said Standard Conditions contain or shall be deemed to contain a Clause giving effect to the provisions of the Hague Rules. In neither case shall the proviso to the first sentence of Article V of the Hague Rules or the Hague Visby Rules apply. The Carrier hereby agrees (i) that to the extent of any inconsistency the said clause shall prevail over the said Standard Conditions in respect of any period to which the Hague Rules or the Hague Visby Rules by their terms apply, and (ii) that for the purpose of the terms of this Contract of Carriage this Waybill falls within the definition of Article 1(b) of the Hague Rules and the Hague Visby Rules.

The shipper accepts the said Standard Conditions on his own behalf and on behalf of the Consignee and the owner of the goods and warrants that he has authority to do so. The consignee by presenting this Waybill and/or requesting delivery of the goods further undertakes all liabilities of the Shipper hereunder, such undertaking being additional and without prejudice to the Shipper's own liability. The benefit of the contract, evidenced by this Waybill shall thereby be transferred to the Consignee or other persons presenting this Waybill.

Notwithstanding anything contained in the said Standard Conditions, the term Carrier in this Waybill shall mean the Carrier named on the front hereof.

A copy of the Carrier's said Standard Conditions applicable hereto may be inspected or will be supplied on request at the office of the Carrier or the Carrier's Principal Agents.

Pre-carriage by*	Place of receipt by pre-carrier*
Vessel	Port of loading
Port of discharge	Place of delivery by on-carrier*

Shipping marks; container number	Number and kind of packages; description of goods	Gross weight	Measurement

Specimen

Freight details; charges etc.

RECEIVED FOR CARRIAGE as above in apparent good order and condition, unless otherwise stated hereon, the goods described in the above particulars.

C of S
SWB
1987

Ocean freight payable at

Place and date of issue

Signature for carrier; carrier's principal place of business

Authorised and licensed by the Chamber of Shipping © 1979/1987

Letter of Credit Presentation Form

(c) BBA/SITPRO 1992

LETTER OF CREDIT PRESENTATION FORM

Principal/exporter	Principal's/exporter's reference(s)	
	Issuing bank L/C no.	Your reference no.
	Issuing bank	
To (bank)	Value of the drawing	

DOCUMENTS ENCLOSED (state no. of copies)

Bill of exchange	Commercial invoice	Certified Consular Invoice	Certificate of origin
Insurance policy/certificate	Transport documents	L/C for endorsement	OTHER DOCUMENTS

OTHER DOCUMENTS: Document | Copies

Dear Sirs,

We have much pleasure in enclosing the above documents relating to the Letter of Credit referred to above.
We trust you will find the documents to be in order and look forward to receiving your settlement as shown below.
Should you discover any discrepancies please contact us as shown below BEFORE taking any action.

Specimen

FOR TERM DRAFTS
We request you to *discount/negotiate (less interest)
Please *retain/return accepted draft(s) to us
*Delete as appropriate

PAYMENT INSTRUCTIONS

For GBP sterling items please remit proceeds to our account no. :
held with :
 :
 :
Sort code no. :

For GBP sterling items please remit proceeds to us by cheque

For currency items - (please specify)
:
:
:
Forward contract reference (if any)
:

OTHER - (please specify)
:
:
:

DISCREPANCIES/SPECIAL INSTRUCTIONS

Contact details (eg. fax, telex nos.)	Company/telephone no.
	Name of signatory
	Place and date
	Signature

SITPRO Licensee No. 000.

Bill of Lading

Shipper	**Bill of Lading**
	for Combined Transport or port to port shipment or through carriage. Not negotiable unless consigned "to order".
	B/L No.
Consignee (if "to Order" so indicate)	*New Brunswick Container Line*
Notify address (No claim shall attach for failure to notify)	NBCL
	H. & E. Brunswick GmbH & Co.

Place of receipt	
Ocean vessel	Voy No.	Port of loading
Port of discharge	Place of delivery

Marks and numbers;	Number and kind of packages or shipping units	Description of goods said to contain	Gross weight	Measurement

Specimen

Excess Value Declaration : Refer to Clause 6 (4) (B) + (C) on reverse side   Particulars above declared by shipper

Freight and charges	RECEIVED by the Carrier the goods in apparent good order and condition and, as far as ascertained by reasonable means of checking, as specified above unless otherwise stated, to be transported to such place as agreed, authorised or permitted herein and subject to all the terms and conditions appearing on the front and reverse of this Bill of Lading to which the Merchant agrees by accepting this Bill of Lading, any local privileges and customs notwithstanding.
	The particulars given above as stated by the shipper and the weight, measure, quantity, condition, contents and value of the Goods are unknown to the Carrier.
	One of the Bs/L must be surrendered duly endorsed in exchange for the goods or delivery order.
For the release of goods apply to :	IN WITNESS whereof the number of original Bills of Lading stated below have been signed, all of this tenor and date, one of which being accomplished, the others to be void.

	Freight payable at	Place and date of issue
	Number of original Bs/L	Signed as carrier
		H. & E. Brunswick GmbH & Co.

Forwarder's Certificate of Receipt

Lieferanten bzw. Auftraggeber des Spediteurs
Suppliers or Forwarders Principals

FIATA FCR
BSL
**Forwarders
Certificate of Receipt**
ORIGINAL

No   DE

Ref. No.

Empfänger
Consignee

Die Durchf... des Auftrages erfolgt auf Grund der umseitig abgedruckten Allge...en Bedingungen.
The goods and instructions are accepted and dealt with subject to the General Con...tions printed overleaf.

Zeichen und Nummern; | Anzahl/Verpackungsart
Marks and numbers; | *Number and kind of packages*

Inhalt
Description of goods

Bruttogewicht
Gross weight

Maß
Measurement

Specimen

FIATA

laut Angaben des Versenders
according to the declaration of the consignor

SVS/RVS   Wert/Value
(§§ 39 ff ADSp) DM

327515

FIATA Reg. No. A

Wir bescheinigen hiermit die oben bezeichnete Sendung in äußerlich
guter Beschaffenheit übernommen zu haben

We certify having assumed control of the above mentioned consignment
in external apparent good order and condition

zur Verfügung des Empfängers
at the disposal of the consignee ☐

mit der unwiderruflichen Weisung*
with irrevocable instructions

zum Versand an den Empfänger
to be forwarded to the consignee ☐

(falls erforderlich, Angaben über den Transportweg und Transportmittel)
Besondere Angaben
Special remarks

Frankatur- und Spesenvorschrift
Instructions as to freight and charges

* Die Weisung zur Beförderung kann nur gegen Rückgabe der Original-Bescheinigung widerrufen oder abgeändert werden, und nur soweit und solange als der ausstellende Spediteur noch ein Verfügungsrecht über die bezeichnete Sendung besitzt.

Die Weisung zur Verfügungsstellung an den angegebenen Dritten kann nur gegen Rückgabe der Original-Bescheinigung widerrufen oder abgeändert werden, und nur solange, als die Verfügung, des begünstigten Dritten noch nicht beim ausstellenden Spediteur eingegangen ist.

* Forwarding instructions can only be cancelled or altered if the original Certificate is surrendered to us, and then only provided we are still in a position to comply with such cancellation or alteration.
Instructions authorizing disposal by a third party can only be cancelled or altered if the original Certificate of Receipt is surrendered to us, and then only provided we have not yet received instructions under the original authority.

Ort und Datum / *Place and date of issue*

Stempel und rechtsgültige Unterschrift
Stamp and authorized signature

Bill of Exchange

_____, the_____   For _____
Place and date of issuance   Amount in figures

At / On _____
Maturity

pay this _____ Bill of Exchange (_____ unpaid) to the order of _____

_____ the sum of

_____
Amount in words

To _____
Drawee

_____

at _____

| payable at _____ |
| Place |
| _____ |
| with _____ |
| Name and address of the bank   to the debit of account No. |

Specimen

Drawer's signature and full address

Acknowledgements

The authors and publishers are grateful to the following copyright owners for permission to reproduce documents.

The names of persons and companies used in the book are fictitious. Any similarities to existing persons are purely unintentional.

The letterheads and logos may not be copied or used otherwise.

p 310–316 SITPRO, London, UK
p 317 H. & E. Brunswick GmbH & Co., Hamburg, Germany
p 318 Verein Hamburger Spediteure e. V., Hamburg, Germany